Garfield Travel Adventures

by

JIM DAVIS

Ballantine Books • New York

A Ballantine Book
Published by The Random House Publishing Group

GARFIELD IN THE ROUGH: copyright © 1984 by Paws, Inc.
GARFIELD IN PARADISE: copyright © 1986 by Paws, Inc.
GARFIELD GOES HOLLYWOOD: copyright © 1987 by Paws, Inc.

Ballantine and colophon are registered trademarks of Random House, Inc.

"GARFIELD" and the GARFIELD characters are registered and unregistered trademarks of Paws, Inc.

This work was originally published as three separate titles: *Garfield in the Rough*, *Garfield in Paradise*, and *Garfield Goes Hollywood*.

GARFIELD IN THE ROUGH is based on the television special produced by United Media Productions. Jay Poynor, Executive Producer, written by Jim Davis. © 1984 Paws, Inc.
GARFIELD IN PARADISE is based on the television special produced by United Media Productions. Jay Poynor, Executive Producer, in association with Lee Mendelson and Phil Roman. Created by Jim Davis. Designed by Gary Barker © 1986 Paws, Inc.
GARFIELD GOES HOLLYWOOD is based on the television special written by Jim Davis, directed by Phil Roman, in association with United Media-Mendelson Productions © 1987 Paws, Inc.

www.ballantinebooks.com

Library of Congress Control Number: 2004095966

ISBN 0-345-48087-2

Manufactured in the United States of America

9 8 7 6 5 4 3 2 1

First Edition: February 2005

Garfield in the Rough

by Jim Davis

CAMPING SUPPLY GUIDE

50 lb. bag of kitty litter — no fuss, no muss — sanitized and completely biodegradable.

Fully stocked refrigerator — camping is always more fun when you take your best friend.

Garlic clove talisman — to insure the campers "King of the Hill" superiority in the food chain cycle.

Microwave oven — plus 200 miles of extension cord.

Credit cards — for the motel in case the weather is anything but perfect.

Telephone — camper can constantly stay in touch with his agent, lawyer, accountant, broker, pizzeria, and suicide prevention hotline.

Inflatable easy chair.

AM/FM cassette forest blaster — to assist the New Wave camper in break dancing across the forest floor.

Campers own bed…to insure that no roots, rocks, sticks, or stems interfere with a good weekend's sleep.

Headphone set — to tune out those distracting sounds of nature.

Gas grill — for barbecuing small woodland creatures that forage too close to the camp site.

Pocket coffee maker — this compact morning eye-opener is also wash 'n' wear.

Pocket blender — for blending roots, herbs, and berries with your favorite ice cream.

Electric can opener — a must for the campers who can't hunt, fish, or trap.

Color TV — for tuning in old Tarzan movies to enhance the camping experience.

HO HUM. DOUBLE HO HUM, HECK WITH IT! LET'S SHOOT THE WORKS. TRIPLE HO HUM. HERE I AM, WAKING UP IN THE SAME OLD BED

FACING THE SAME OLD MORNING ROUTINE

STUCK IN THE SAME OLD STRETCH

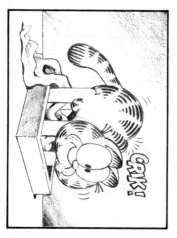

CRIK!

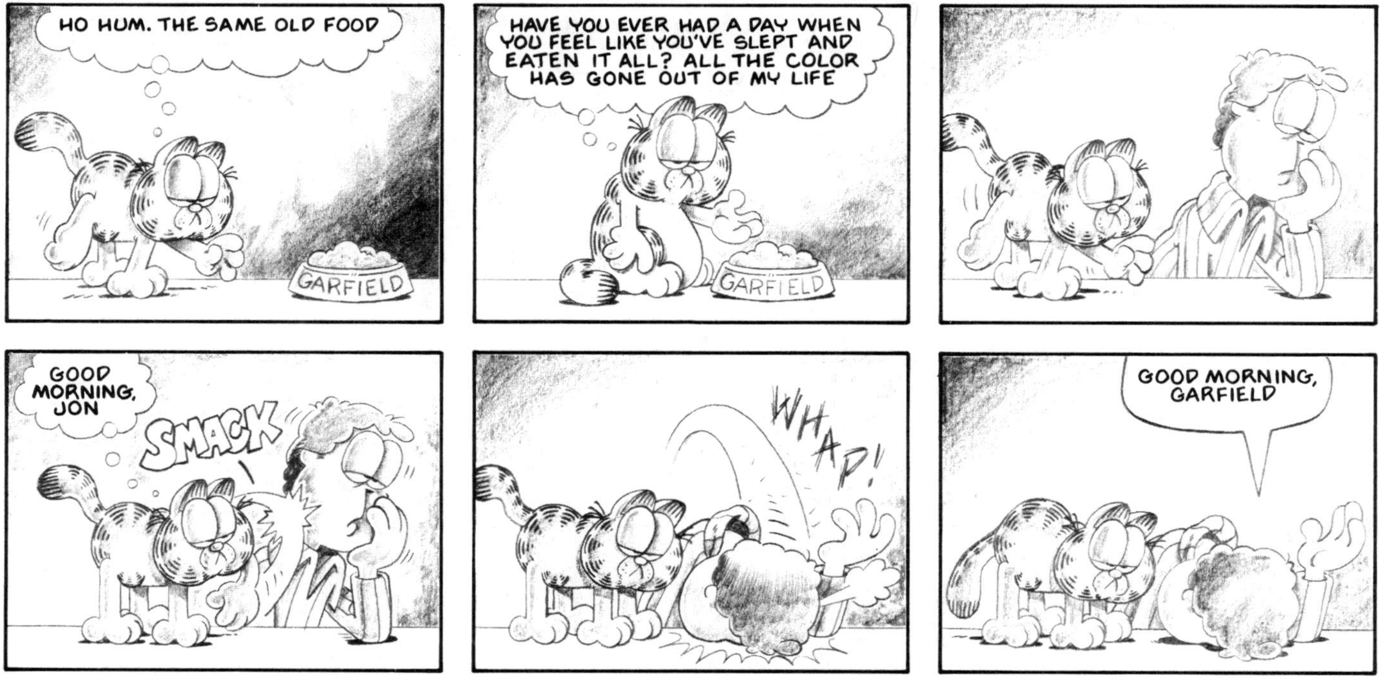
HO HUM. THE SAME OLD FOOD
GARFIELD
HAVE YOU EVER HAD A DAY WHEN YOU FEEL LIKE YOU'VE SLEPT AND EATEN IT ALL? ALL THE COLOR HAS GONE OUT OF MY LIFE
GARFIELD
GOOD MORNING, JON
SMACK
WHAP!
GOOD MORNING, GARFIELD

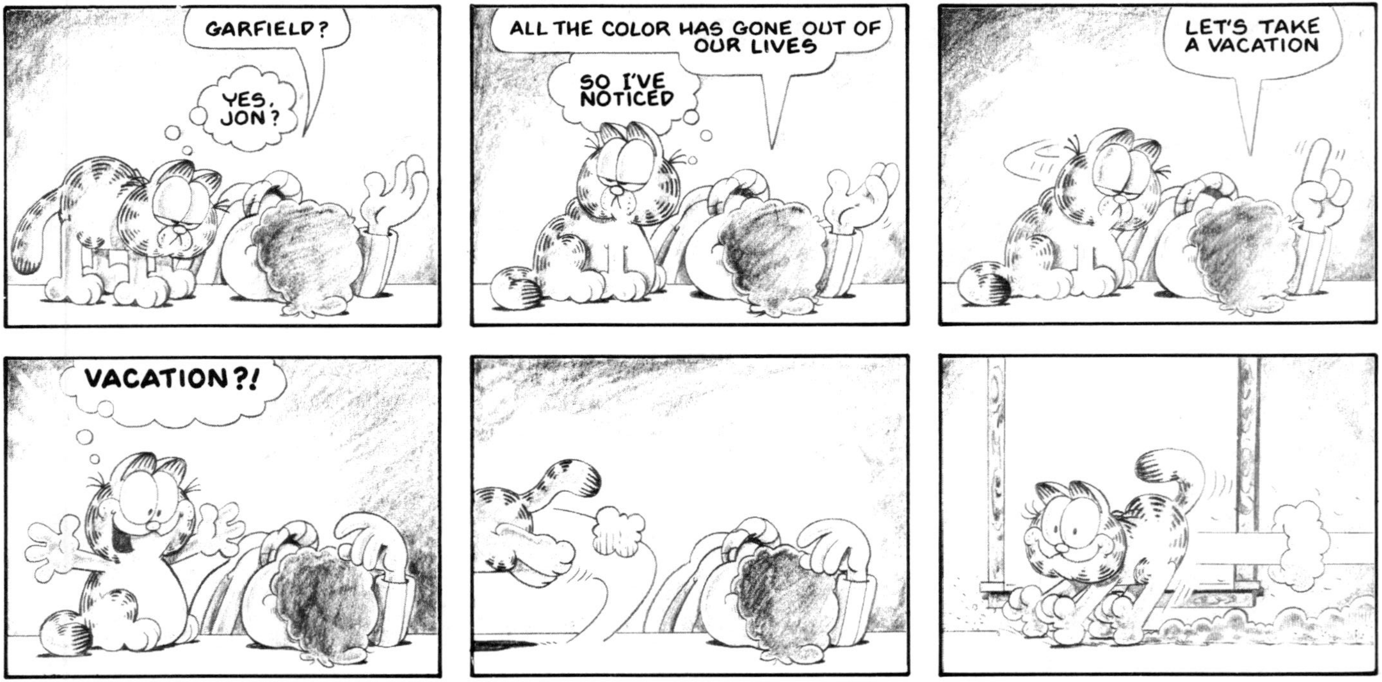
GARFIELD?
YES, JON?
ALL THE COLOR HAS GONE OUT OF OUR LIVES
SO I'VE NOTICED
LET'S TAKE A VACATION
VACATION?!

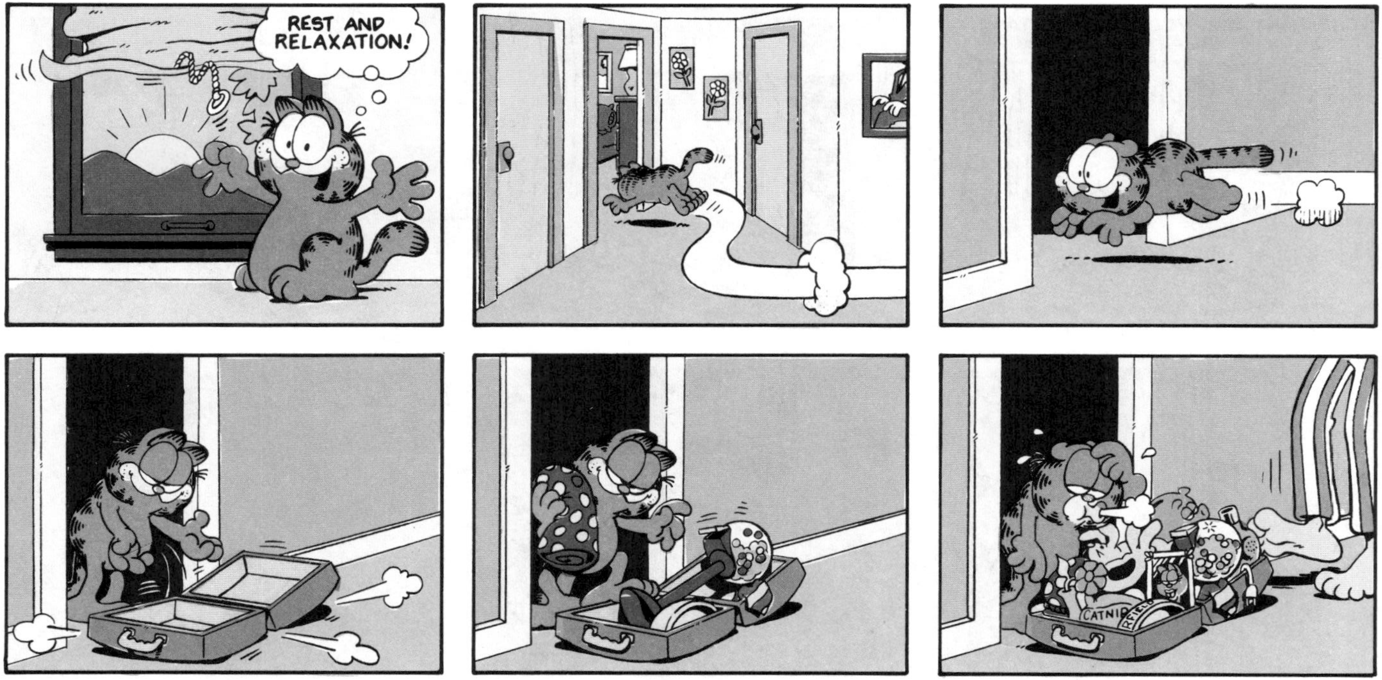
REST AND RELAXATION!
CATNIP

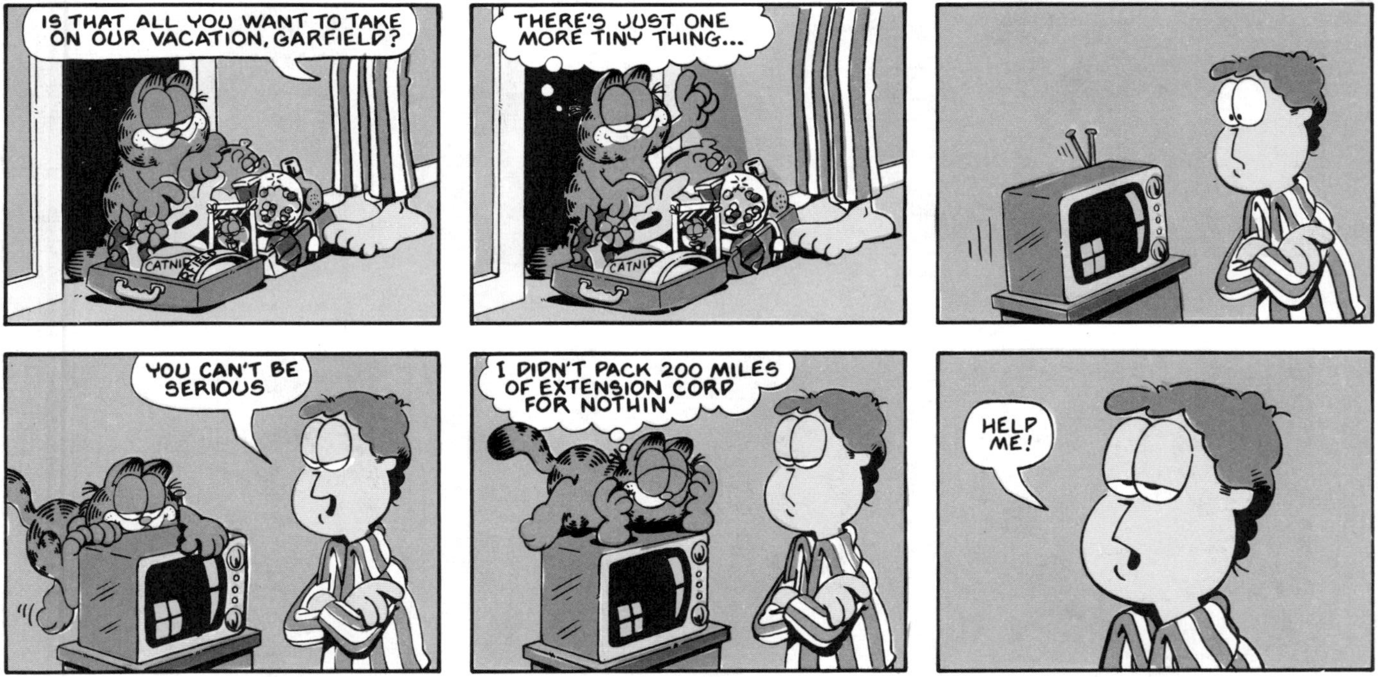
IS THAT ALL YOU WANT TO TAKE ON OUR VACATION, GARFIELD?
THERE'S JUST ONE MORE TINY THING...
CATNIP
YOU CAN'T BE SERIOUS
I DIDN'T PACK 200 MILES OF EXTENSION CORD FOR NOTHIN'
HELP ME!

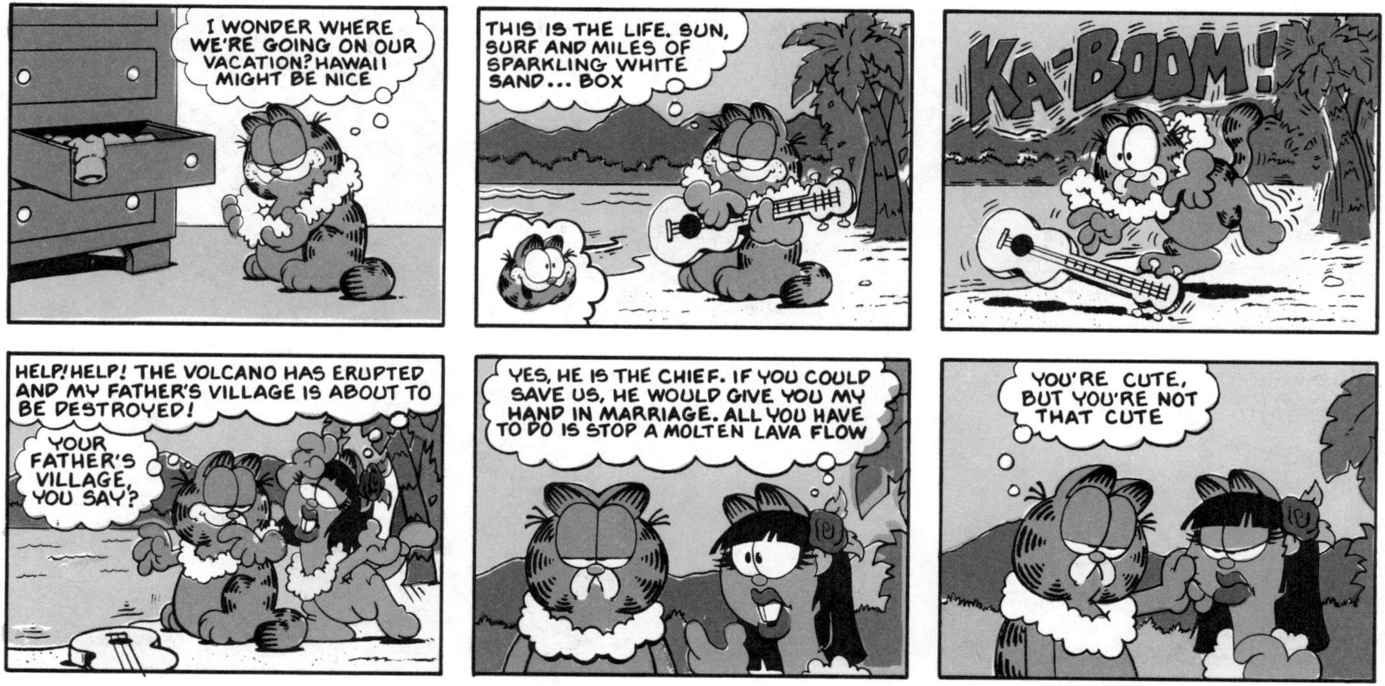
I WONDER WHERE WE'RE GOING ON OUR VACATION? HAWAII MIGHT BE NICE
THIS IS THE LIFE. SUN, SURF AND MILES OF SPARKLING WHITE SAND... BOX
KA-BOOM!
HELP! HELP! THE VOLCANO HAS ERUPTED AND MY FATHER'S VILLAGE IS ABOUT TO BE DESTROYED!
YOUR FATHER'S VILLAGE, YOU SAY?
YES, HE IS THE CHIEF. IF YOU COULD SAVE US, HE WOULD GIVE YOU MY HAND IN MARRIAGE. ALL YOU HAVE TO DO IS STOP A MOLTEN LAVA FLOW
YOU'RE CUTE, BUT YOU'RE NOT THAT CUTE

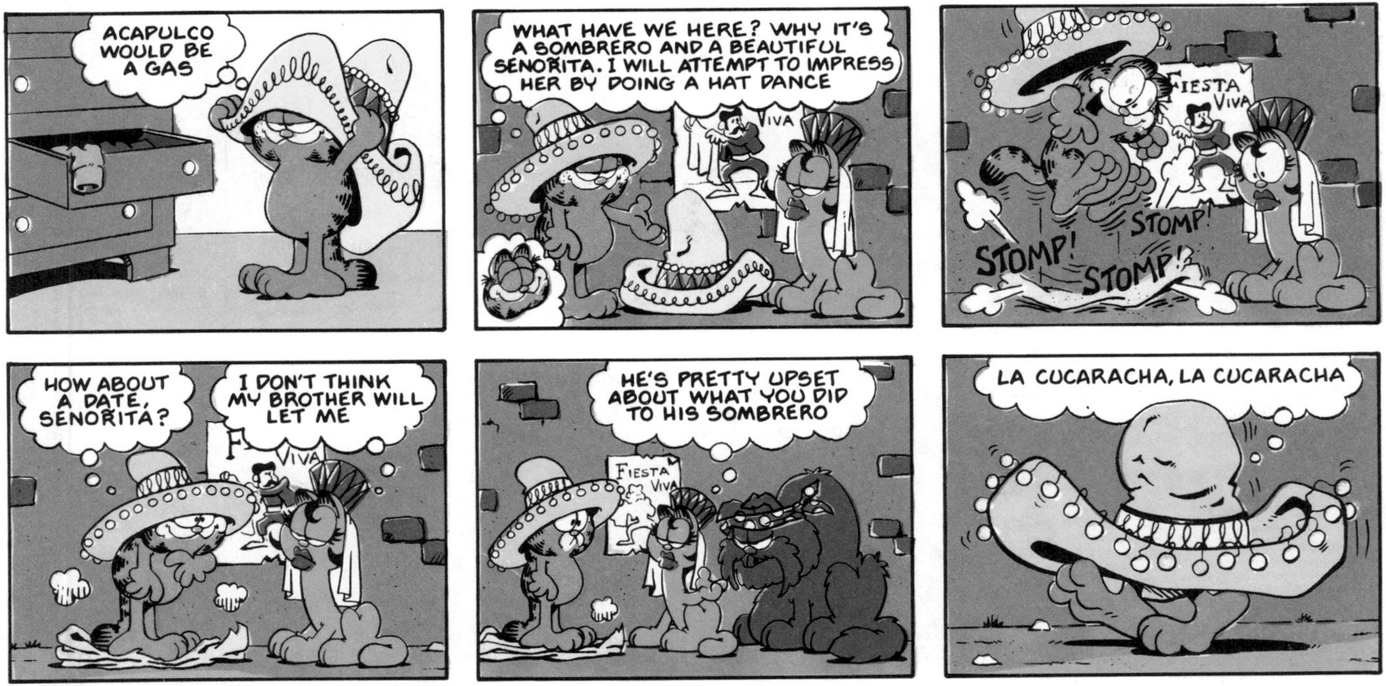
ACAPULCO WOULD BE A GAS
WHAT HAVE WE HERE? WHY IT'S A SOMBRERO AND A BEAUTIFUL SEÑORITA. I WILL ATTEMPT TO IMPRESS HER BY DOING A HAT DANCE
VIVA
FIESTA VIVA
STOMP! STOMP! STOMP!
HOW ABOUT A DATE, SEÑORITA?
I DON'T THINK MY BROTHER WILL LET ME
VIVA
FIESTA VIVA
HE'S PRETTY UPSET ABOUT WHAT YOU DID TO HIS SOMBRERO
LA CUCARACHA, LA CUCARACHA

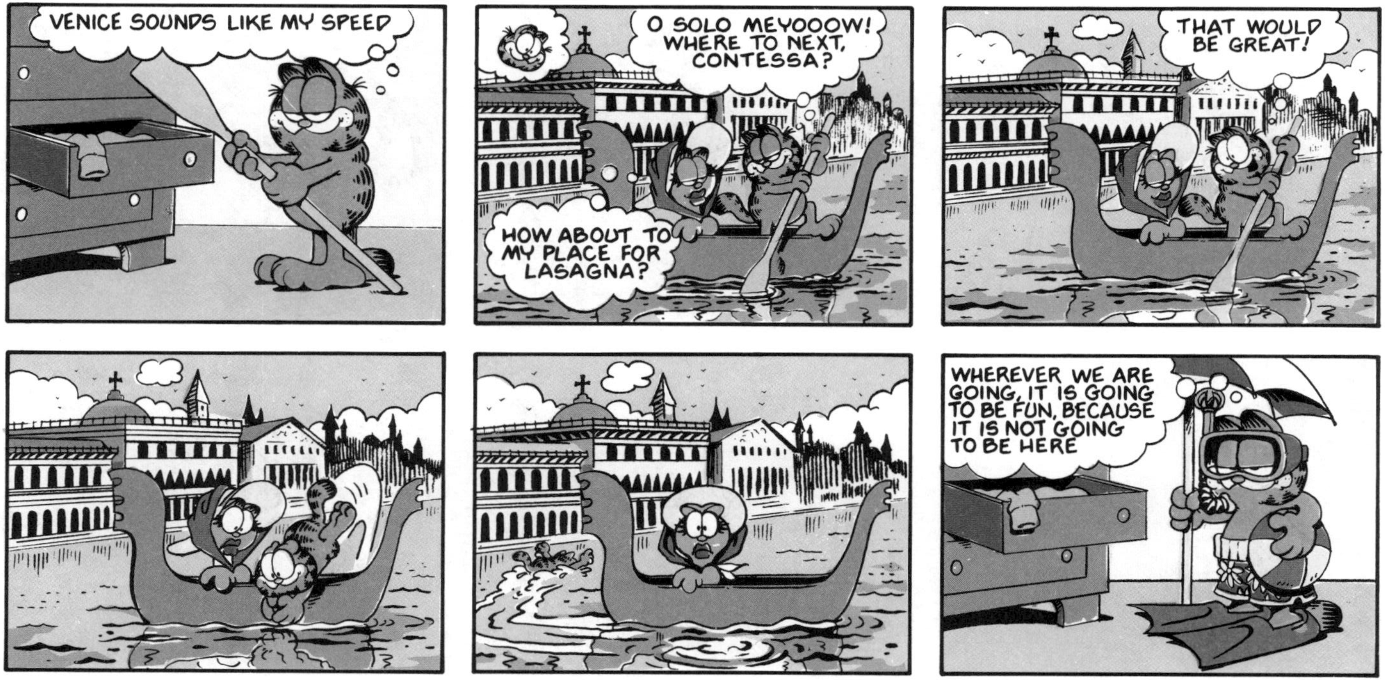
VENICE SOUNDS LIKE MY SPEED
O SOLO MEYOOOW! WHERE TO NEXT, CONTESSA?
HOW ABOUT TO MY PLACE FOR LASAGNA?
THAT WOULD BE GREAT!
WHEREVER WE ARE GOING, IT IS GOING TO BE FUN, BECAUSE IT IS NOT GOING TO BE HERE

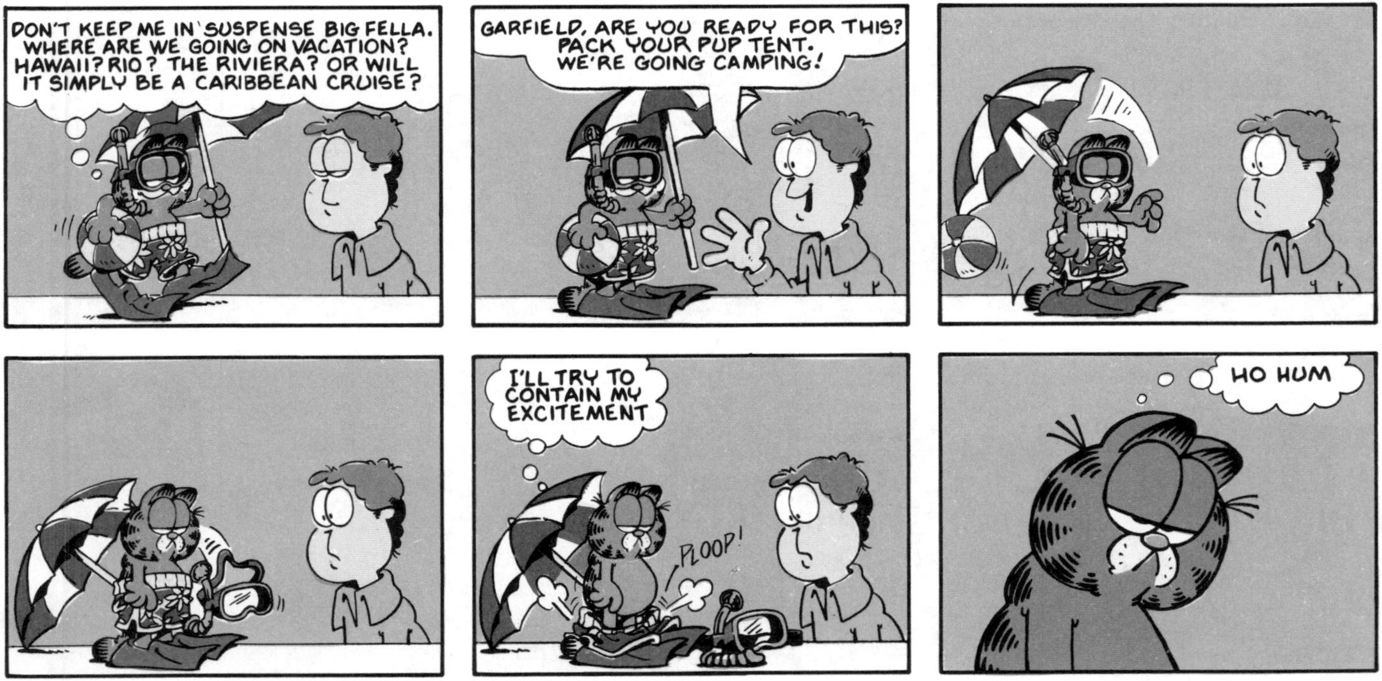
DON'T KEEP ME IN SUSPENSE BIG FELLA. WHERE ARE WE GOING ON VACATION? HAWAII? RIO? THE RIVIERA? OR WILL IT SIMPLY BE A CARIBBEAN CRUISE?
GARFIELD, ARE YOU READY FOR THIS? PACK YOUR PUP TENT. WE'RE GOING CAMPING!
I'LL TRY TO CONTAIN MY EXCITEMENT
PLOOP!
HO HUM

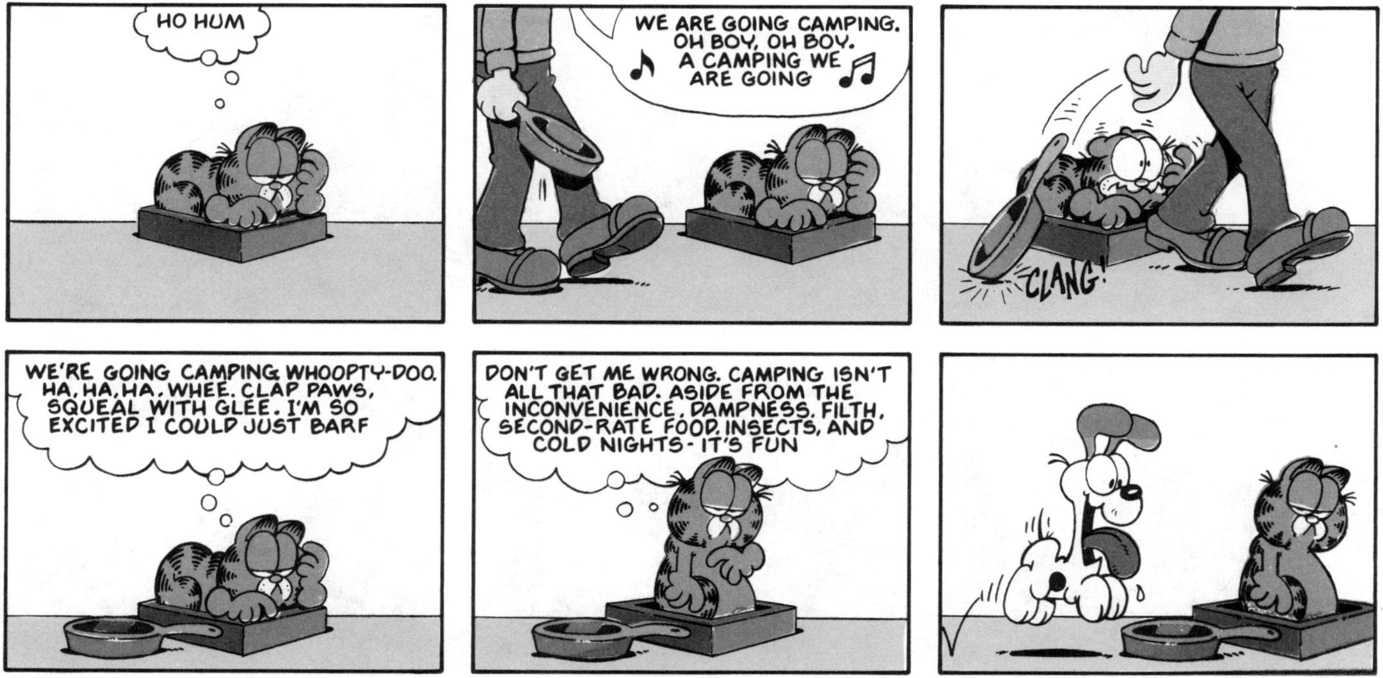
HO HUM
WE ARE GOING CAMPING. OH BOY, OH BOY. A CAMPING WE ARE GOING
CLANG!
WE'RE GOING CAMPING. WHOOPTY-DOO. HA, HA, HA, WHEE. CLAP PAWS, SQUEAL WITH GLEE. I'M SO EXCITED I COULD JUST BARF
DON'T GET ME WRONG. CAMPING ISN'T ALL THAT BAD. ASIDE FROM THE INCONVENIENCE, DAMPNESS, FILTH, SECOND-RATE FOOD, INSECTS, AND COLD NIGHTS - IT'S FUN

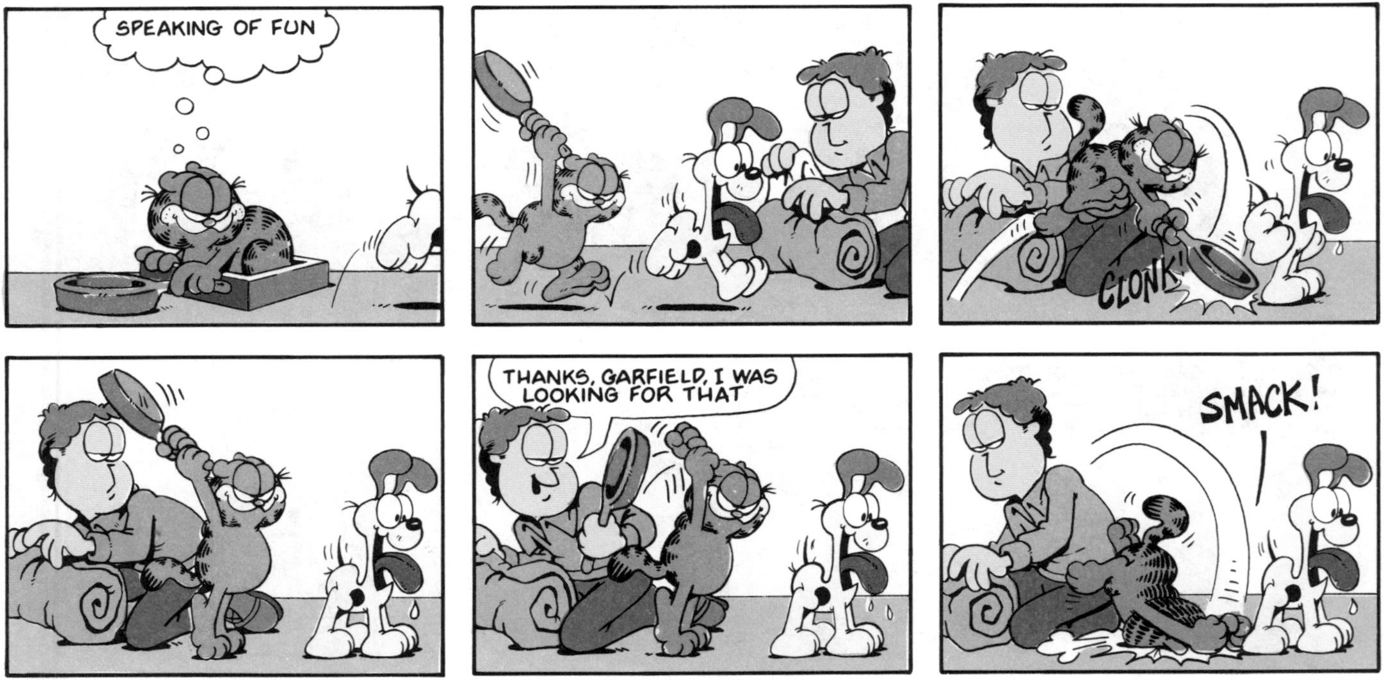
SPEAKING OF FUN
CLONK!
THANKS, GARFIELD, I WAS LOOKING FOR THAT
SMACK!

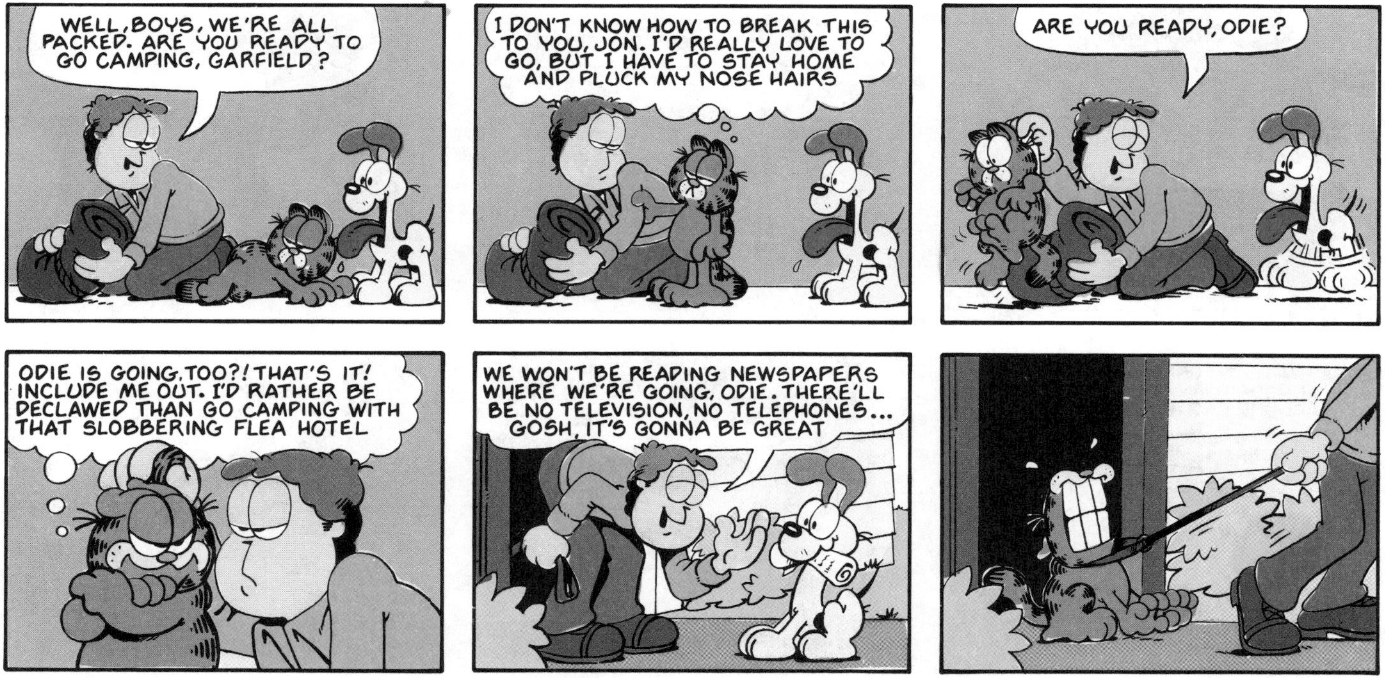
WELL, BOYS, WE'RE ALL PACKED. ARE YOU READY TO GO CAMPING, GARFIELD?
I DON'T KNOW HOW TO BREAK THIS TO YOU, JON. I'D REALLY LOVE TO GO, BUT I HAVE TO STAY HOME AND PLUCK MY NOSE HAIRS
ARE YOU READY, ODIE?
ODIE IS GOING, TOO?! THAT'S IT! INCLUDE ME OUT. I'D RATHER BE DECLAWED THAN GO CAMPING WITH THAT SLOBBERING FLEA HOTEL
WE WON'T BE READING NEWSPAPERS WHERE WE'RE GOING, ODIE. THERE'LL BE NO TELEVISION, NO TELEPHONES... GOSH, IT'S GONNA BE GREAT

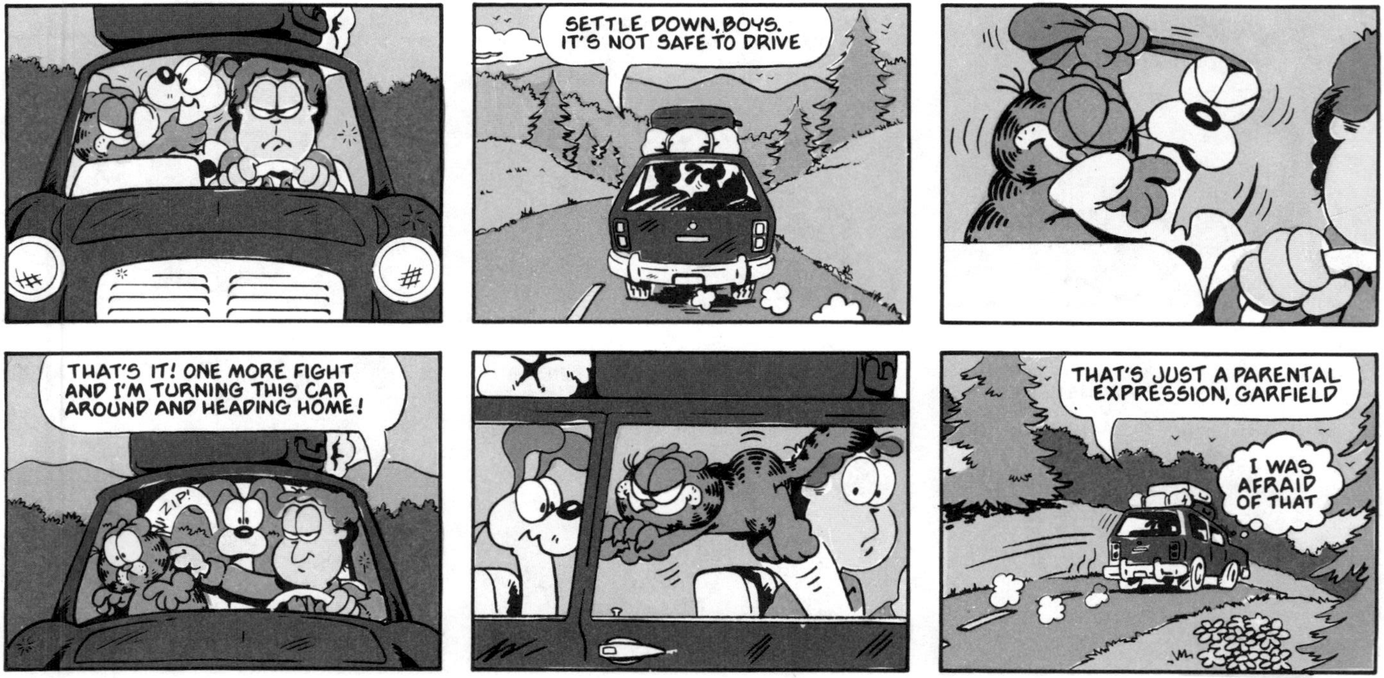
SETTLE DOWN, BOYS. IT'S NOT SAFE TO DRIVE
THAT'S IT! ONE MORE FIGHT AND I'M TURNING THIS CAR AROUND AND HEADING HOME!
ZIP!
THAT'S JUST A PARENTAL EXPRESSION, GARFIELD
I WAS AFRAID OF THAT

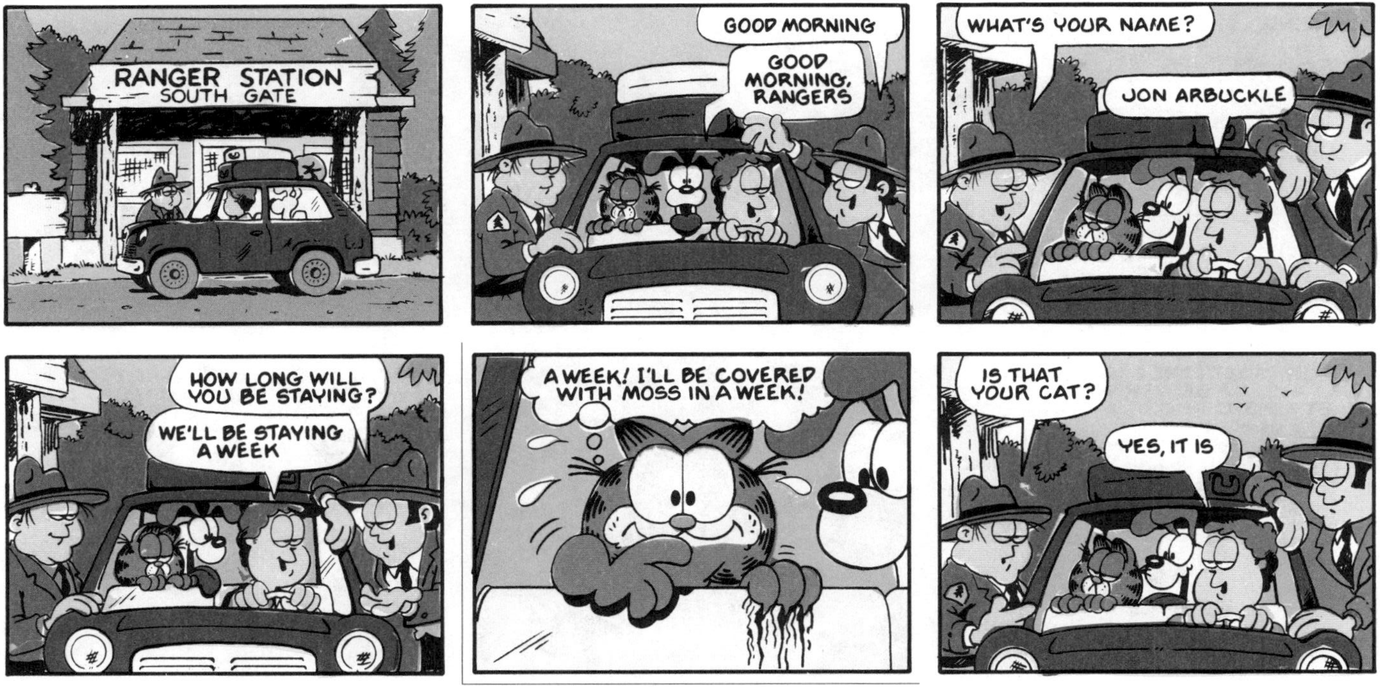
RANGER STATION
SOUTH GATE
GOOD MORNING
GOOD MORNING, RANGERS
WHAT'S YOUR NAME?
JON ARBUCKLE
HOW LONG WILL YOU BE STAYING?
WE'LL BE STAYING A WEEK
A WEEK! I'LL BE COVERED WITH MOSS IN A WEEK!
IS THAT YOUR CAT?
YES, IT IS

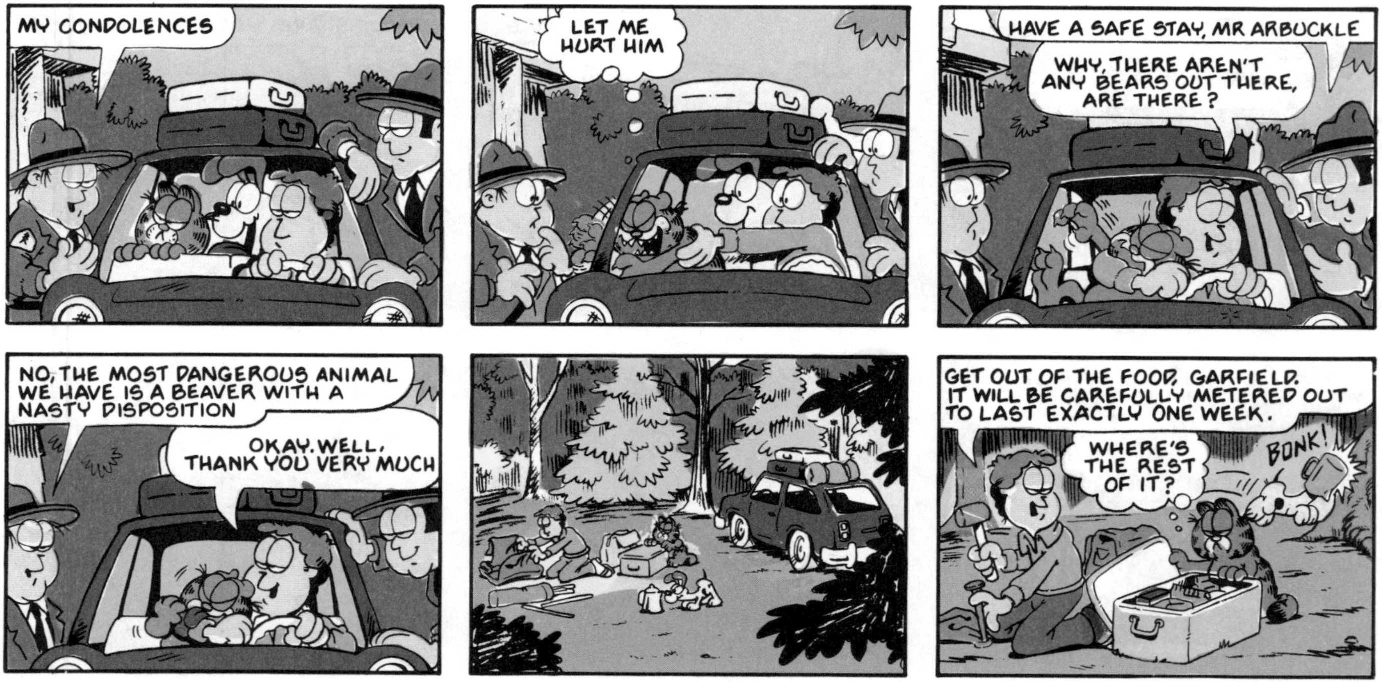
MY CONDOLENCES
LET ME HURT HIM
HAVE A SAFE STAY, MR ARBUCKLE
WHY, THERE AREN'T ANY BEARS OUT THERE, ARE THERE?
NO, THE MOST DANGEROUS ANIMAL WE HAVE IS A BEAVER WITH A NASTY DISPOSITION
OKAY. WELL, THANK YOU VERY MUCH
GET OUT OF THE FOOD, GARFIELD. IT WILL BE CAREFULLY METERED OUT TO LAST EXACTLY ONE WEEK.
WHERE'S THE REST OF IT?
BONK!

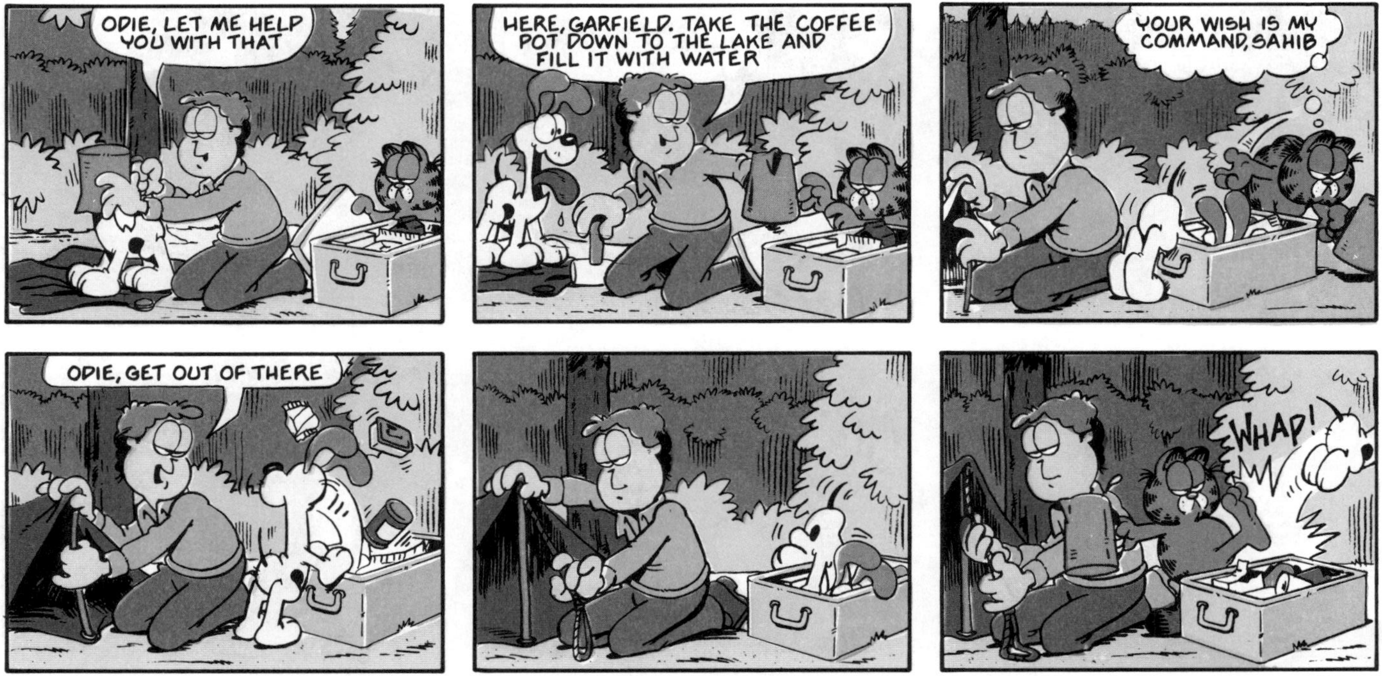
ODIE, LET ME HELP YOU WITH THAT
HERE, GARFIELD. TAKE THE COFFEE POT DOWN TO THE LAKE AND FILL IT WITH WATER
YOUR WISH IS MY COMMAND, SAHIB
ODIE, GET OUT OF THERE
WHAP!

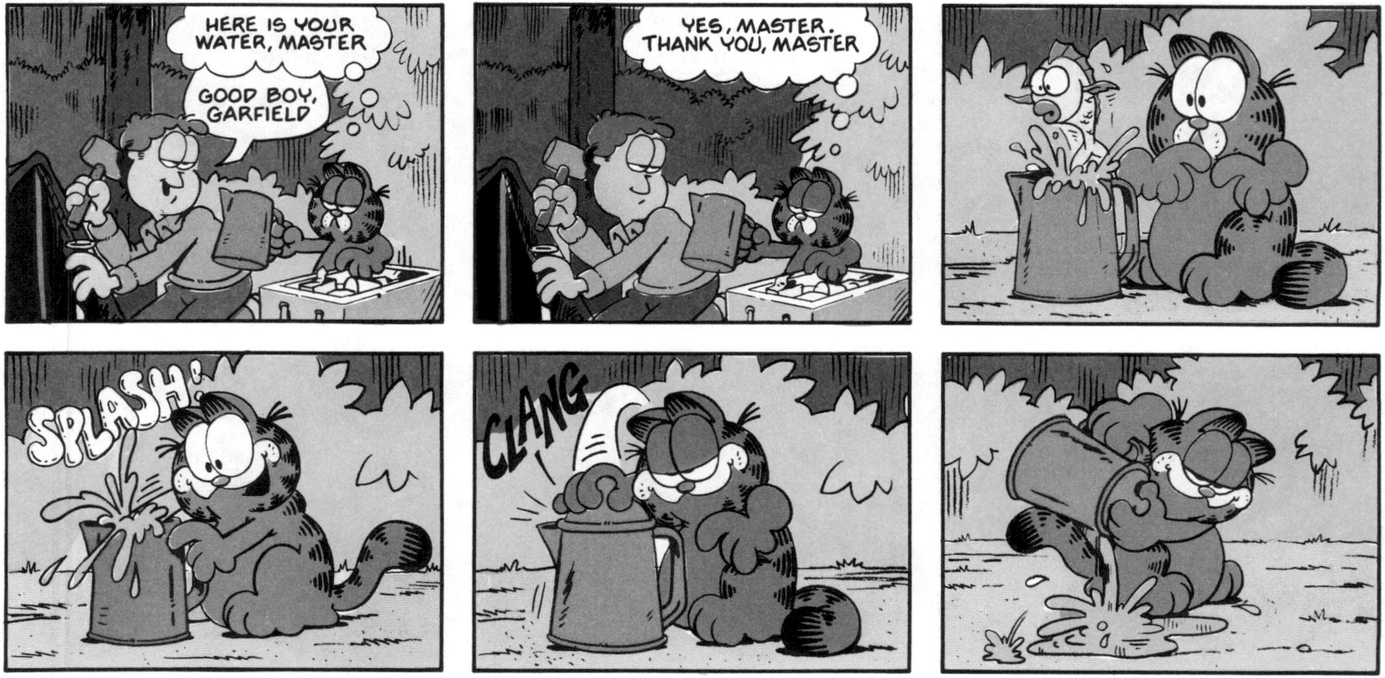
HERE IS YOUR WATER, MASTER
GOOD BOY, GARFIELD
YES, MASTER. THANK YOU, MASTER
SPLASH!
CLANG

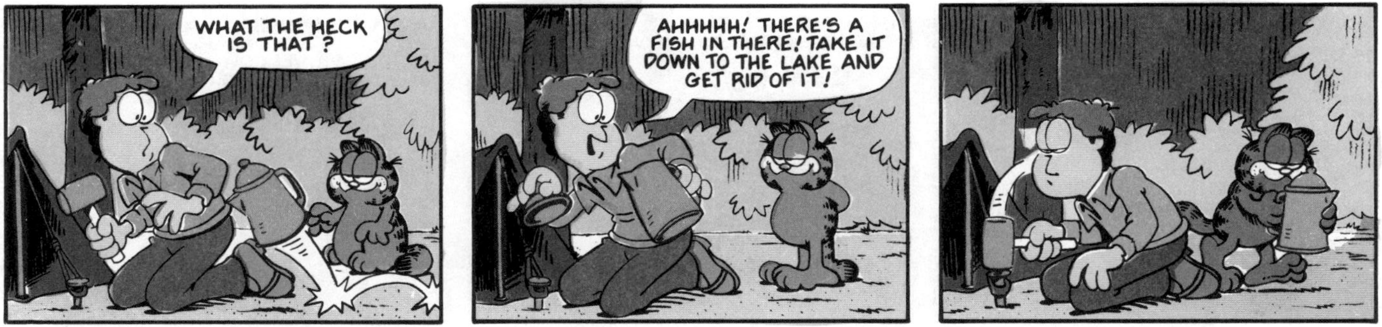
WHAT THE HECK IS THAT ?
AHHHHH! THERE'S A FISH IN THERE! TAKE IT DOWN TO THE LAKE AND GET RID OF IT!
THAT DIDN'T TAKE LONG
THE LAKE ISN'T (BURP) FAR

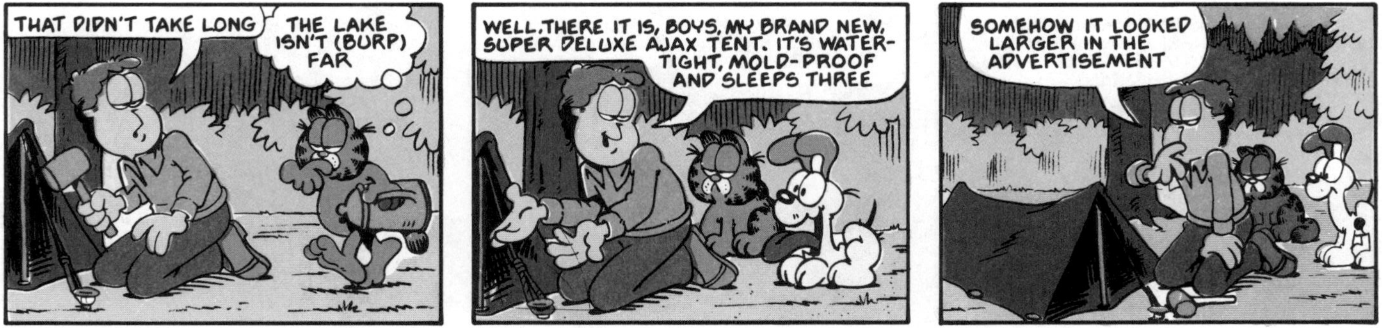
WELL, THERE IT IS, BOYS, MY BRAND NEW, SUPER DELUXE AJAX TENT. IT'S WATER-TIGHT, MOLD-PROOF AND SLEEPS THREE
SOMEHOW IT LOOKED LARGER IN THE ADVERTISEMENT

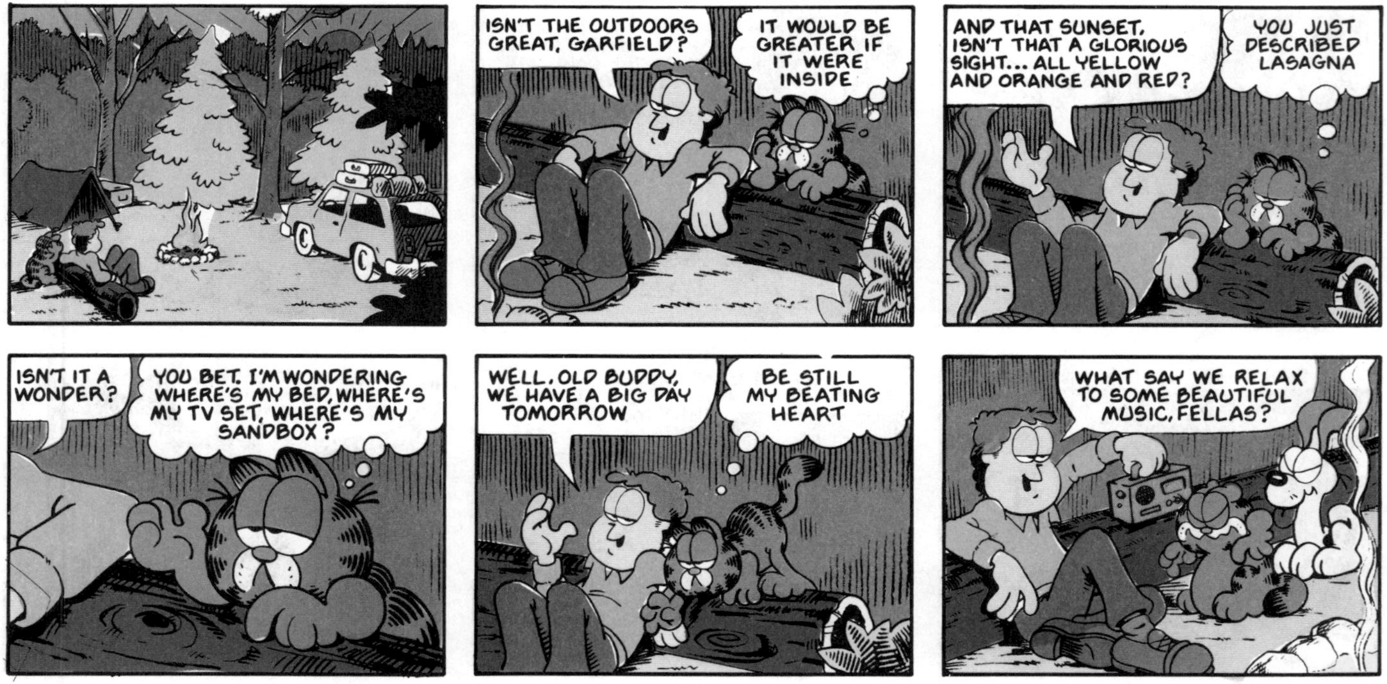
ISN'T THE OUTDOORS GREAT, GARFIELD?
IT WOULD BE GREATER IF IT WERE INSIDE
AND THAT SUNSET, ISN'T THAT A GLORIOUS SIGHT... ALL YELLOW AND ORANGE AND RED?
YOU JUST DESCRIBED LASAGNA
ISN'T IT A WONDER?
YOU BET. I'M WONDERING WHERE'S MY BED, WHERE'S MY TV SET, WHERE'S MY SANDBOX?
WELL, OLD BUDDY, WE HAVE A BIG DAY TOMORROW
BE STILL MY BEATING HEART
WHAT SAY WE RELAX TO SOME BEAUTIFUL MUSIC, FELLAS?

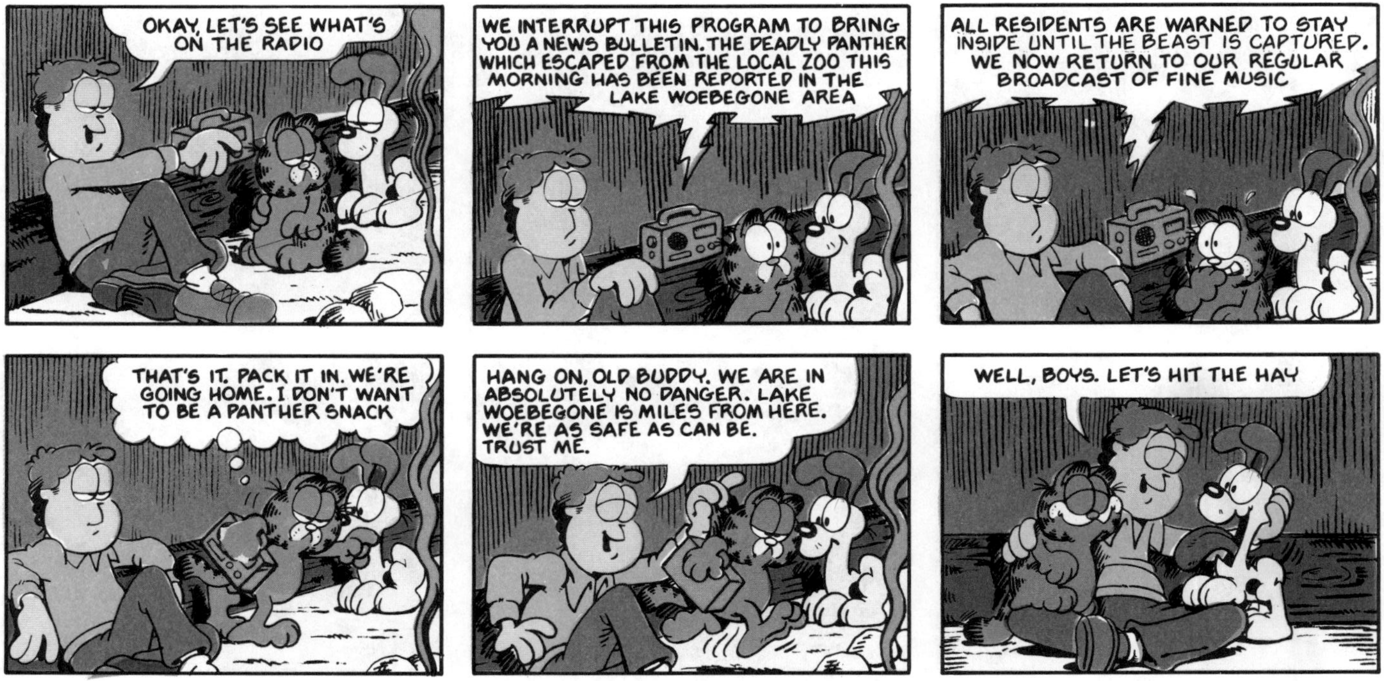
OKAY, LET'S SEE WHAT'S ON THE RADIO
WE INTERRUPT THIS PROGRAM TO BRING YOU A NEWS BULLETIN. THE DEADLY PANTHER WHICH ESCAPED FROM THE LOCAL ZOO THIS MORNING HAS BEEN REPORTED IN THE LAKE WOEBEGONE AREA
ALL RESIDENTS ARE WARNED TO STAY INSIDE UNTIL THE BEAST IS CAPTURED. WE NOW RETURN TO OUR REGULAR BROADCAST OF FINE MUSIC
THAT'S IT. PACK IT IN. WE'RE GOING HOME. I DON'T WANT TO BE A PANTHER SNACK
HANG ON, OLD BUDDY. WE ARE IN ABSOLUTELY NO DANGER. LAKE WOEBEGONE IS MILES FROM HERE. WE'RE AS SAFE AS CAN BE. TRUST ME.
WELL, BOYS. LET'S HIT THE HAY

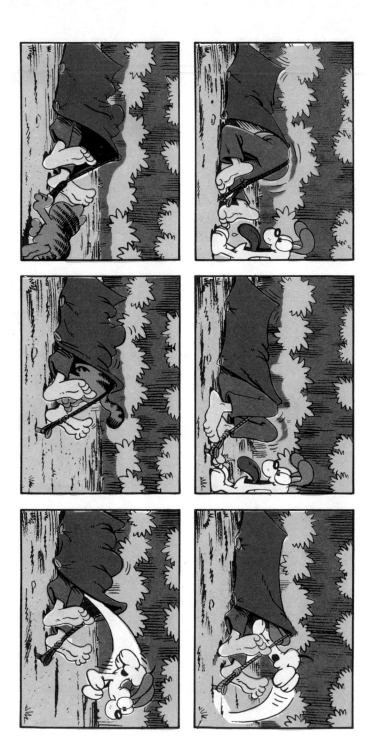

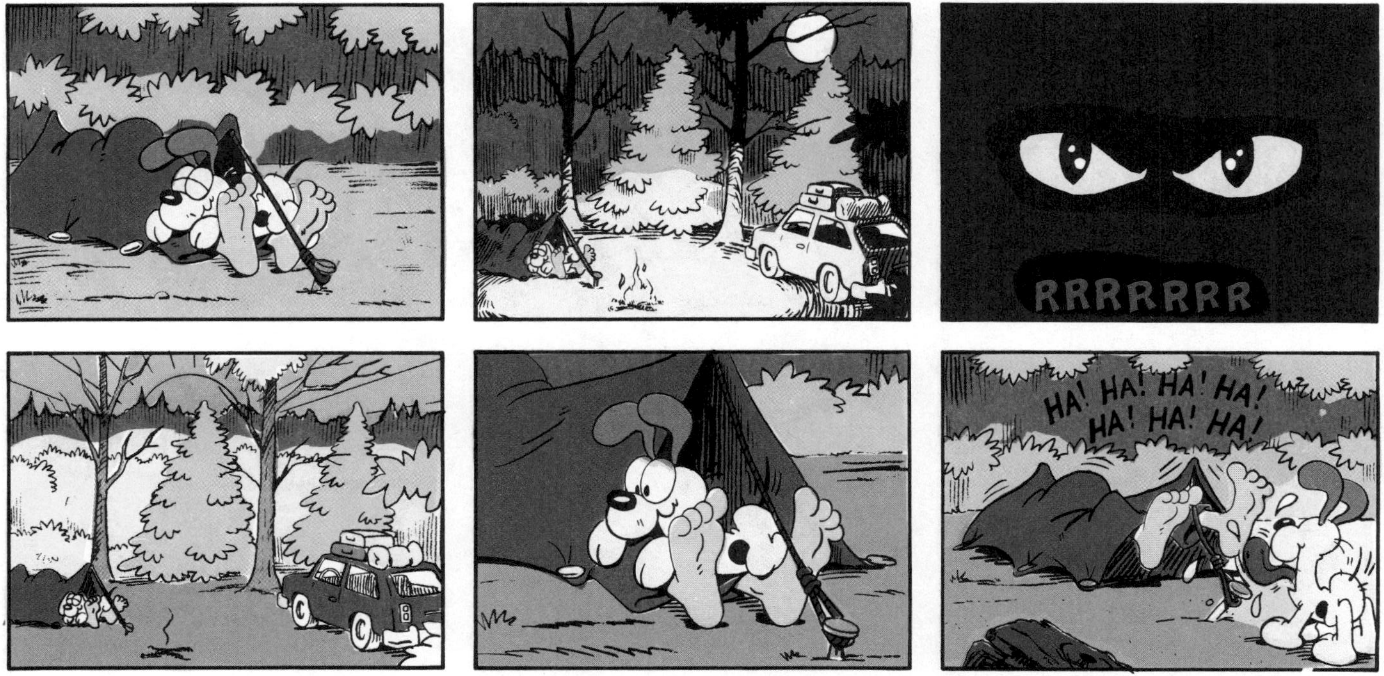
RRRRRRR
HA! HA! HA! HA!
HA! HA! HA!

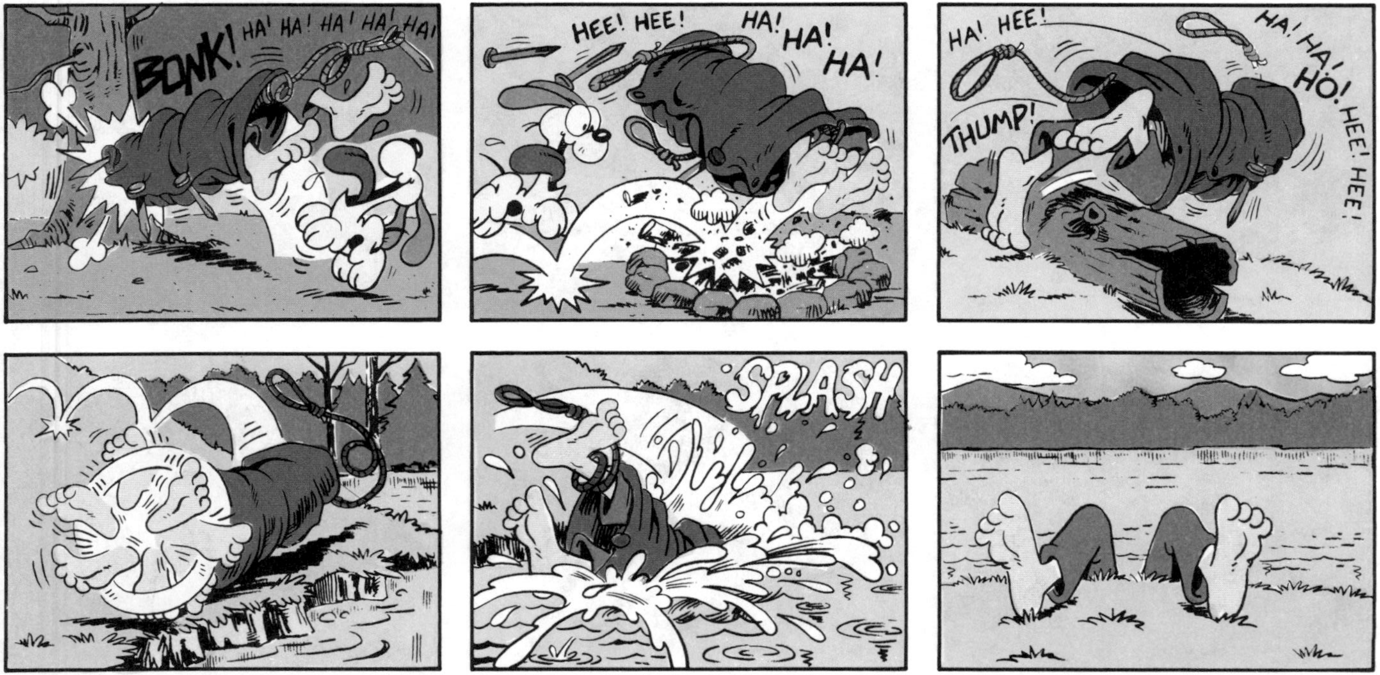
BONK!
HA! HA! HA! HA! HA!
HEE! HEE!
HA! HA! HA!
HA! HEE!
THUMP!
HA! HA! HO! HEE! HEE!
SPLASH

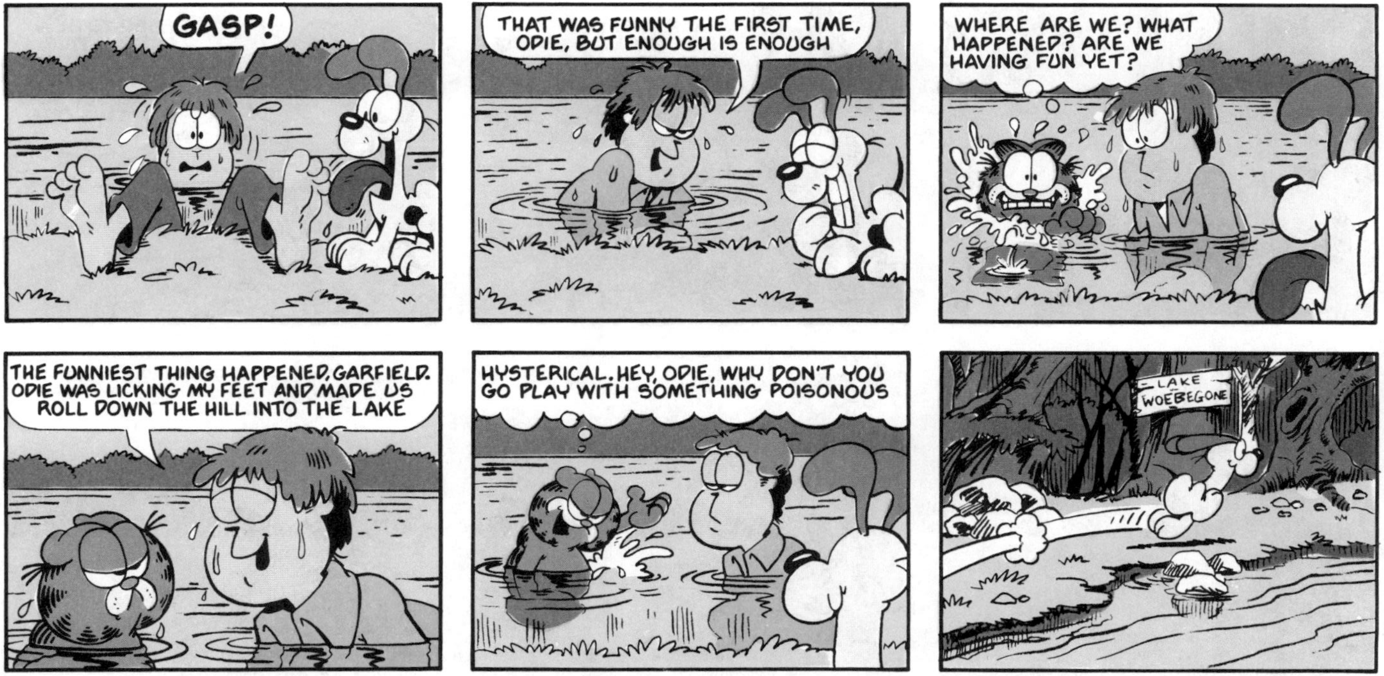
GASP!
THAT WAS FUNNY THE FIRST TIME, ODIE, BUT ENOUGH IS ENOUGH
WHERE ARE WE? WHAT HAPPENED? ARE WE HAVING FUN YET?
THE FUNNIEST THING HAPPENED, GARFIELD. ODIE WAS LICKING MY FEET AND MADE US ROLL DOWN THE HILL INTO THE LAKE
HYSTERICAL. HEY, ODIE, WHY DON'T YOU GO PLAY WITH SOMETHING POISONOUS
LAKE WOEBEGONE

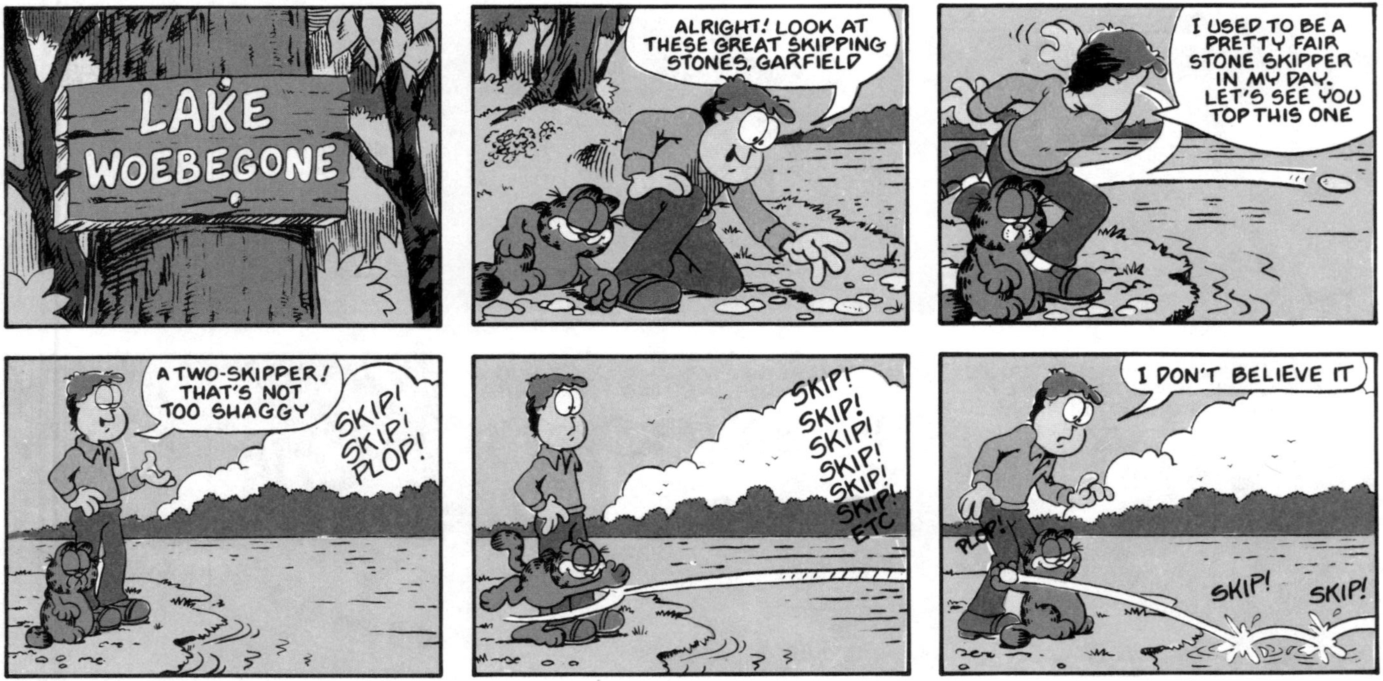
LAKE WOEBEGONE
ALRIGHT! LOOK AT THESE GREAT SKIPPING STONES, GARFIELD
I USED TO BE A PRETTY FAIR STONE SKIPPER IN MY DAY. LET'S SEE YOU TOP THIS ONE
A TWO-SKIPPER! THAT'S NOT TOO SHAGGY
SKIP! SKIP! PLOP!
SKIP! SKIP! SKIP! SKIP! SKIP! SKIP! ETC
I DON'T BELIEVE IT
PLOP!
SKIP!
SKIP!

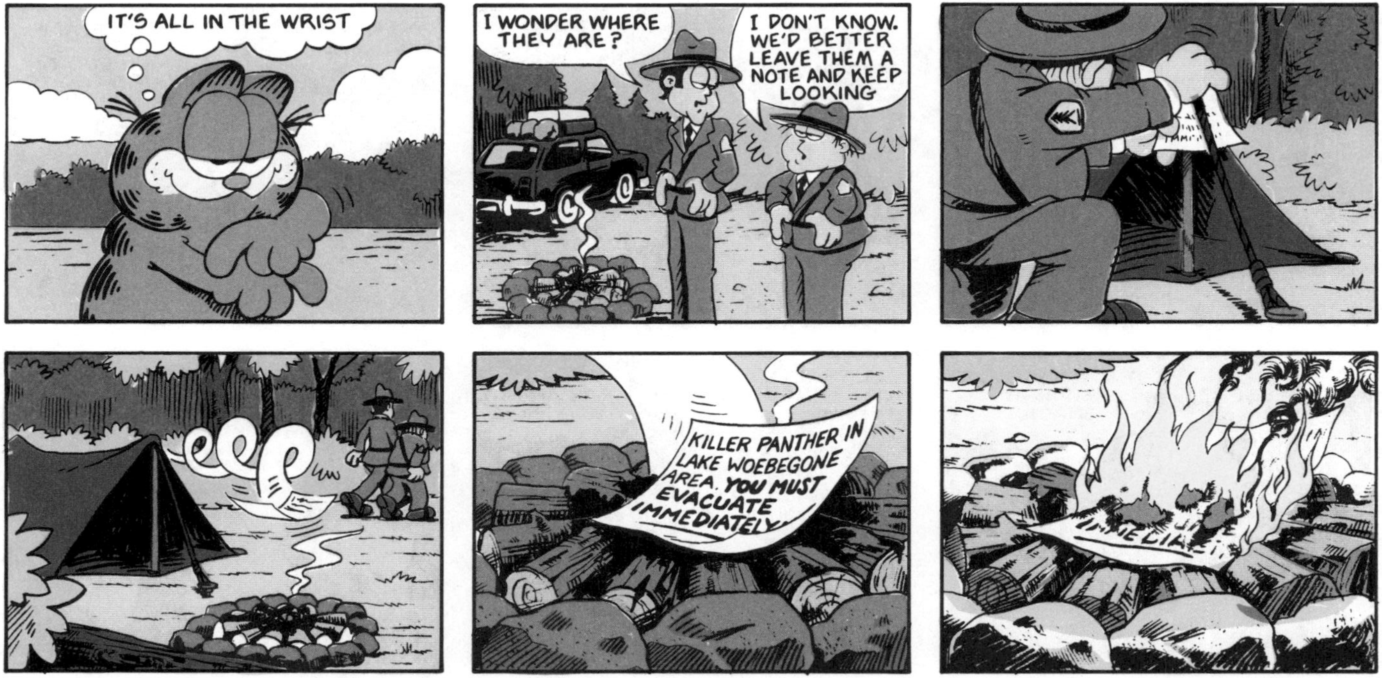
IT'S ALL IN THE WRIST
I WONDER WHERE THEY ARE?
I DON'T KNOW. WE'D BETTER LEAVE THEM A NOTE AND KEEP LOOKING
KILLER PANTHER IN LAKE WOEBEGONE AREA. YOU MUST EVACUATE IMMEDIATELY
IMMEDIA

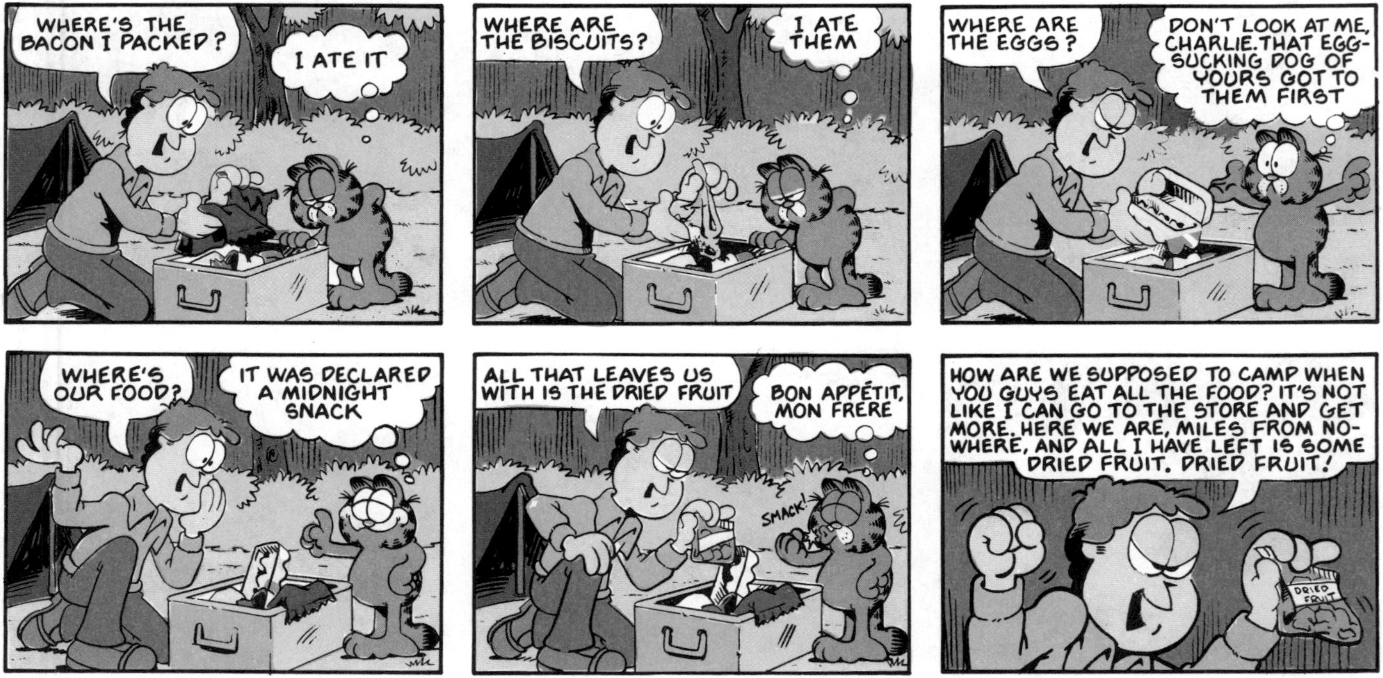
WHERE'S THE BACON I PACKED?
I ATE IT
WHERE ARE THE BISCUITS?
I ATE THEM
WHERE ARE THE EGGS?
DON'T LOOK AT ME, CHARLIE. THAT EGG-SUCKING DOG OF YOURS GOT TO THEM FIRST
WHERE'S OUR FOOD?
IT WAS DECLARED A MIDNIGHT SNACK
ALL THAT LEAVES US WITH IS THE DRIED FRUIT
BON APPÉTIT, MON FRERE
SMACK!
HOW ARE WE SUPPOSED TO CAMP WHEN YOU GUYS EAT ALL THE FOOD? IT'S NOT LIKE I CAN GO TO THE STORE AND GET MORE. HERE WE ARE, MILES FROM NO-WHERE, AND ALL I HAVE LEFT IS SOME DRIED FRUIT. DRIED FRUIT!
DRIED FRUIT

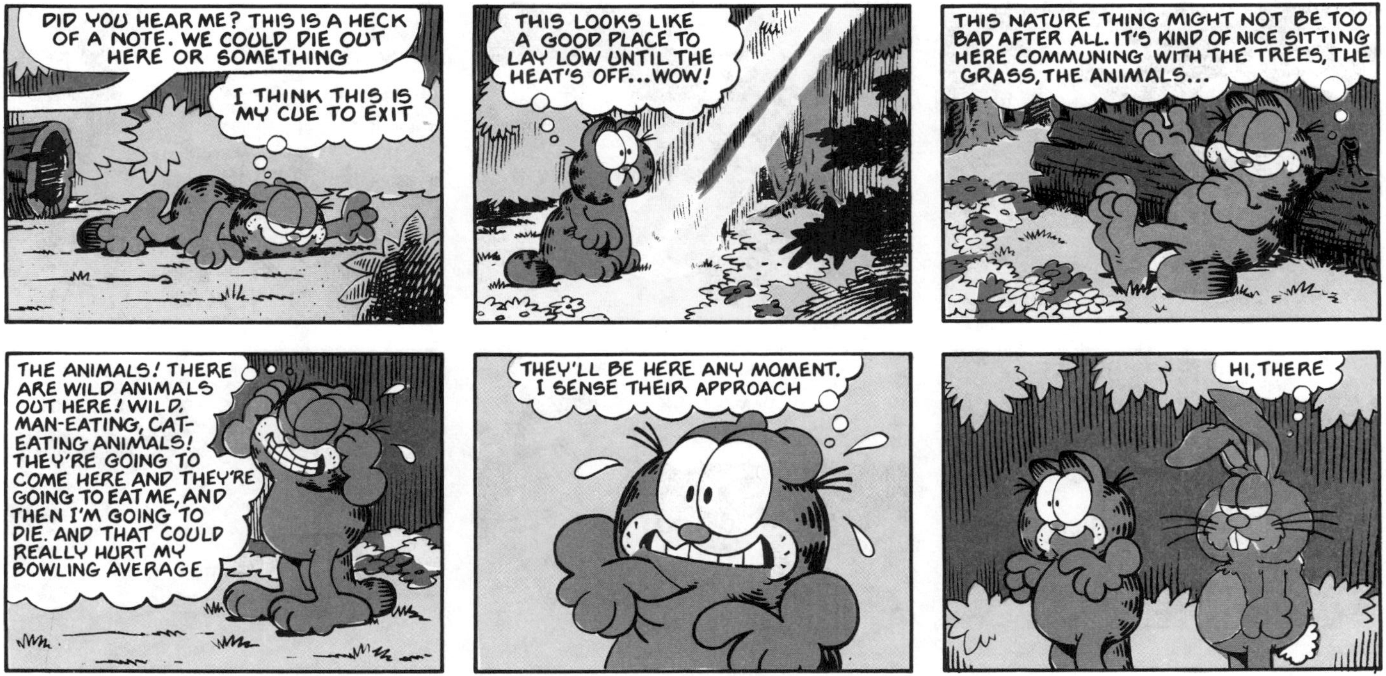
DID YOU HEAR ME? THIS IS A HECK OF A NOTE. WE COULD DIE OUT HERE OR SOMETHING
I THINK THIS IS MY CUE TO EXIT
THIS LOOKS LIKE A GOOD PLACE TO LAY LOW UNTIL THE HEAT'S OFF...WOW!
THIS NATURE THING MIGHT NOT BE TOO BAD AFTER ALL. IT'S KIND OF NICE SITTING HERE COMMUNING WITH THE TREES, THE GRASS, THE ANIMALS...
THE ANIMALS! THERE ARE WILD ANIMALS OUT HERE! WILD, MAN-EATING, CAT-EATING ANIMALS! THEY'RE GOING TO COME HERE AND THEY'RE GOING TO EAT ME, AND THEN I'M GOING TO DIE. AND THAT COULD REALLY HURT MY BOWLING AVERAGE
THEY'LL BE HERE ANY MOMENT. I SENSE THEIR APPROACH
HI, THERE

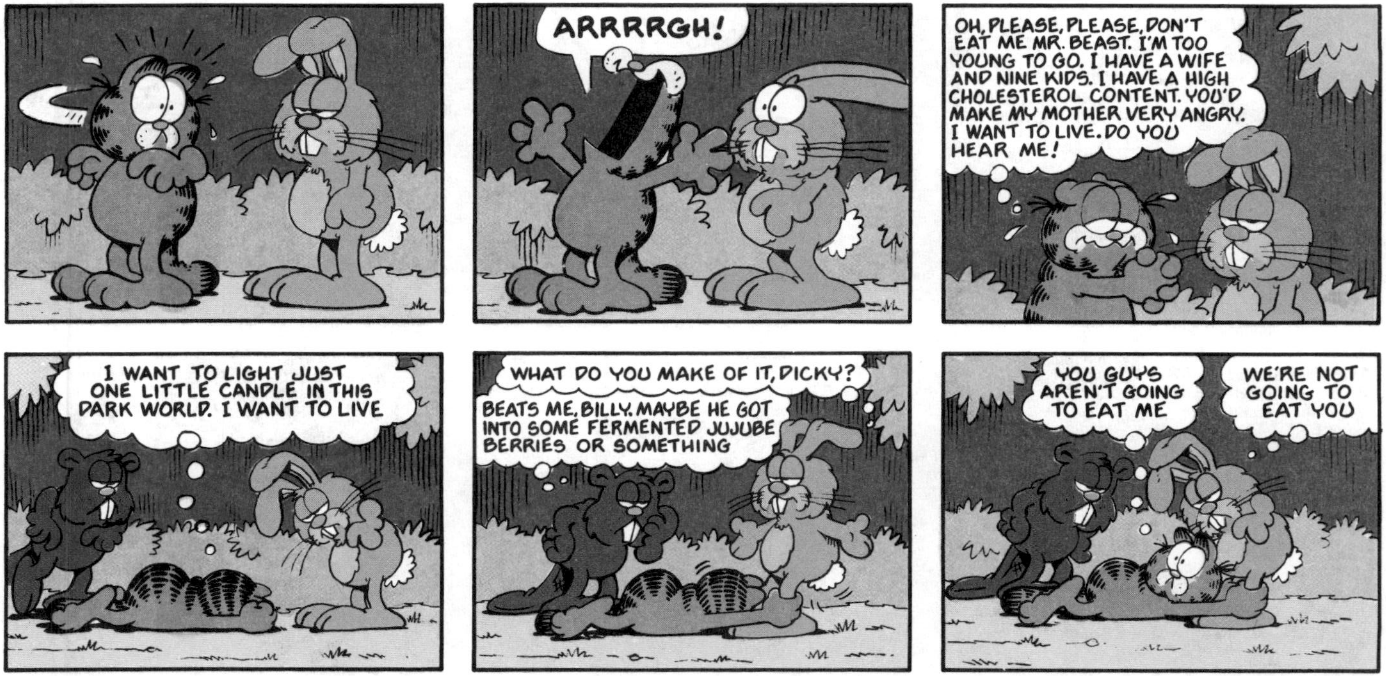
ARRRRGH!
OH, PLEASE, PLEASE, DON'T EAT ME MR. BEAST. I'M TOO YOUNG TO GO. I HAVE A WIFE AND NINE KIDS. I HAVE A HIGH CHOLESTEROL CONTENT. YOU'D MAKE MY MOTHER VERY ANGRY. I WANT TO LIVE. DO YOU HEAR ME!
I WANT TO LIGHT JUST ONE LITTLE CANDLE IN THIS DARK WORLD. I WANT TO LIVE
WHAT DO YOU MAKE OF IT, DICKY?
BEATS ME, BILLY. MAYBE HE GOT INTO SOME FERMENTED JUJUBE BERRIES OR SOMETHING
YOU GUYS AREN'T GOING TO EAT ME
WE'RE NOT GOING TO EAT YOU

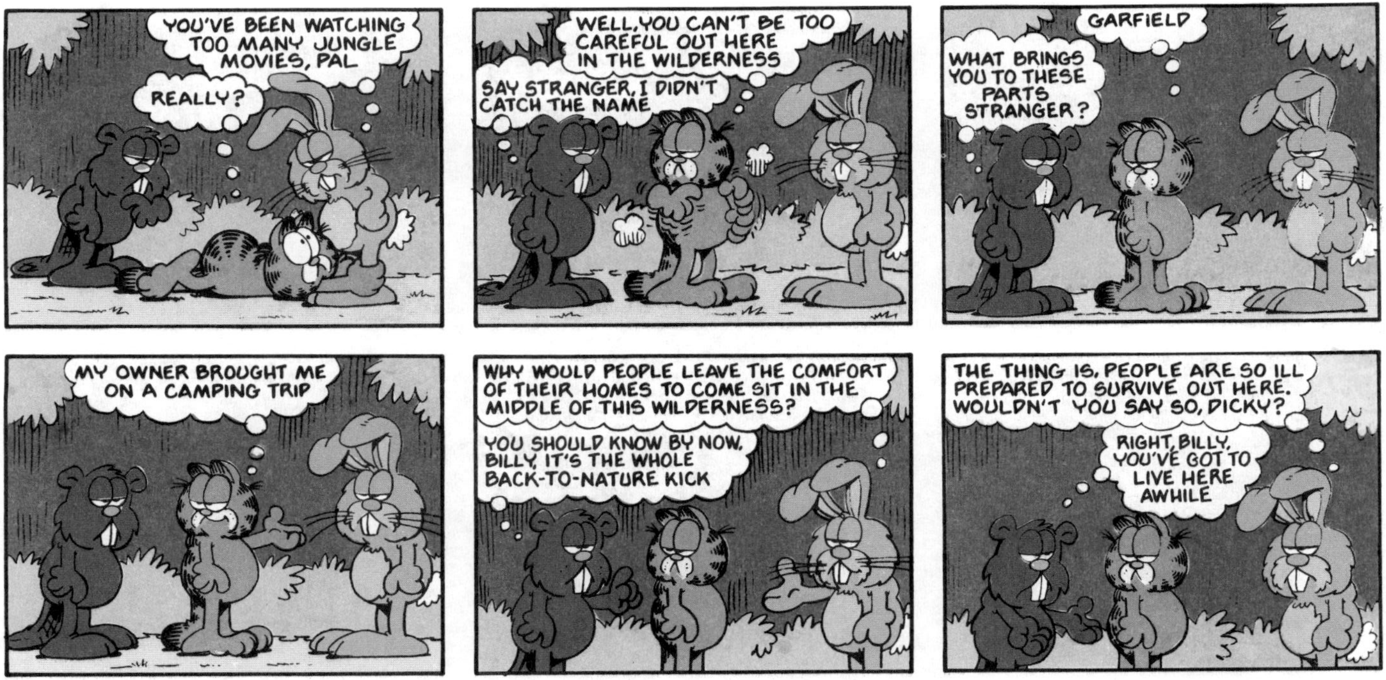
YOU'VE BEEN WATCHING TOO MANY JUNGLE MOVIES, PAL
REALLY?
SAY STRANGER, I DIDN'T CATCH THE NAME
WELL, YOU CAN'T BE TOO CAREFUL OUT HERE IN THE WILDERNESS
WHAT BRINGS YOU TO THESE PARTS STRANGER?
GARFIELD
MY OWNER BROUGHT ME ON A CAMPING TRIP
WHY WOULD PEOPLE LEAVE THE COMFORT OF THEIR HOMES TO COME SIT IN THE MIDDLE OF THIS WILDERNESS?
YOU SHOULD KNOW BY NOW, BILLY, IT'S THE WHOLE BACK-TO-NATURE KICK
THE THING IS, PEOPLE ARE SO ILL PREPARED TO SURVIVE OUT HERE. WOULDN'T YOU SAY SO, DICKY?
RIGHT, BILLY, YOU'VE GOT TO LIVE HERE AWHILE

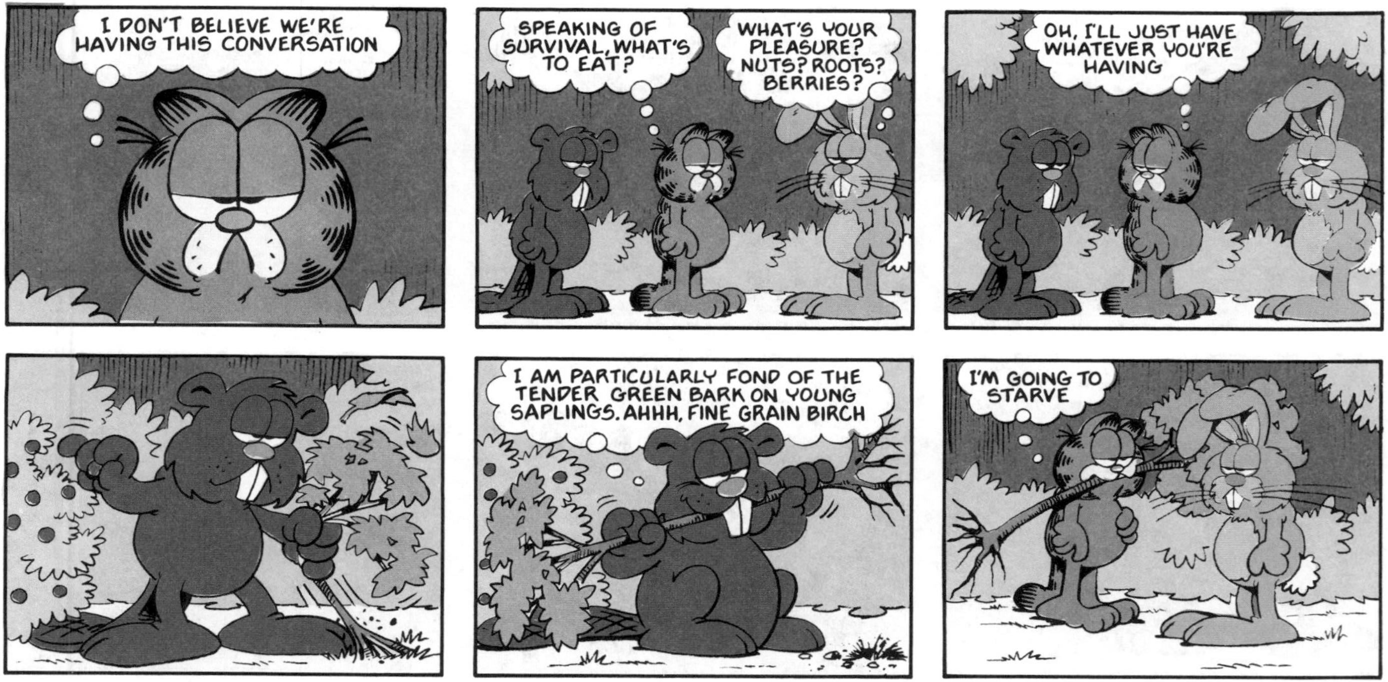
I DON'T BELIEVE WE'RE HAVING THIS CONVERSATION
SPEAKING OF SURVIVAL, WHAT'S TO EAT?
WHAT'S YOUR PLEASURE? NUTS? ROOTS? BERRIES?
OH, I'LL JUST HAVE WHATEVER YOU'RE HAVING
I AM PARTICULARLY FOND OF THE TENDER GREEN BARK ON YOUNG SAPLINGS. AHHH, FINE GRAIN BIRCH
I'M GOING TO STARVE

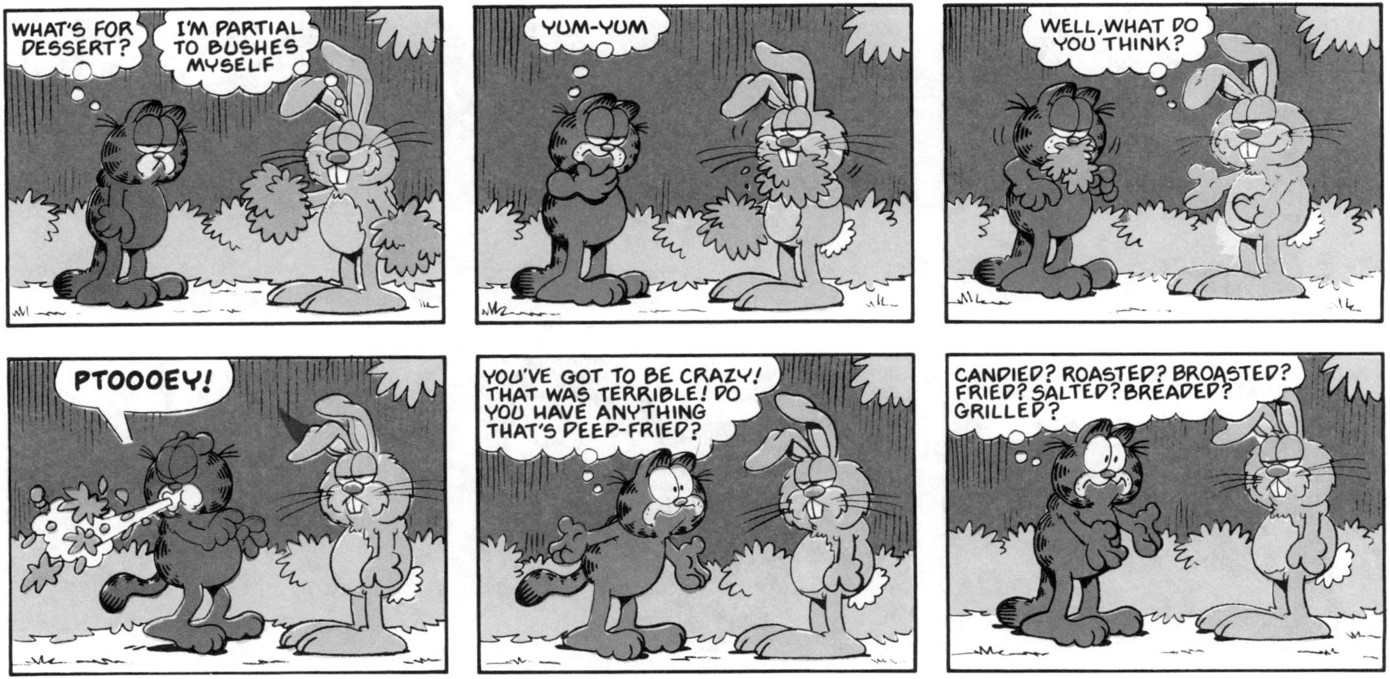
WHAT'S FOR DESSERT?
I'M PARTIAL TO BUSHES MYSELF
YUM-YUM
WELL, WHAT DO YOU THINK?
PTOOOEY!
YOU'VE GOT TO BE CRAZY! THAT WAS TERRIBLE! DO YOU HAVE ANYTHING THAT'S DEEP-FRIED?
CANDIED? ROASTED? BROASTED? FRIED? SALTED? BREADED? GRILLED?

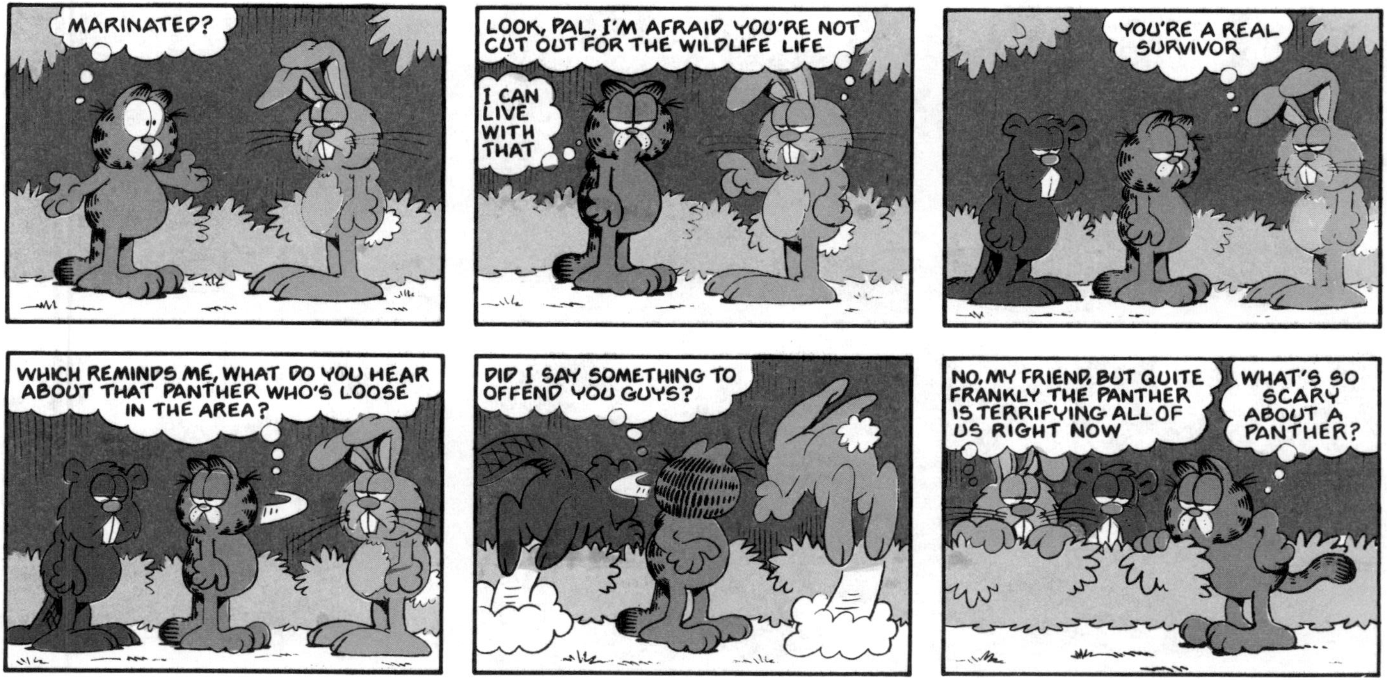
MARINATED?
LOOK, PAL, I'M AFRAID YOU'RE NOT CUT OUT FOR THE WILDLIFE LIFE
I CAN LIVE WITH THAT
YOU'RE A REAL SURVIVOR
WHICH REMINDS ME, WHAT DO YOU HEAR ABOUT THAT PANTHER WHO'S LOOSE IN THE AREA?
DID I SAY SOMETHING TO OFFEND YOU GUYS?
NO, MY FRIEND, BUT QUITE FRANKLY THE PANTHER IS TERRIFYING ALL OF US RIGHT NOW
WHAT'S SO SCARY ABOUT A PANTHER?

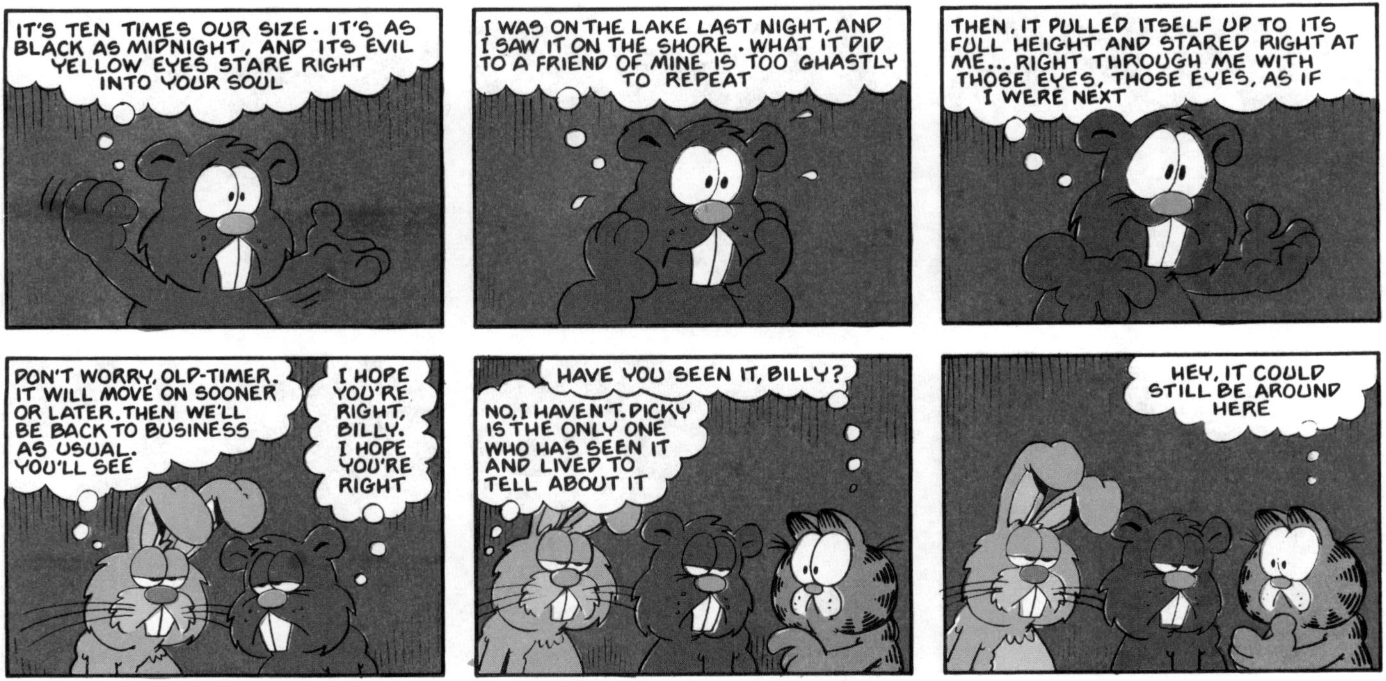
IT'S TEN TIMES OUR SIZE. IT'S AS BLACK AS MIDNIGHT, AND ITS EVIL YELLOW EYES STARE RIGHT INTO YOUR SOUL
I WAS ON THE LAKE LAST NIGHT, AND I SAW IT ON THE SHORE. WHAT IT DID TO A FRIEND OF MINE IS TOO GHASTLY TO REPEAT
THEN, IT PULLED ITSELF UP TO ITS FULL HEIGHT AND STARED RIGHT AT ME... RIGHT THROUGH ME WITH THOSE EYES, THOSE EYES, AS IF I WERE NEXT
DON'T WORRY, OLD-TIMER. IT WILL MOVE ON SOONER OR LATER. THEN WE'LL BE BACK TO BUSINESS AS USUAL. YOU'LL SEE
I HOPE YOU'RE RIGHT, BILLY. I HOPE YOU'RE RIGHT
HAVE YOU SEEN IT, BILLY?
NO, I HAVEN'T. DICKY IS THE ONLY ONE WHO HAS SEEN IT AND LIVED TO TELL ABOUT IT
HEY, IT COULD STILL BE AROUND HERE

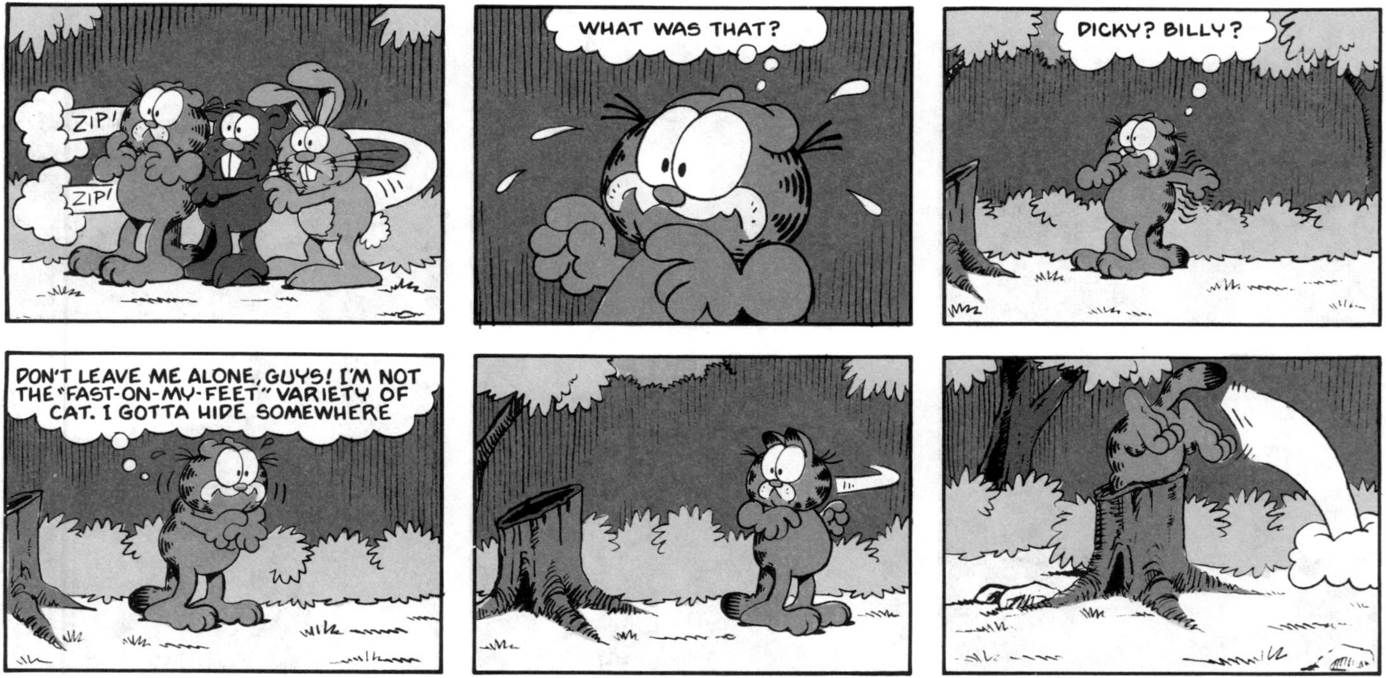
ZIP!
ZIP!
WHAT WAS THAT?
DICKY? BILLY?
DON'T LEAVE ME ALONE, GUYS! I'M NOT THE "FAST-ON-MY-FEET" VARIETY OF CAT. I GOTTA HIDE SOMEWHERE

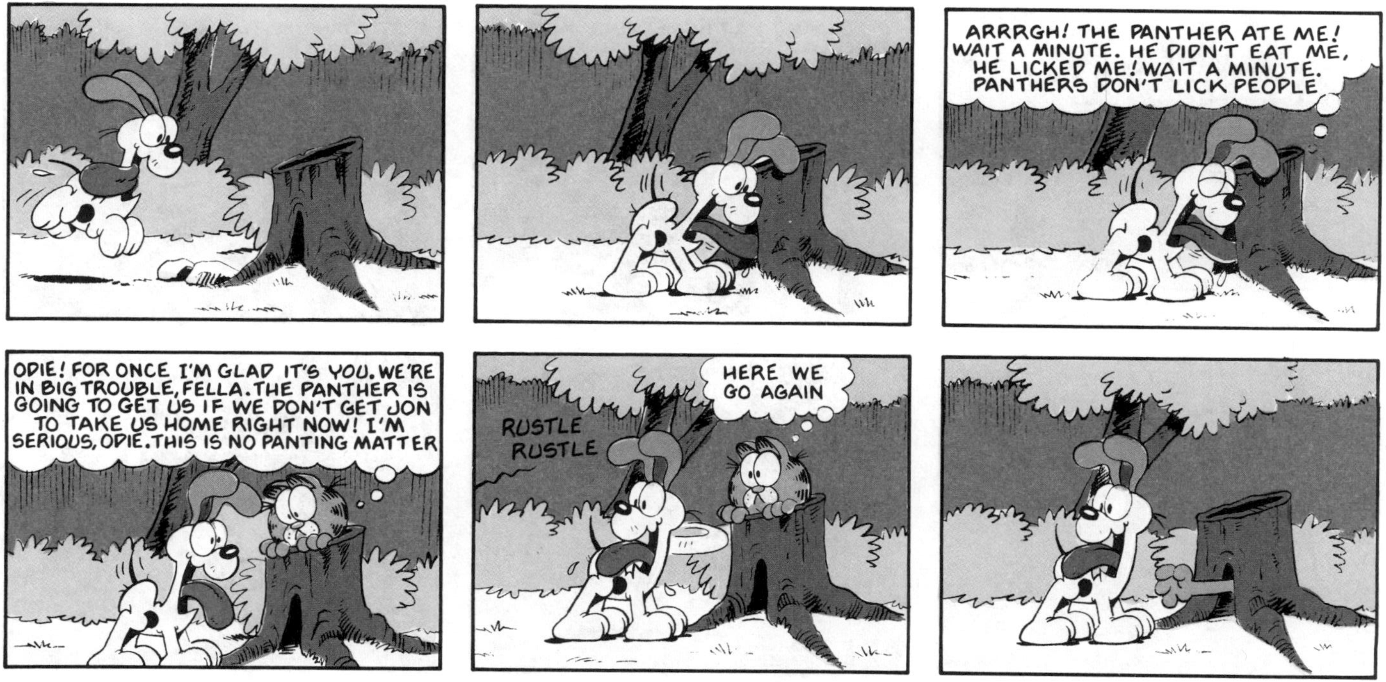
ARRRGH! THE PANTHER ATE ME! WAIT A MINUTE. HE DIDN'T EAT ME, HE LICKED ME! WAIT A MINUTE. PANTHERS DON'T LICK PEOPLE
ODIE! FOR ONCE I'M GLAD IT'S YOU. WE'RE IN BIG TROUBLE, FELLA. THE PANTHER IS GOING TO GET US IF WE DON'T GET JON TO TAKE US HOME RIGHT NOW! I'M SERIOUS, ODIE. THIS IS NO PANTING MATTER
RUSTLE RUSTLE
HERE WE GO AGAIN

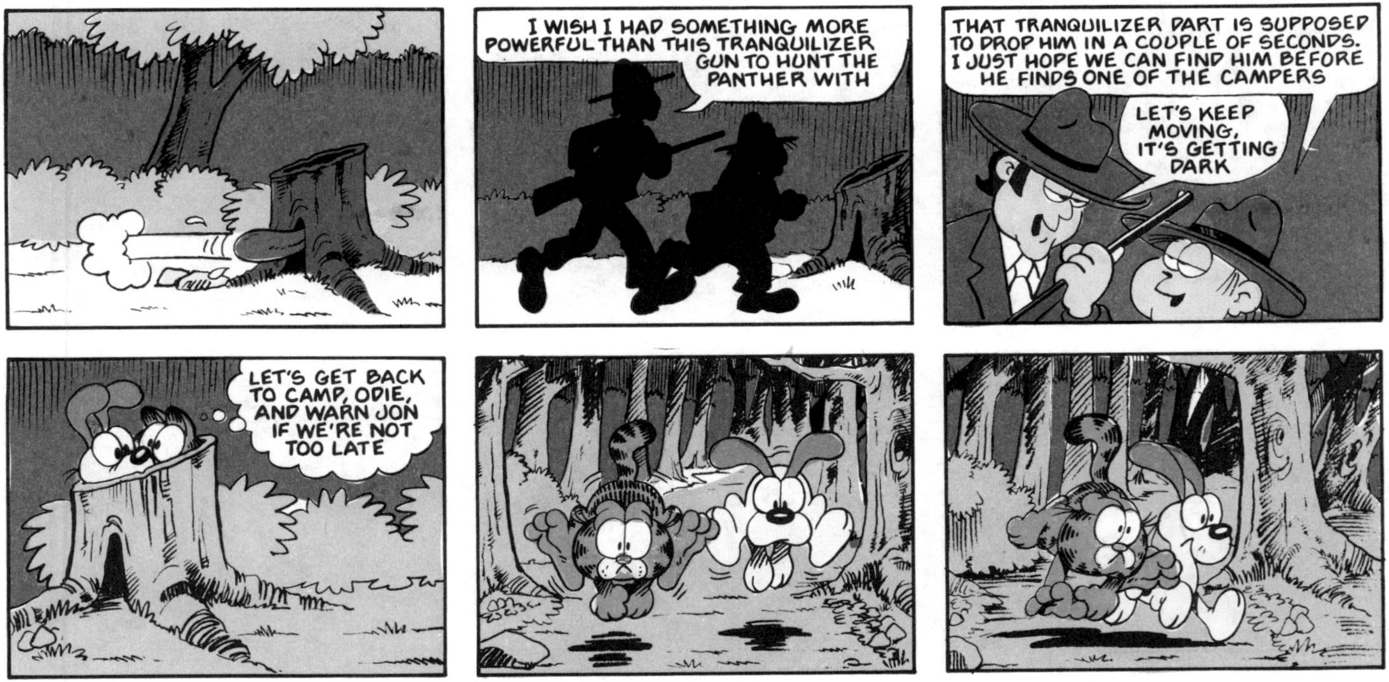
I WISH I HAD SOMETHING MORE POWERFUL THAN THIS TRANQUILIZER GUN TO HUNT THE PANTHER WITH
THAT TRANQUILIZER DART IS SUPPOSED TO DROP HIM IN A COUPLE OF SECONDS. I JUST HOPE WE CAN FIND HIM BEFORE HE FINDS ONE OF THE CAMPERS
LET'S KEEP MOVING, IT'S GETTING DARK
LET'S GET BACK TO CAMP, ODIE, AND WARN JON IF WE'RE NOT TOO LATE

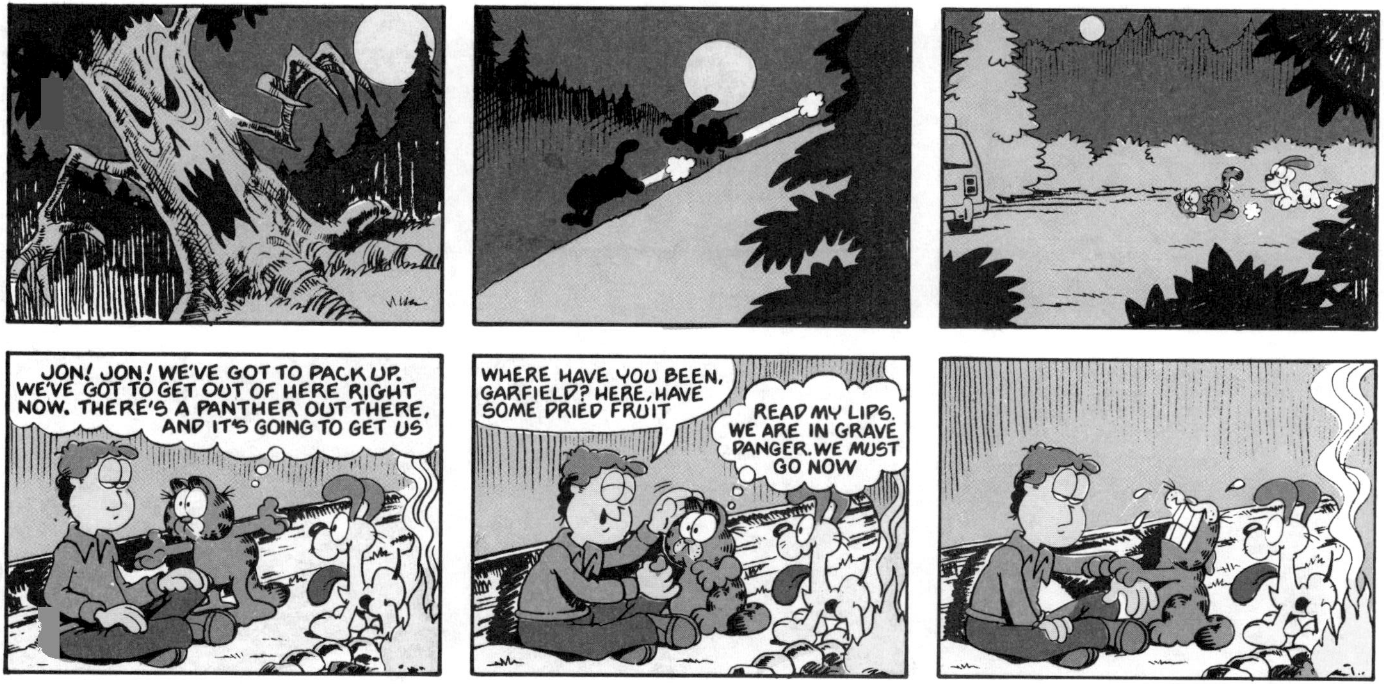

JON! JON! WE'VE GOT TO PACK UP. WE'VE GOT TO GET OUT OF HERE RIGHT NOW. THERE'S A PANTHER OUT THERE, AND IT'S GOING TO GET US
WHERE HAVE YOU BEEN, GARFIELD? HERE, HAVE SOME DRIED FRUIT
READ MY LIPS. WE ARE IN GRAVE DANGER. WE MUST GO NOW

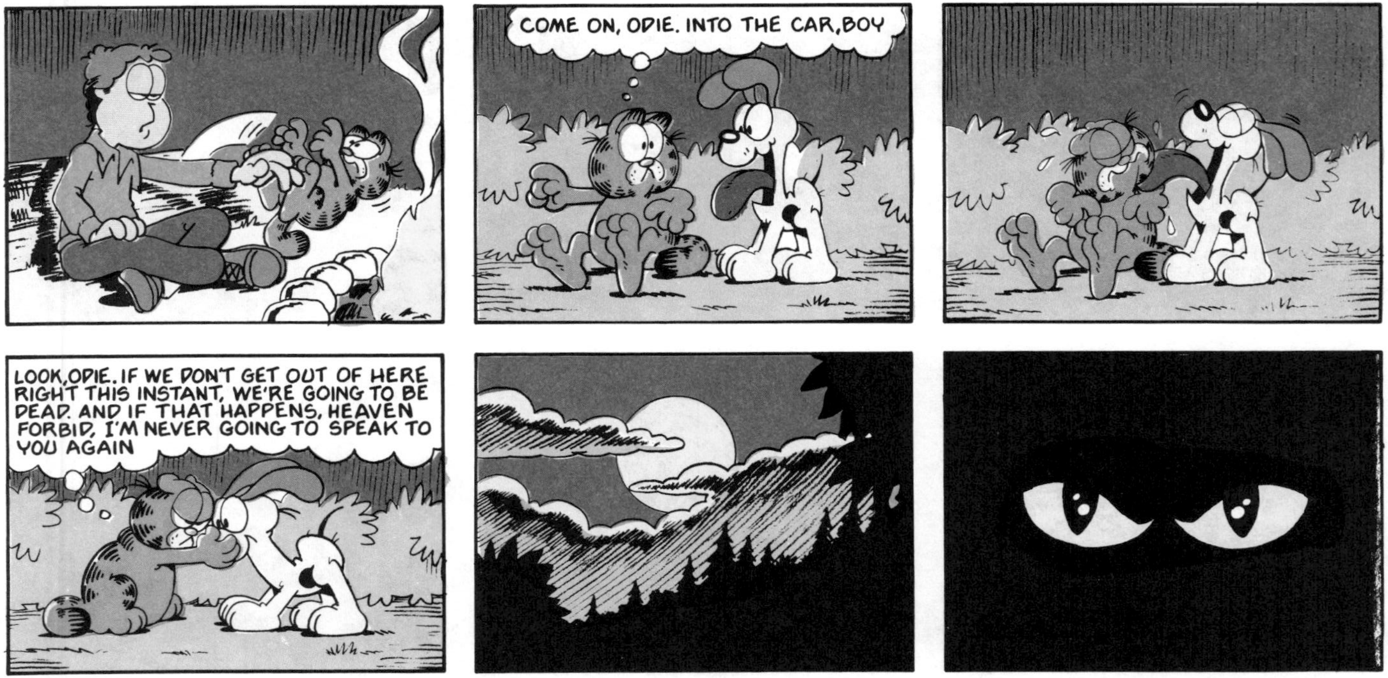
COME ON, ODIE. INTO THE CAR, BOY
LOOK, ODIE. IF WE DON'T GET OUT OF HERE RIGHT THIS INSTANT, WE'RE GOING TO BE DEAD. AND IF THAT HAPPENS, HEAVEN FORBID, I'M NEVER GOING TO SPEAK TO YOU AGAIN

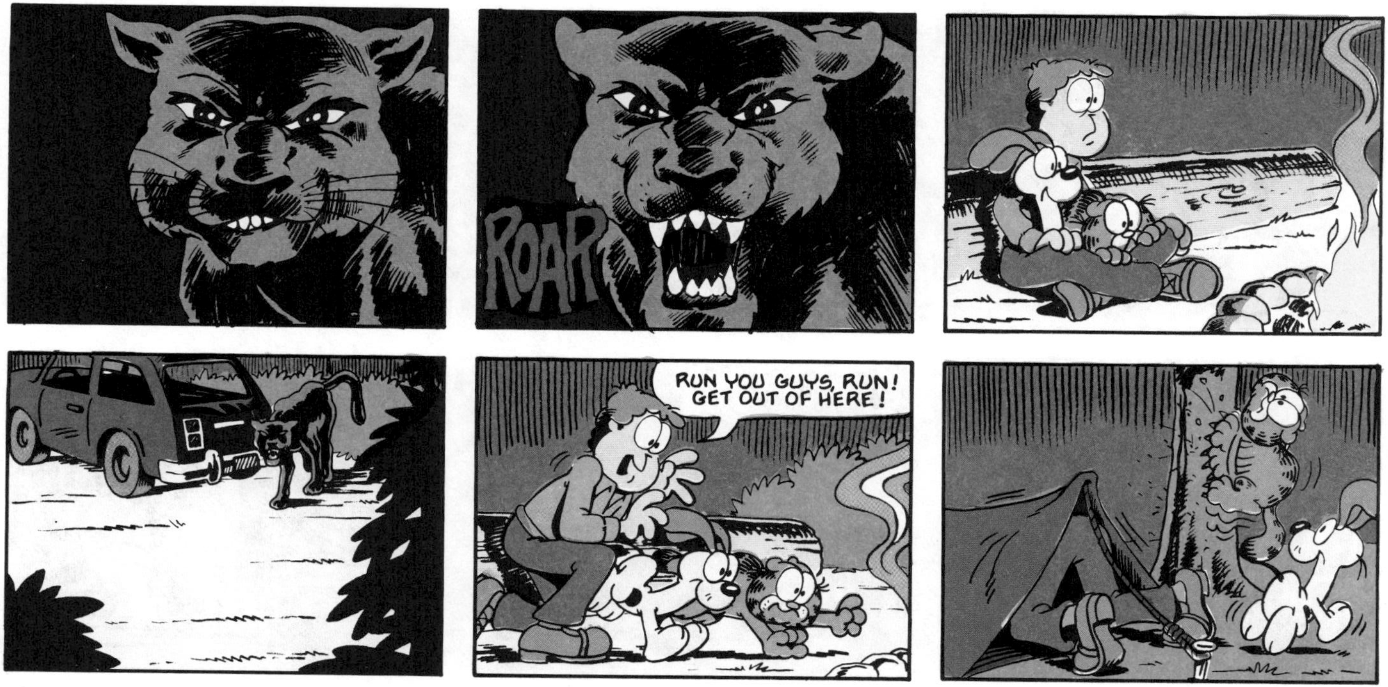
ROAR
RUN YOU GUYS, RUN! GET OUT OF HERE!

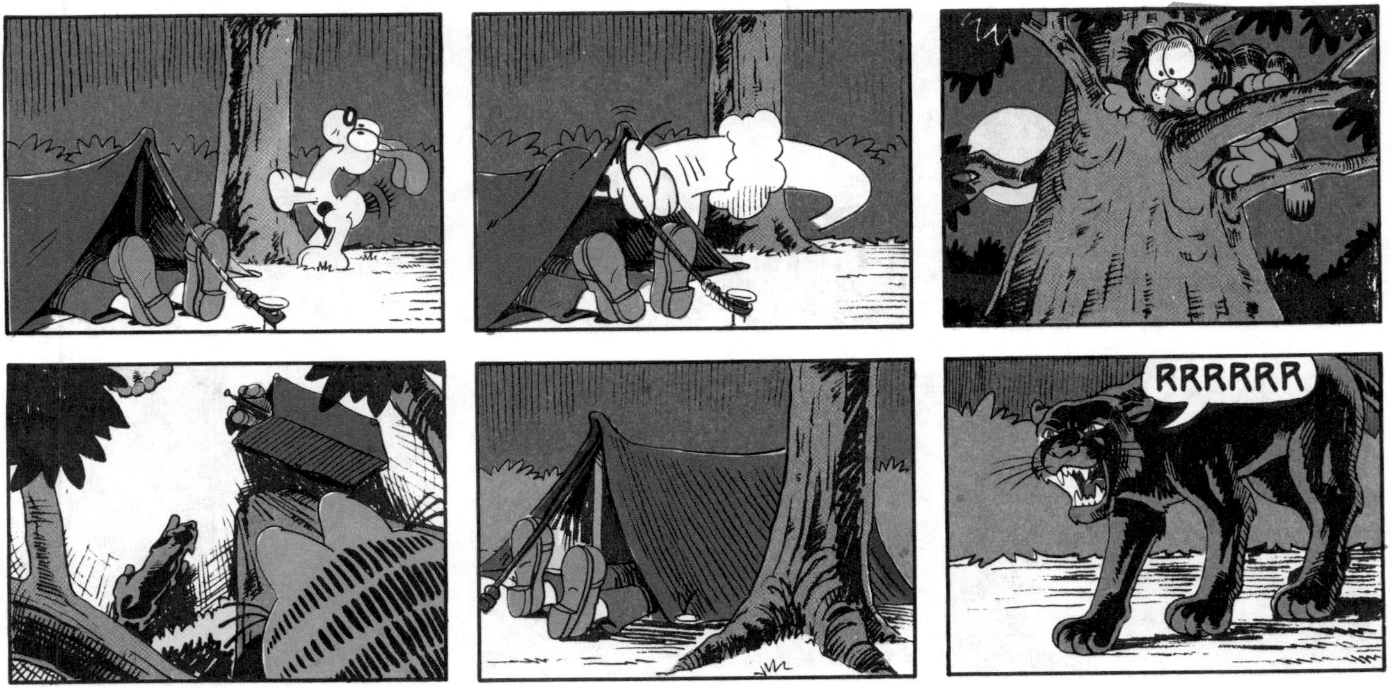
RRRRRR

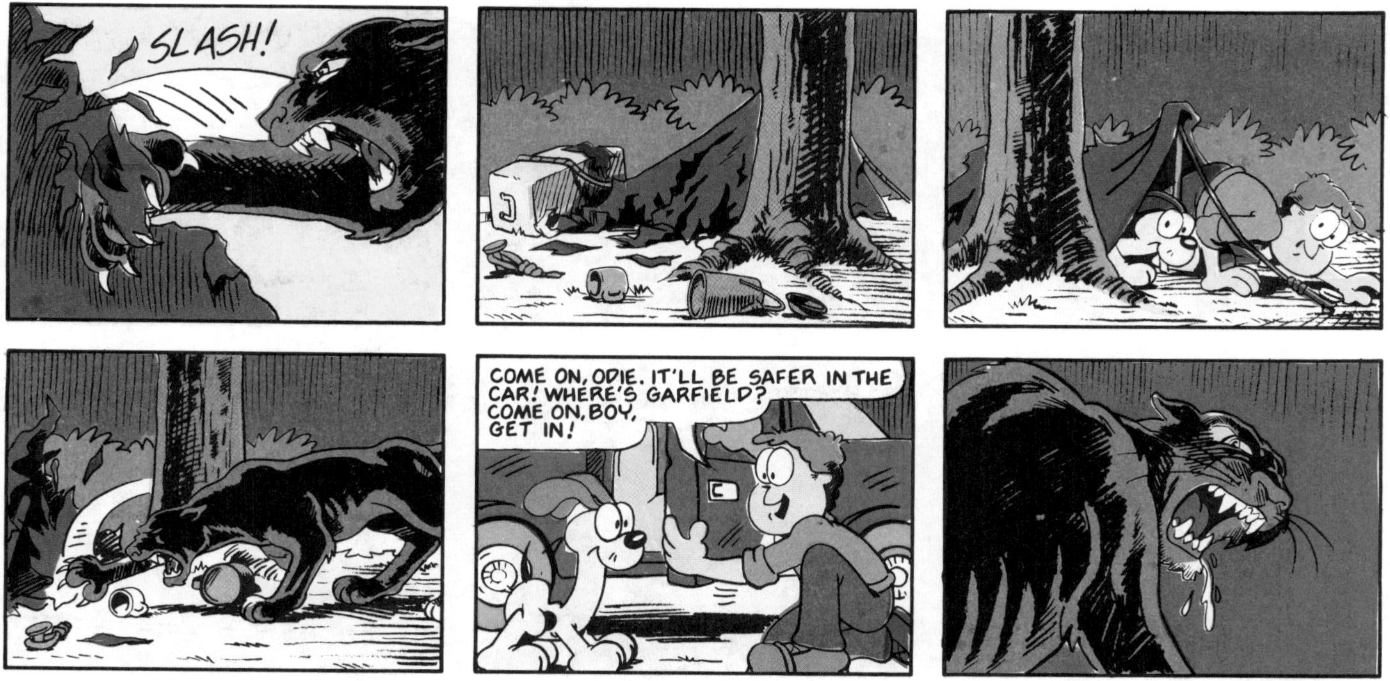
SLASH!
COME ON, ODIE. IT'LL BE SAFER IN THE CAR! WHERE'S GARFIELD? COME ON, BOY, GET IN!

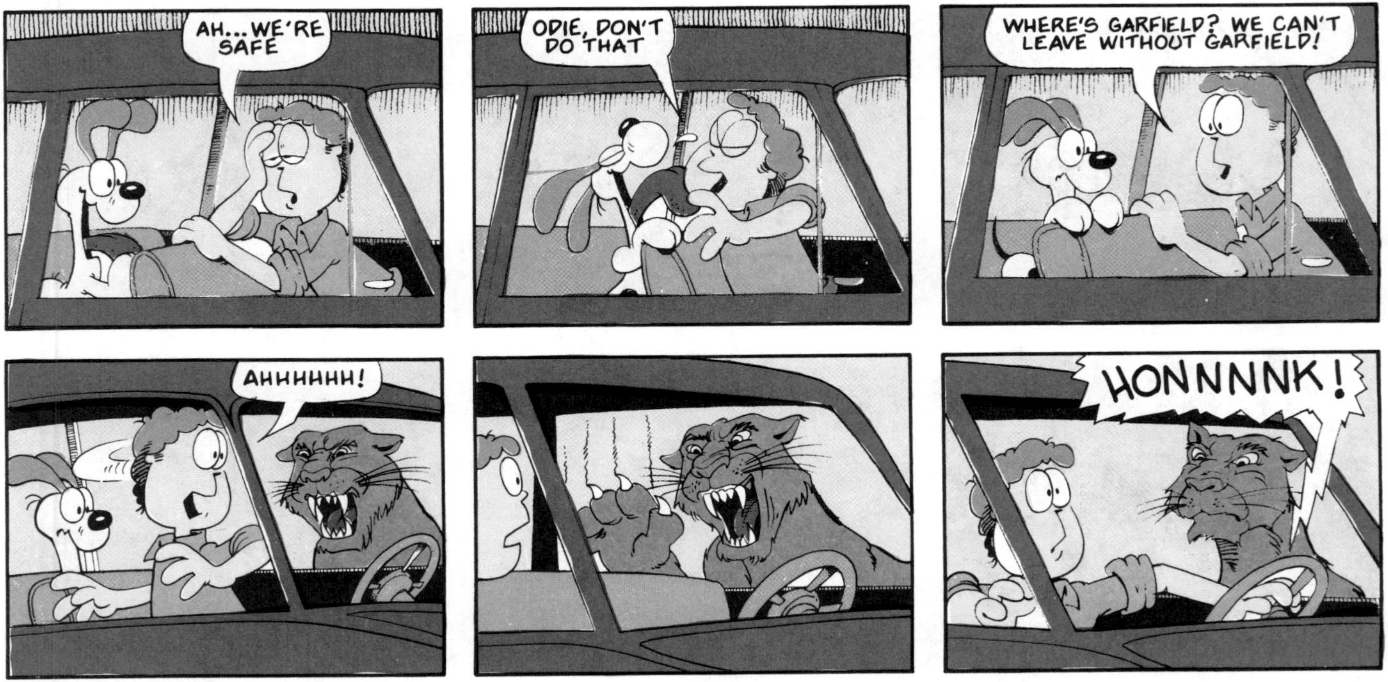
AH...WE'RE SAFE
ODIE, DON'T DO THAT
WHERE'S GARFIELD? WE CAN'T LEAVE WITHOUT GARFIELD!
AHHHHHH!
HONNNNK!

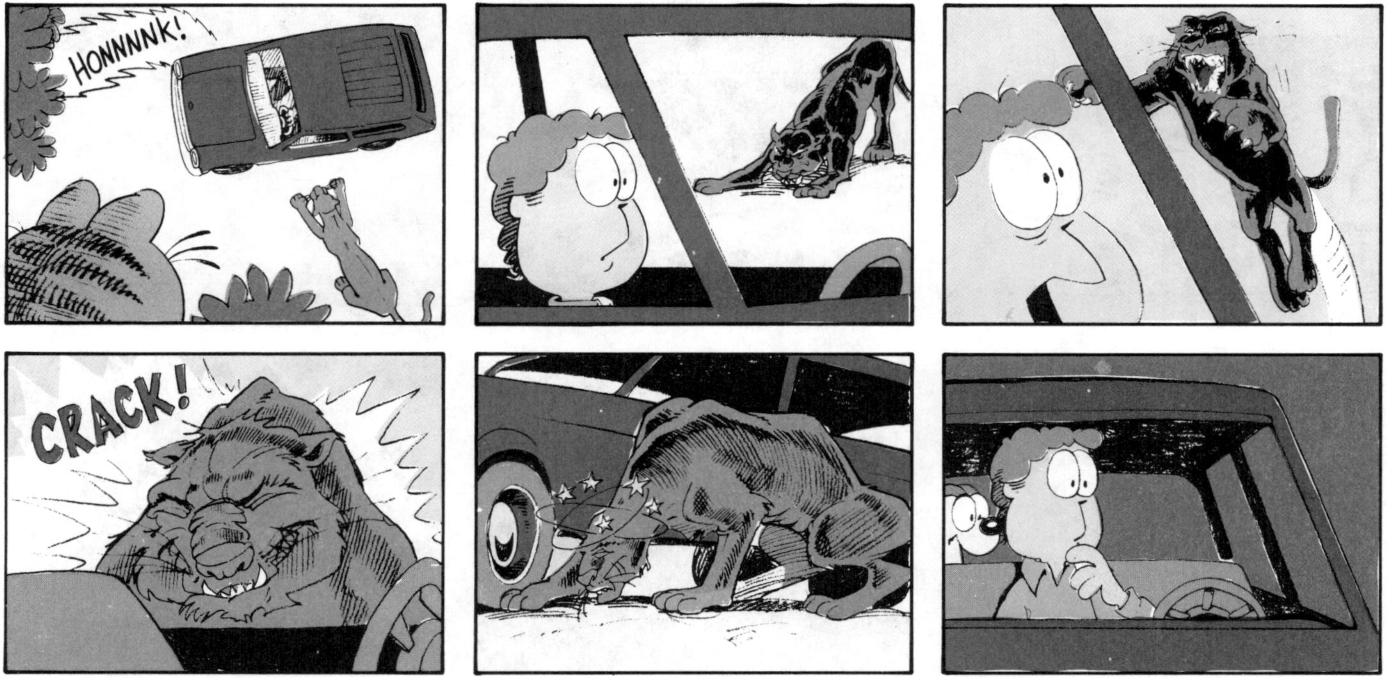
HONNNNK!
CRACK!

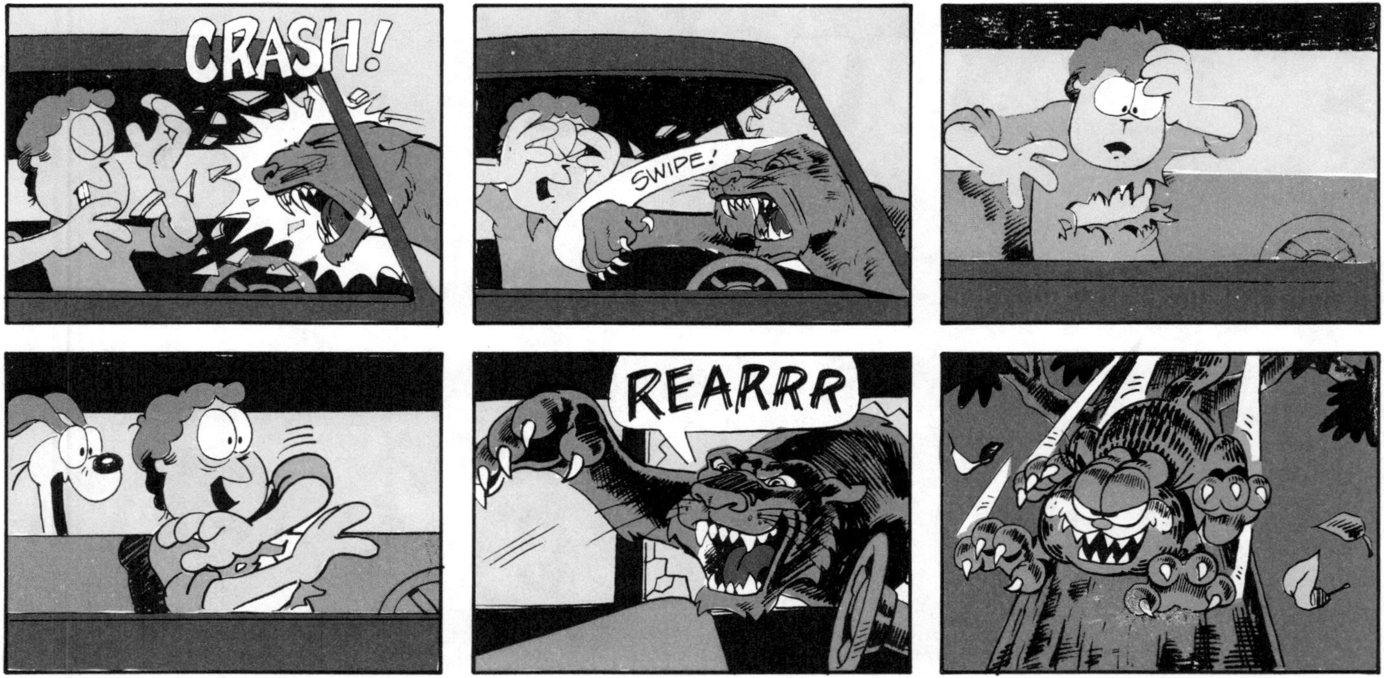
CRASH!
SWIPE!
REARRR

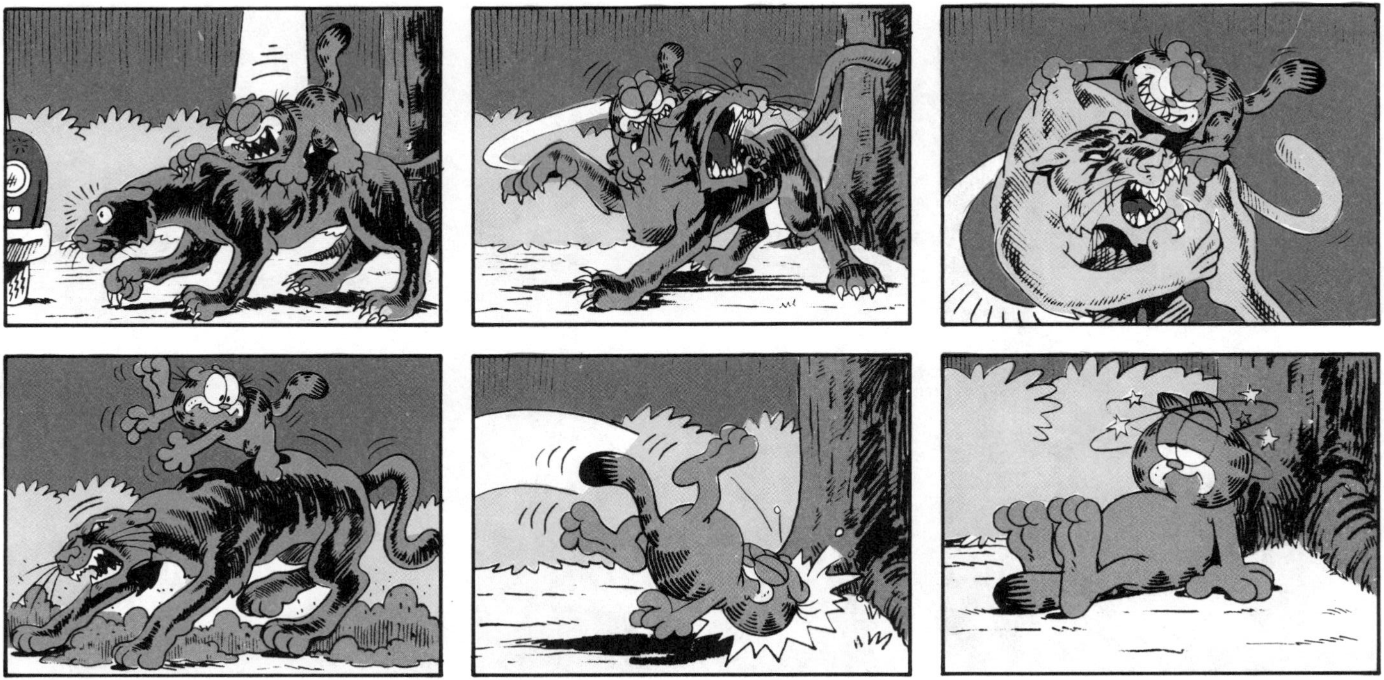

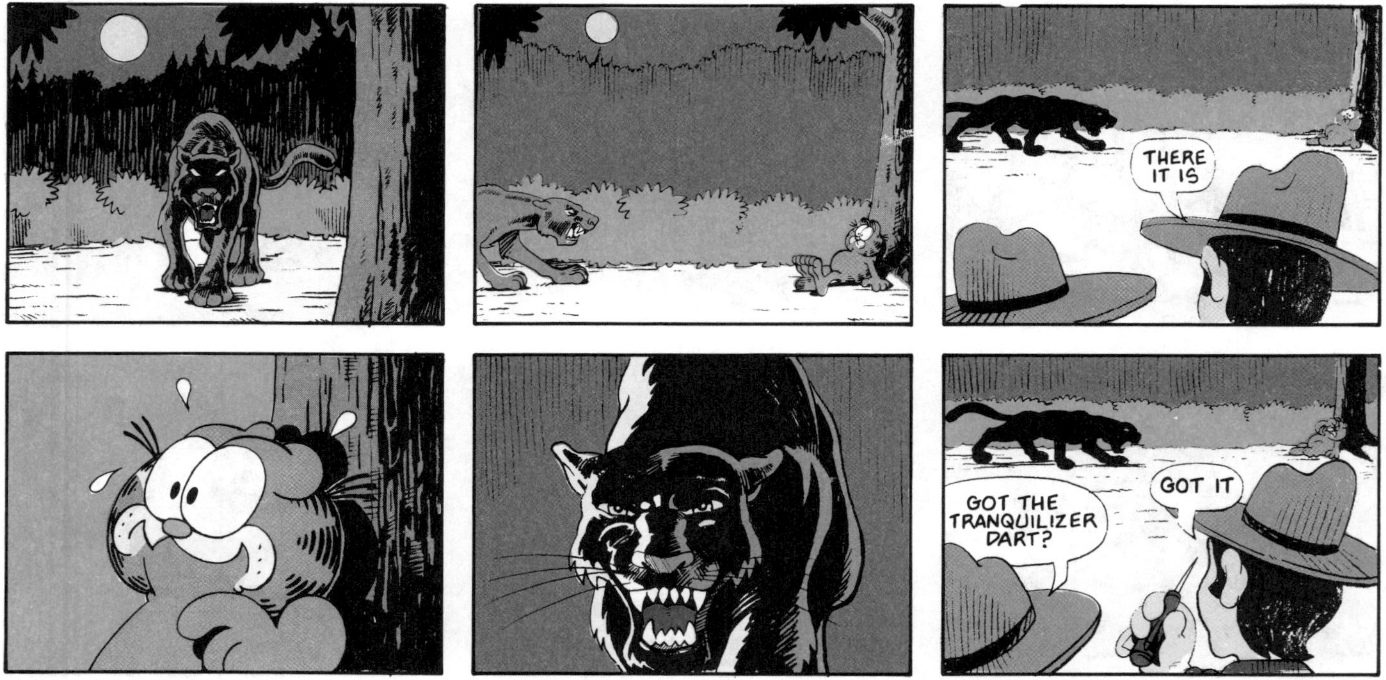
THERE IT IS
GOT THE TRANQUILIZER DART?
GOT IT

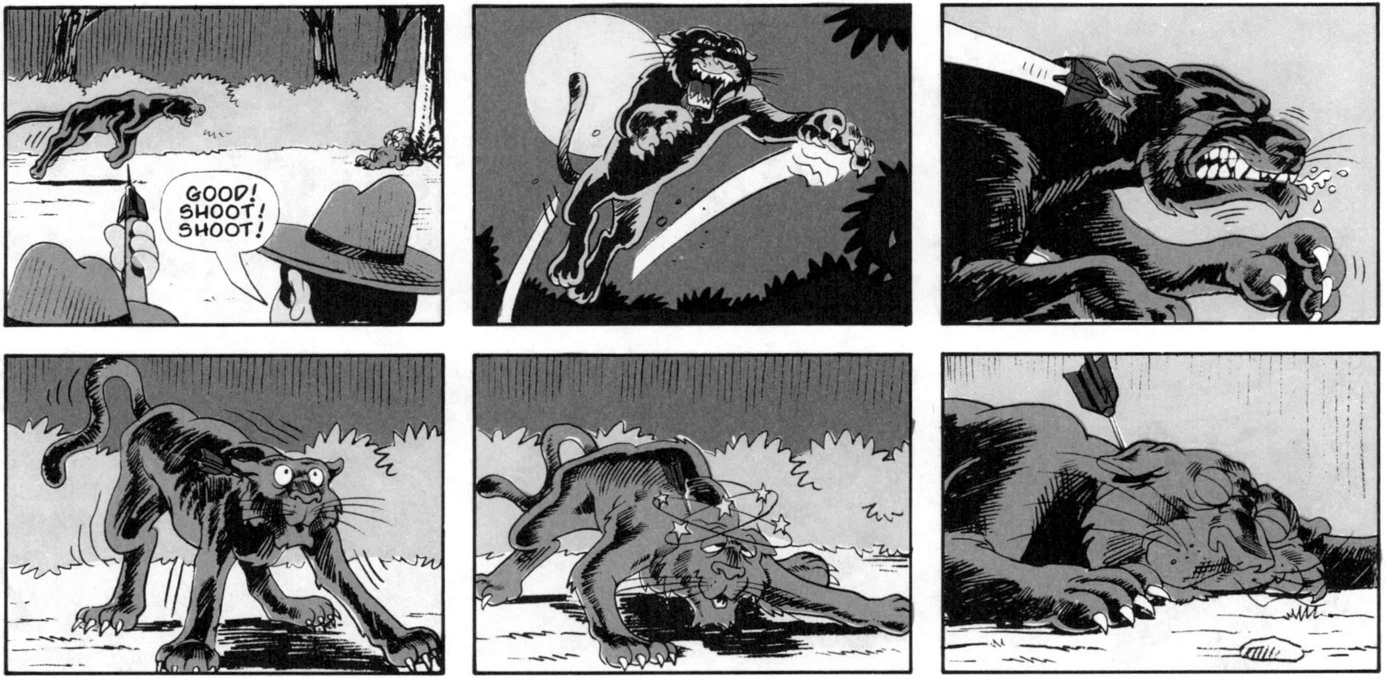
GOOD! SHOOT! SHOOT!

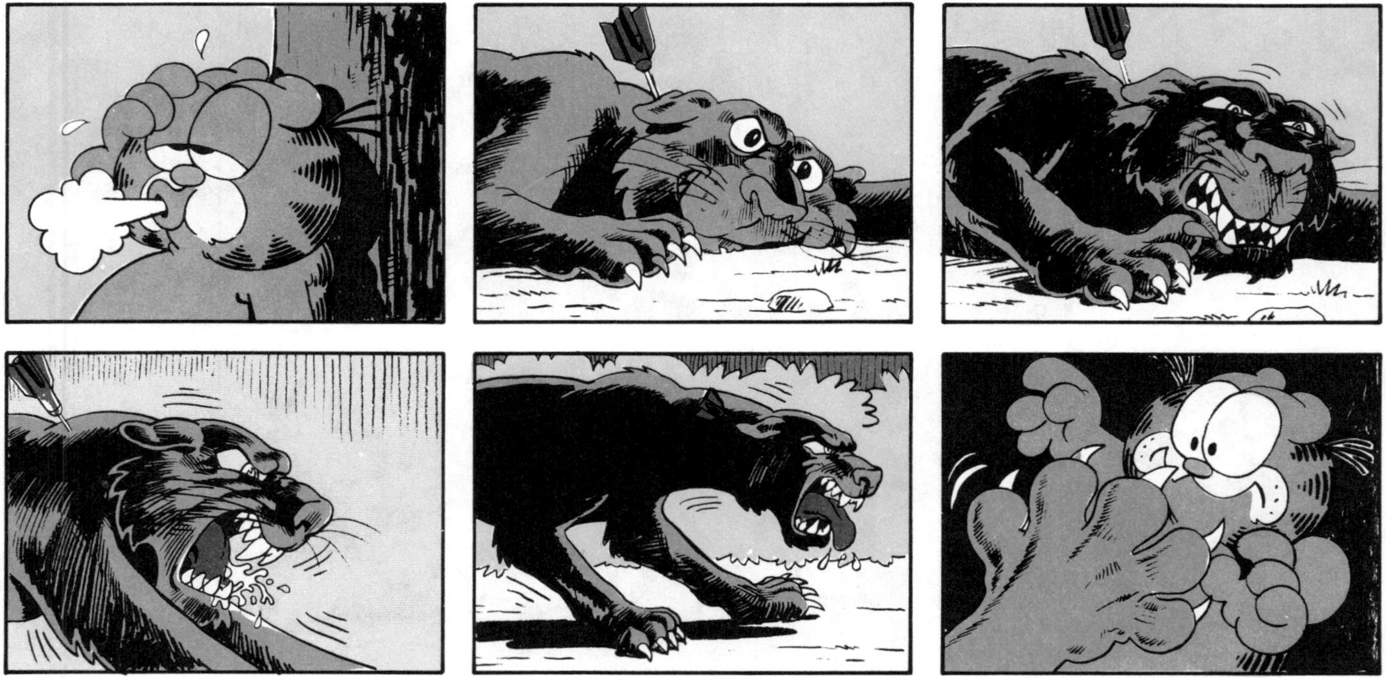

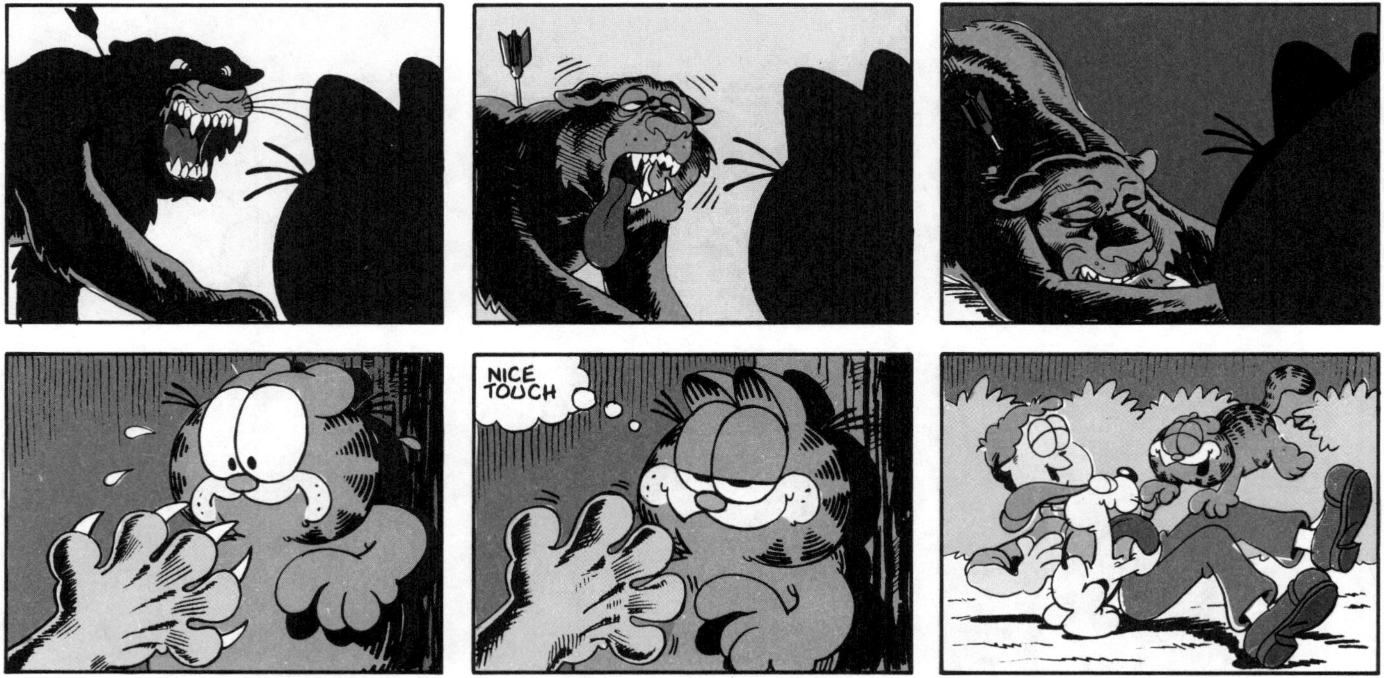
NICE TOUCH

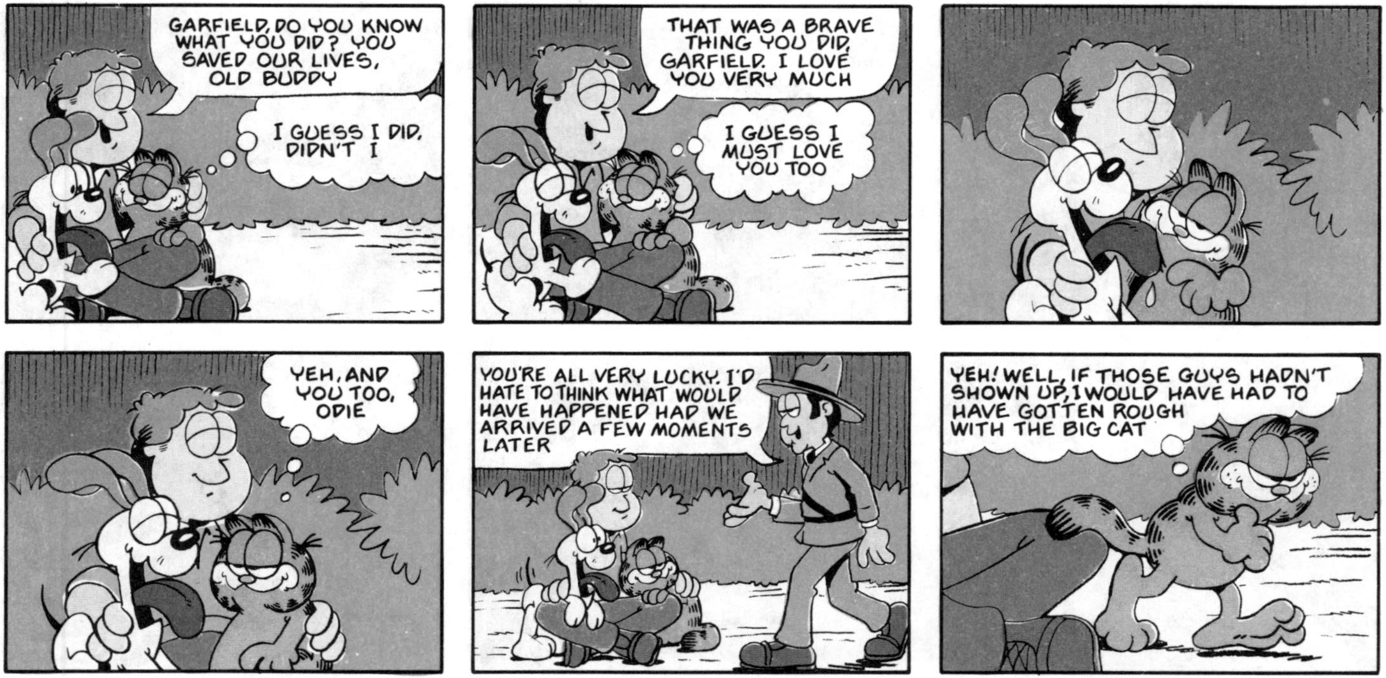
GARFIELD, DO YOU KNOW WHAT YOU DID? YOU SAVED OUR LIVES, OLD BUDDY
I GUESS I DID, DIDN'T I
THAT WAS A BRAVE THING YOU DID, GARFIELD. I LOVE YOU VERY MUCH
I GUESS I MUST LOVE YOU TOO
YEH, AND YOU TOO, ODIE
YOU'RE ALL VERY LUCKY. I'D HATE TO THINK WHAT WOULD HAVE HAPPENED HAD WE ARRIVED A FEW MOMENTS LATER
YEH! WELL, IF THOSE GUYS HADN'T SHOWN UP, I WOULD HAVE HAD TO HAVE GOTTEN ROUGH WITH THE BIG CAT

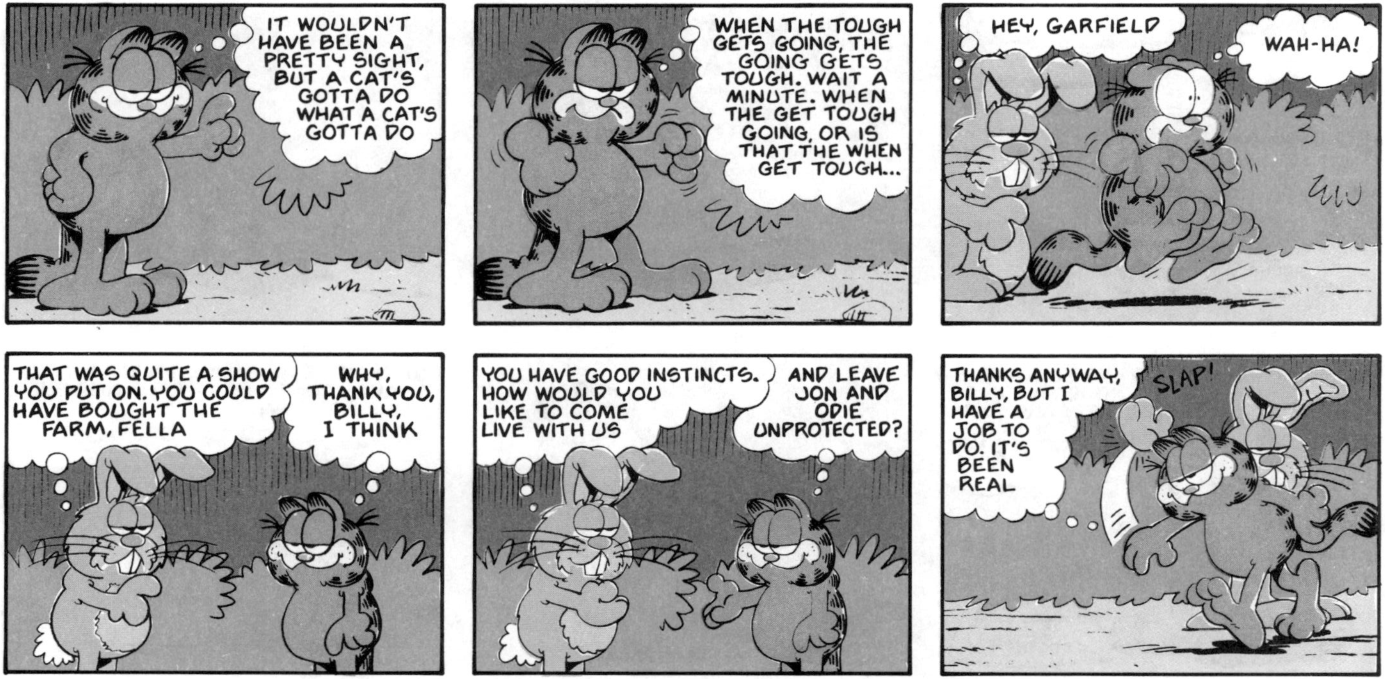
IT WOULDN'T HAVE BEEN A PRETTY SIGHT, BUT A CAT'S GOTTA DO WHAT A CAT'S GOTTA DO
WHEN THE TOUGH GETS GOING, THE GOING GETS TOUGH. WAIT A MINUTE. WHEN THE GET TOUGH GOING, OR IS THAT THE WHEN GET TOUGH...
HEY, GARFIELD
WAH-HA!
THAT WAS QUITE A SHOW YOU PUT ON. YOU COULD HAVE BOUGHT THE FARM, FELLA
WHY, THANK YOU, BILLY, I THINK
YOU HAVE GOOD INSTINCTS. HOW WOULD YOU LIKE TO COME LIVE WITH US
AND LEAVE JON AND ODIE UNPROTECTED?
THANKS ANYWAY, BILLY, BUT I HAVE A JOB TO DO. IT'S BEEN REAL
SLAP!

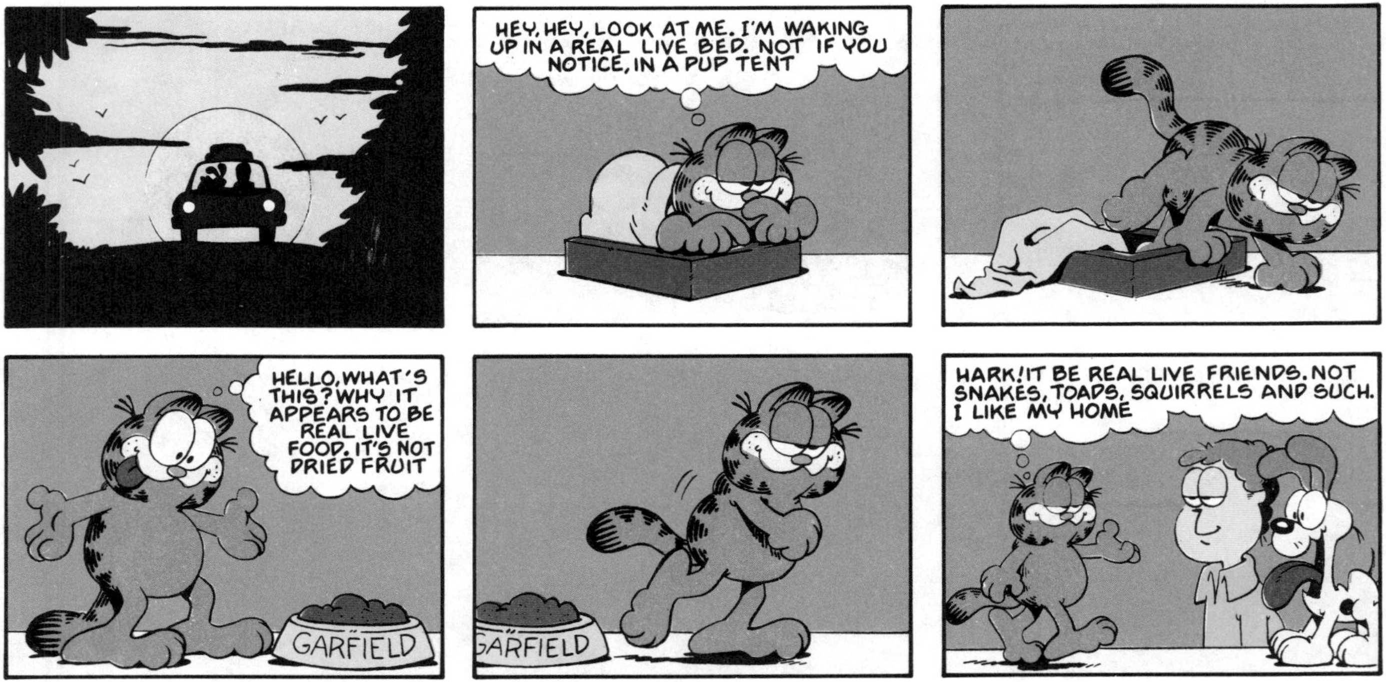
HEY, HEY, LOOK AT ME. I'M WAKING UP IN A REAL LIVE BED. NOT IF YOU NOTICE, IN A PUP TENT
HELLO, WHAT'S THIS? WHY IT APPEARS TO BE REAL LIVE FOOD. IT'S NOT DRIED FRUIT
GARFIELD
GARFIELD
HARK! IT BE REAL LIVE FRIENDS. NOT SNAKES, TOADS, SQUIRRELS AND SUCH. I LIKE MY HOME

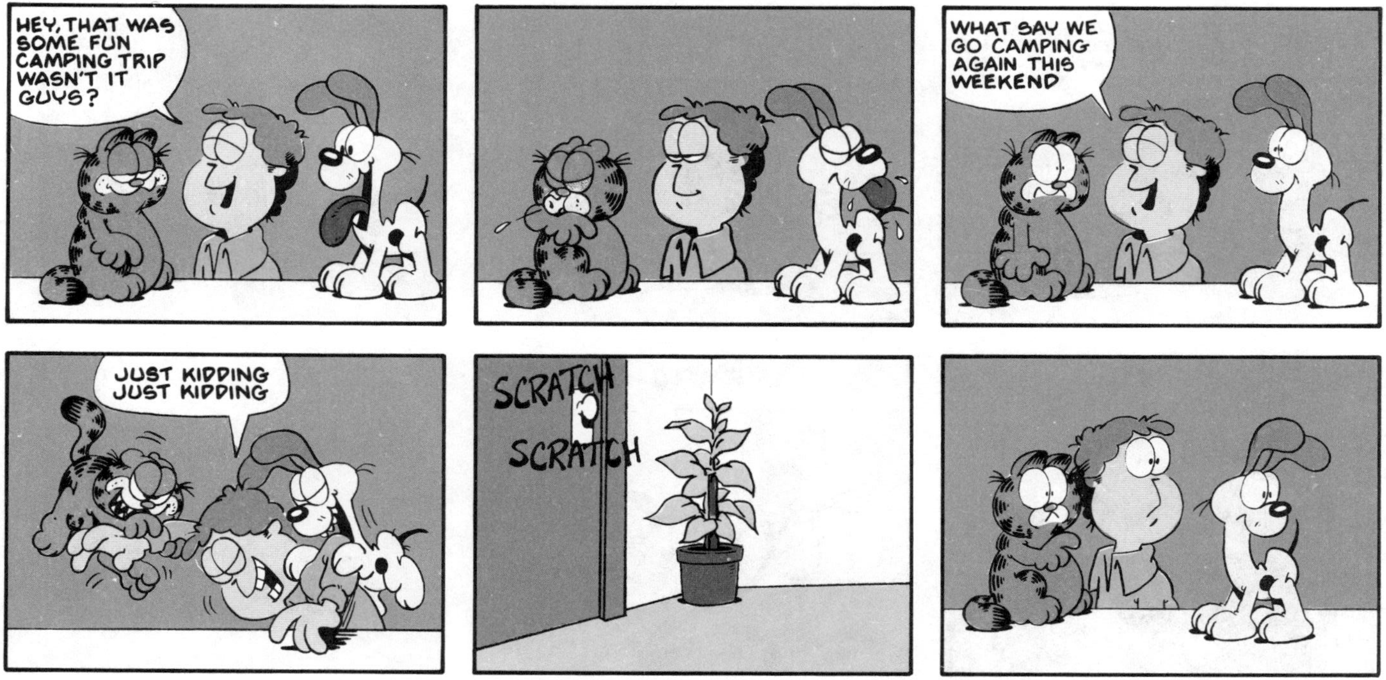
HEY, THAT WAS SOME FUN CAMPING TRIP WASN'T IT GUYS?
WHAT SAY WE GO CAMPING AGAIN THIS WEEKEND
JUST KIDDING JUST KIDDING
SCRATCH
SCRATCH

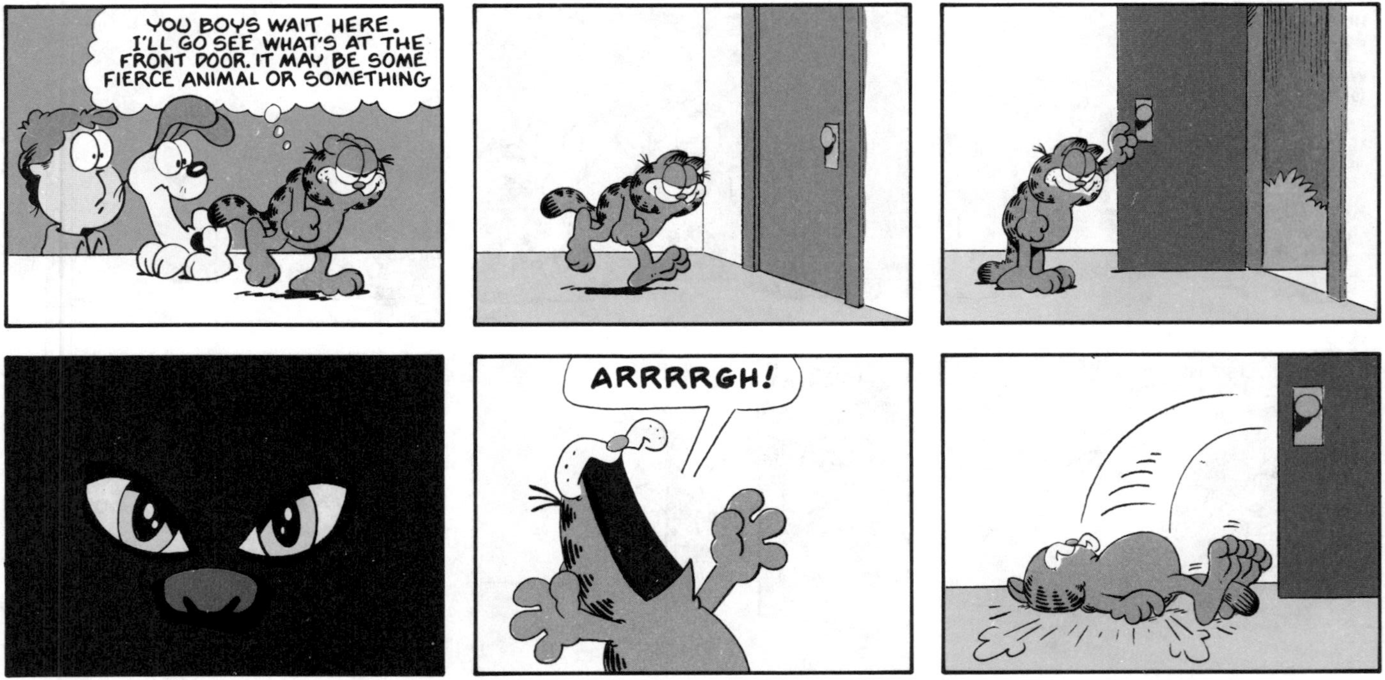
YOU BOYS WAIT HERE. I'LL GO SEE WHAT'S AT THE FRONT DOOR. IT MAY BE SOME FIERCE ANIMAL OR SOMETHING
ARRRRGH!

WHAT WAS AT THE DOOR, GARFIELD?
A HUMBLING EXPERIENCE, MY FRIEND
FINE, NOW HOW ABOUT THIS CAMPING TRIP?

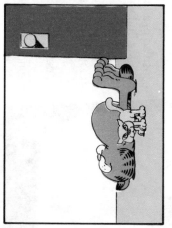

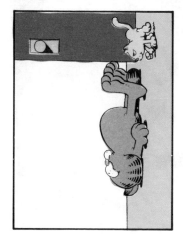

Steps in Making an

1. *Story:* The writer selects a theme (Christmas, camping, etc.) and develops the story. The characters are introduced and taken through the plot in a series of gags and situations. (Everything is resolved in the end.) A finished script is then supplied to the producer.

2. *Storyboard:* A storyboard artist draws the story in a form similar to a comic strip and establishes story continuity, action, long shots, closeups, etc.

3. *Recording of Voices and Songs:* After selecting the proper voices for the characters and the songs to be used, they are recorded on ½ inch magnetic tape.

3A: *Reading the dialogue and music:* The tracks are transferred from ½ inch tape to 35 mm magnetic film. A film editor "reads" the track frame by frame to indicate the position of each letter and word or music beat.

4: *Directing:* The director times the picture out scene by scene to the required length. Using the track readings supplied by the film editor, he makes out exposure sheets in preparing the scenes for the animators. The required action and dialogue is indicated on the sheets frame by frame.

5. *Layout:* The layout artist designs the picture. He or she establishes the style of design to be used. Using the storyboard as a guide, the layout artist composes each scene regarding the characters' relationship to the background, props, etc.

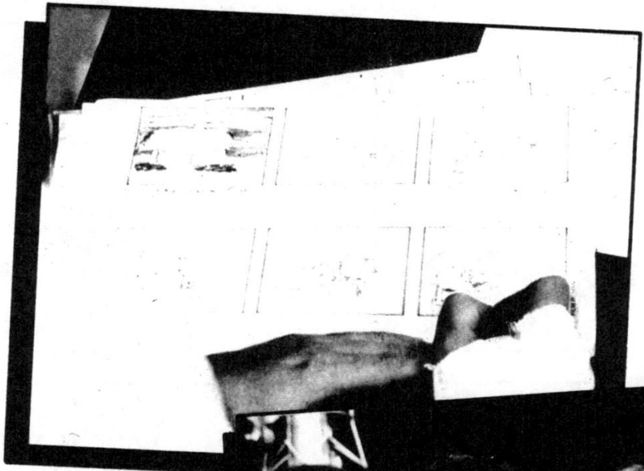

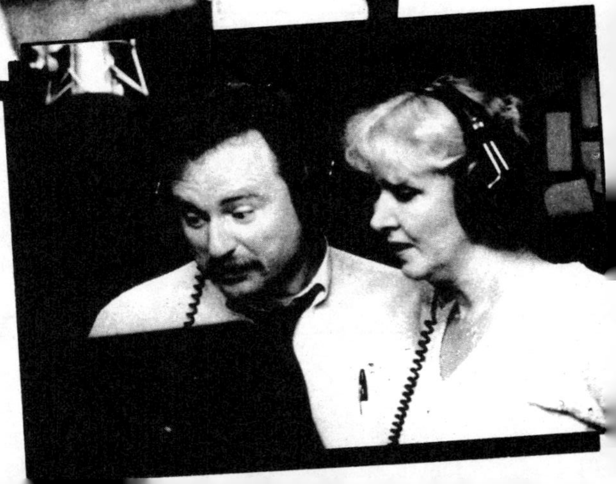

Animated Film

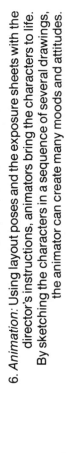

6. *Animation:* Using layout poses and the exposure sheets with the director's instructions, animators bring the characters to life. By sketching the characters in a sequence of several drawings, the animator can create many moods and attitudes.

7. *Background:* The background artist renders the layout sketches in full color and sets the color styling.

8. *Checking:* The checker coordinates the animation, layout, and background areas and prepares all animated scenes for ink and paint and for camera.

9. *Ink and Paint:* The animators pencil drawings are transferred on to celluloid sheets (cels) by either Xerox or hand tracing by inkers. These cels are then painted on the reverse side by painters. Putting the drawing on cels allows the background to show through when the cel is superimposed over it.

10. *Camera:* Using the exposure sheet as a guide the cameraman shoots the drawings in each scene on film one frame at a time as indicated by the animator.

11. *Editing:* The film editor assembles the picture as indicated by the director and adds sound effects and background music.

12. *Dubbing* (Mixing): Up to this time there are separate dialogue, music, and effects tracks. Here they are combined into just one track. The dialogue, music, and effects are set at their proper level throughout the picture.

13. *Answer Print:* The film lab issues a final print with fully balanced color and soundtrack.

Garfield in Paradise

by

JIM DAVIS

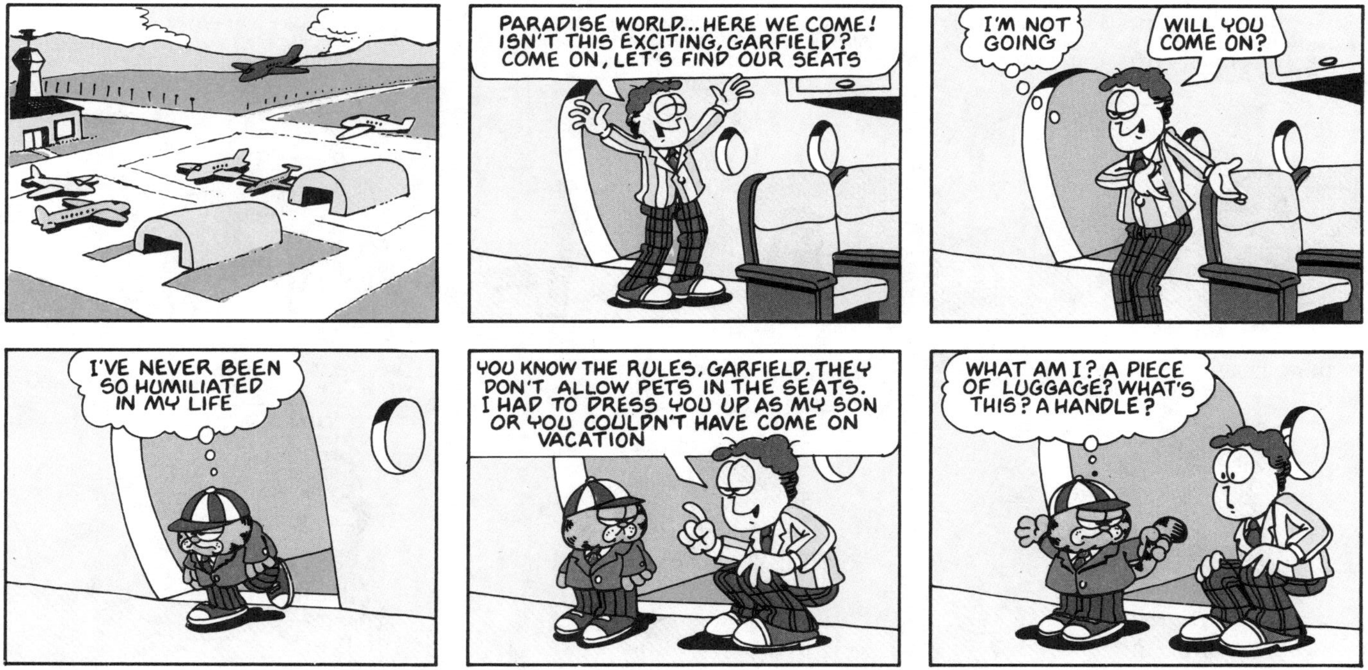
PARADISE WORLD... HERE WE COME! ISN'T THIS EXCITING, GARFIELD? COME ON, LET'S FIND OUR SEATS
I'M NOT GOING
WILL YOU COME ON?
I'VE NEVER BEEN SO HUMILIATED IN MY LIFE
YOU KNOW THE RULES, GARFIELD. THEY DON'T ALLOW PETS IN THE SEATS. I HAD TO DRESS YOU UP AS MY SON OR YOU COULDN'T HAVE COME ON VACATION
WHAT AM I? A PIECE OF LUGGAGE? WHAT'S THIS? A HANDLE?

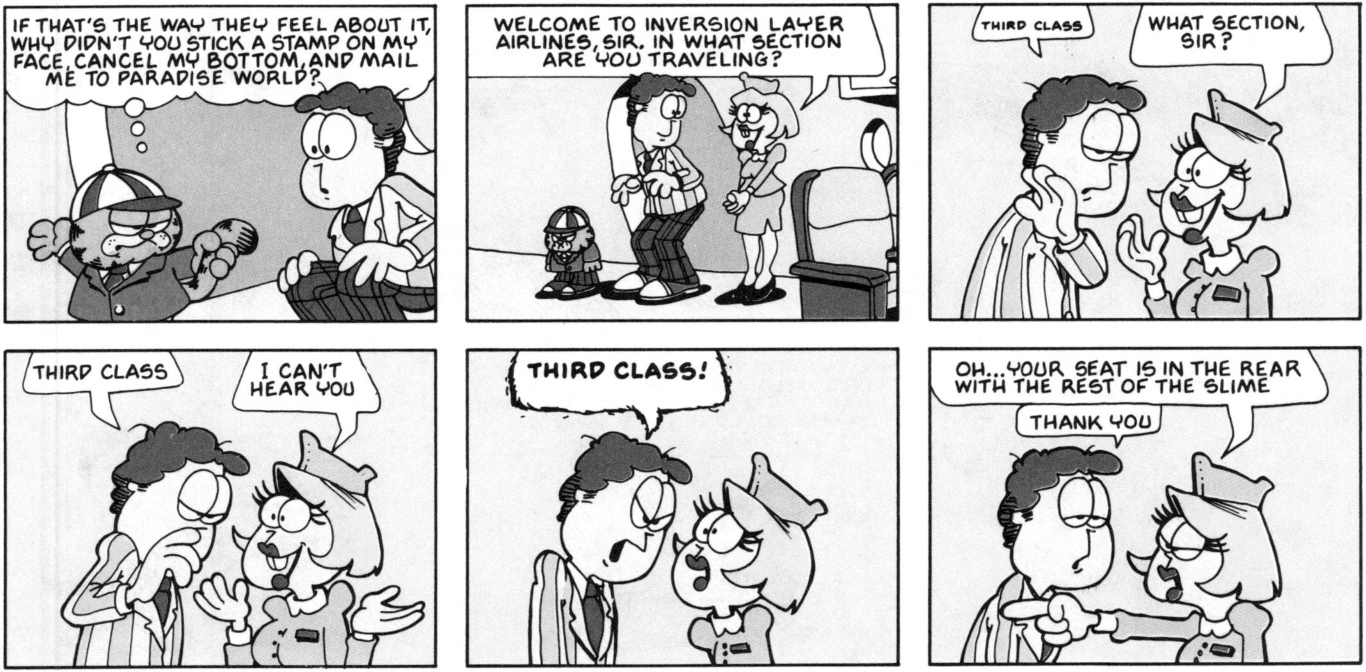
IF THAT'S THE WAY THEY FEEL ABOUT IT, WHY DIDN'T YOU STICK A STAMP ON MY FACE, CANCEL MY BOTTOM, AND MAIL ME TO PARADISE WORLD?
WELCOME TO INVERSION LAYER AIRLINES, SIR. IN WHAT SECTION ARE YOU TRAVELING?
WHAT SECTION, SIR?
THIRD CLASS
I CAN'T HEAR YOU
THIRD CLASS
THIRD CLASS!
OH... YOUR SEAT IS IN THE REAR WITH THE REST OF THE SLIME
THANK YOU

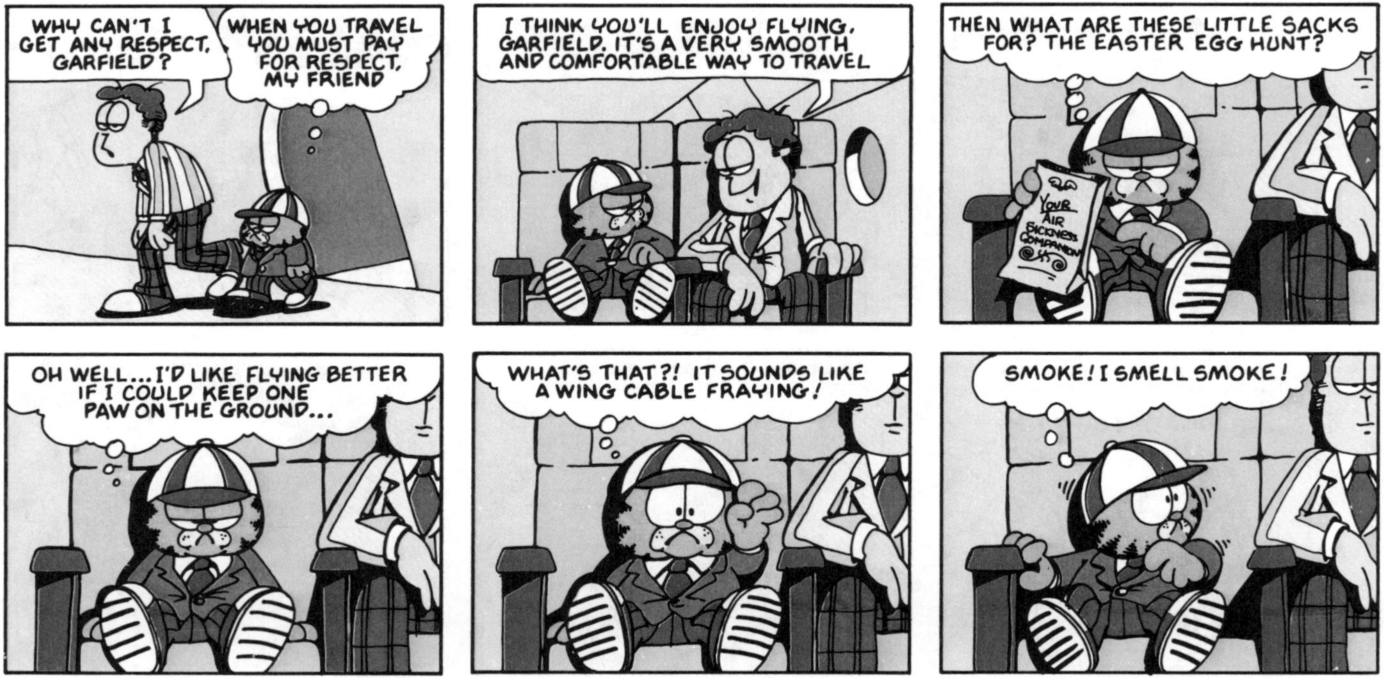
WHY CAN'T I GET ANY RESPECT, GARFIELD?
WHEN YOU TRAVEL YOU MUST PAY FOR RESPECT, MY FRIEND
I THINK YOU'LL ENJOY FLYING, GARFIELD. IT'S A VERY SMOOTH AND COMFORTABLE WAY TO TRAVEL
THEN WHAT ARE THESE LITTLE SACKS FOR? THE EASTER EGG HUNT?
YOUR AIR SICKNESS COMPANION
OH WELL... I'D LIKE FLYING BETTER IF I COULD KEEP ONE PAW ON THE GROUND...
WHAT'S THAT?! IT SOUNDS LIKE A WING CABLE FRAYING!
SMOKE! I SMELL SMOKE!

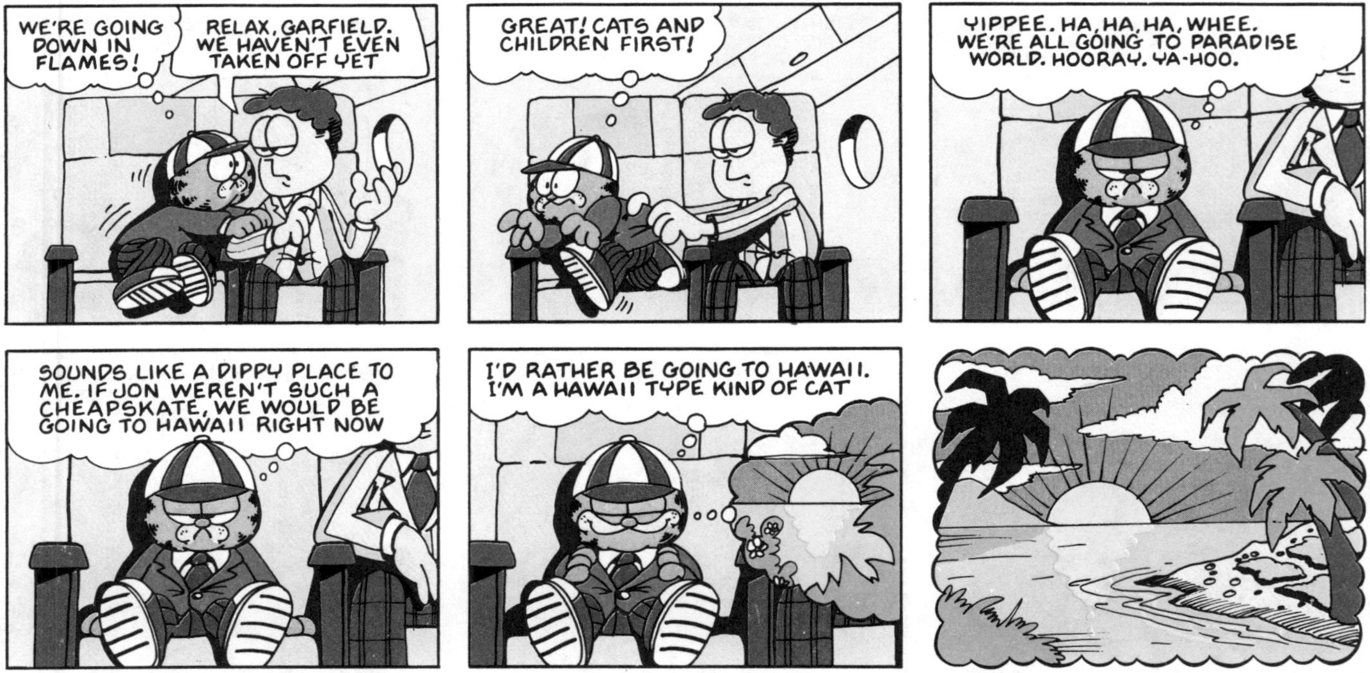
WE'RE GOING DOWN IN FLAMES!
RELAX, GARFIELD. WE HAVEN'T EVEN TAKEN OFF YET
GREAT! CATS AND CHILDREN FIRST!
YIPPEE. HA, HA, HA, WHEE. WE'RE ALL GOING TO PARADISE WORLD. HOORAY. YA-HOO.
SOUNDS LIKE A DIPPY PLACE TO ME. IF JON WEREN'T SUCH A CHEAPSKATE, WE WOULD BE GOING TO HAWAII RIGHT NOW
I'D RATHER BE GOING TO HAWAII. I'M A HAWAII TYPE KIND OF CAT

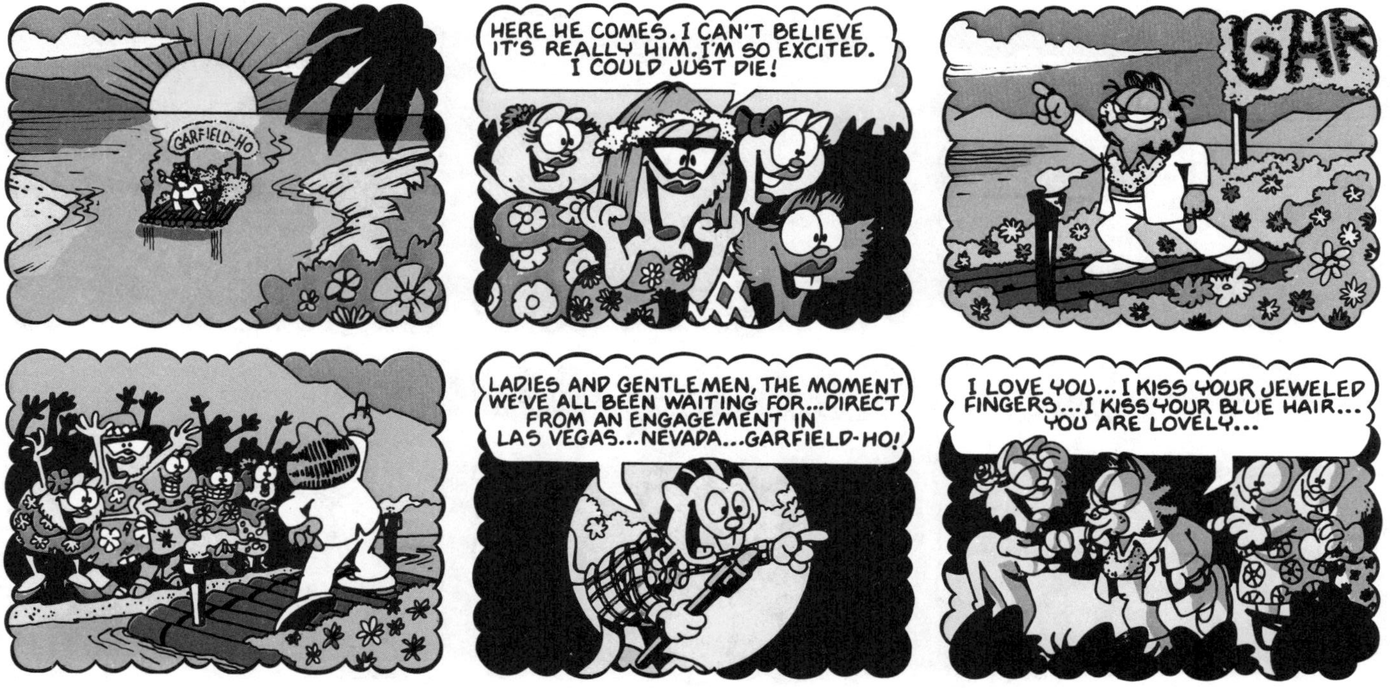
GARFIELD-HO
HERE HE COMES. I CAN'T BELIEVE IT'S REALLY HIM. I'M SO EXCITED. I COULD JUST DIE!
GHR
LADIES AND GENTLEMEN, THE MOMENT WE'VE ALL BEEN WAITING FOR...DIRECT FROM AN ENGAGEMENT IN LAS VEGAS...NEVADA...GARFIELD-HO!
I LOVE YOU... I KISS YOUR JEWELED FINGERS... I KISS YOUR BLUE HAIR... YOU ARE LOVELY...

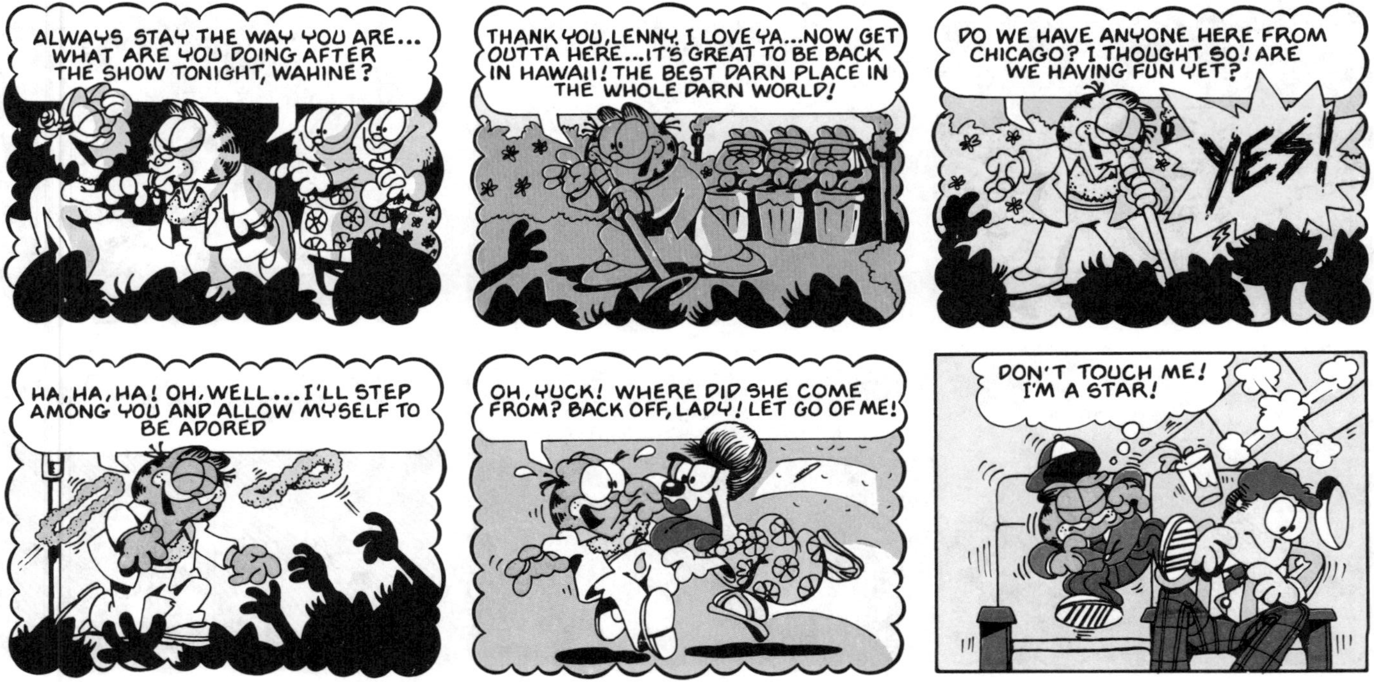
ALWAYS STAY THE WAY YOU ARE... WHAT ARE YOU DOING AFTER THE SHOW TONIGHT, WAHINE?
THANK YOU, LENNY. I LOVE YA...NOW GET OUTTA HERE...IT'S GREAT TO BE BACK IN HAWAII! THE BEST DARN PLACE IN THE WHOLE DARN WORLD!
DO WE HAVE ANYONE HERE FROM CHICAGO? I THOUGHT SO! ARE WE HAVING FUN YET?
YES!
HA, HA, HA! OH, WELL...I'LL STEP AMONG YOU AND ALLOW MYSELF TO BE ADORED
OH, YUCK! WHERE DID SHE COME FROM? BACK OFF, LADY! LET GO OF ME!
DON'T TOUCH ME! I'M A STAR!

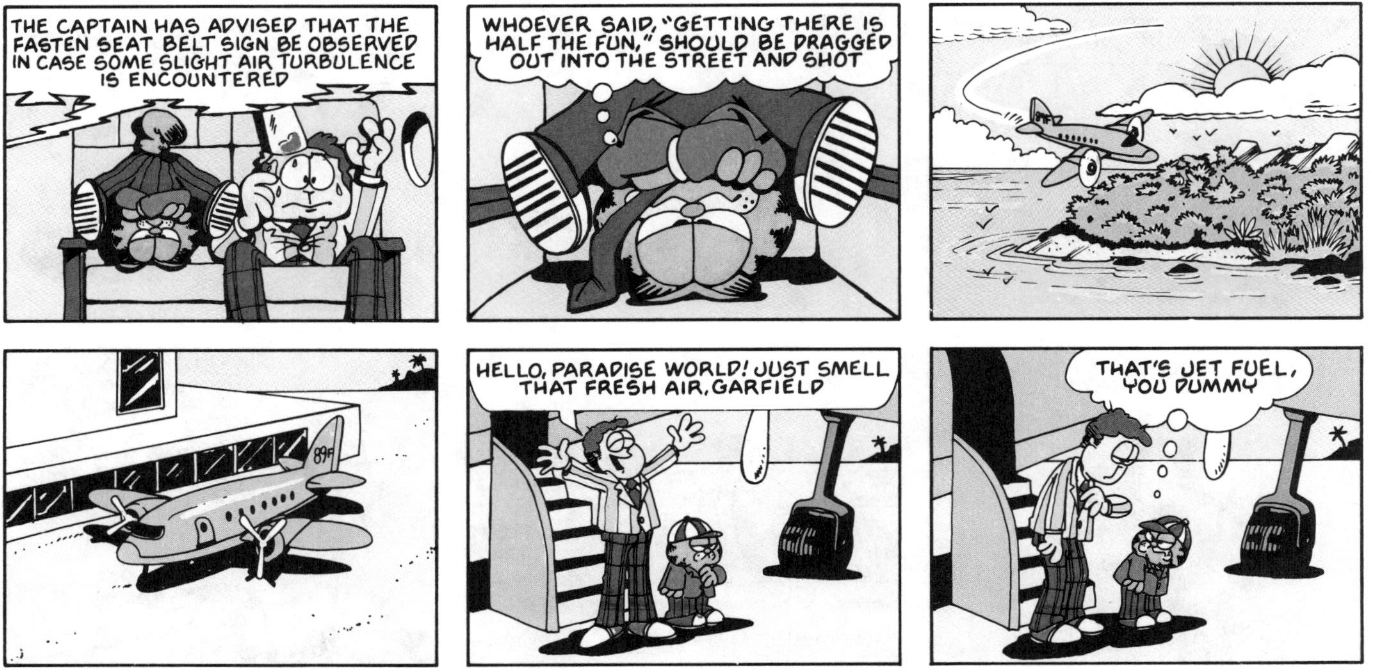
THE CAPTAIN HAS ADVISED THAT THE FASTEN SEAT BELT SIGN BE OBSERVED IN CASE SOME SLIGHT AIR TURBULENCE IS ENCOUNTERED
WHOEVER SAID, "GETTING THERE IS HALF THE FUN," SHOULD BE DRAGGED OUT INTO THE STREET AND SHOT
89F
HELLO, PARADISE WORLD! JUST SMELL THAT FRESH AIR, GARFIELD
THAT'S JET FUEL, YOU DUMMY

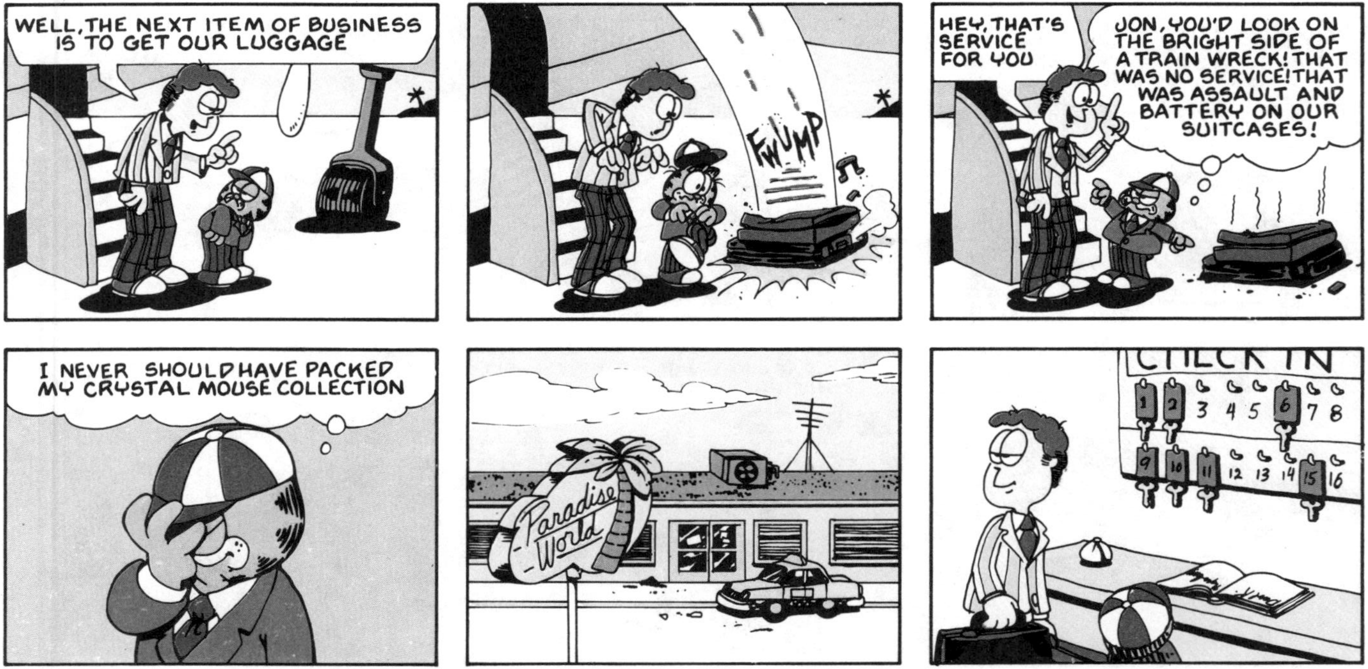
WELL, THE NEXT ITEM OF BUSINESS IS TO GET OUR LUGGAGE
FWUMP
HEY, THAT'S SERVICE FOR YOU
JON, YOU'D LOOK ON THE BRIGHT SIDE OF A TRAIN WRECK! THAT WAS NO SERVICE! THAT WAS ASSAULT AND BATTERY ON OUR SUITCASES!
I NEVER SHOULD HAVE PACKED MY CRYSTAL MOUSE COLLECTION
Paradise World
CHECK IN

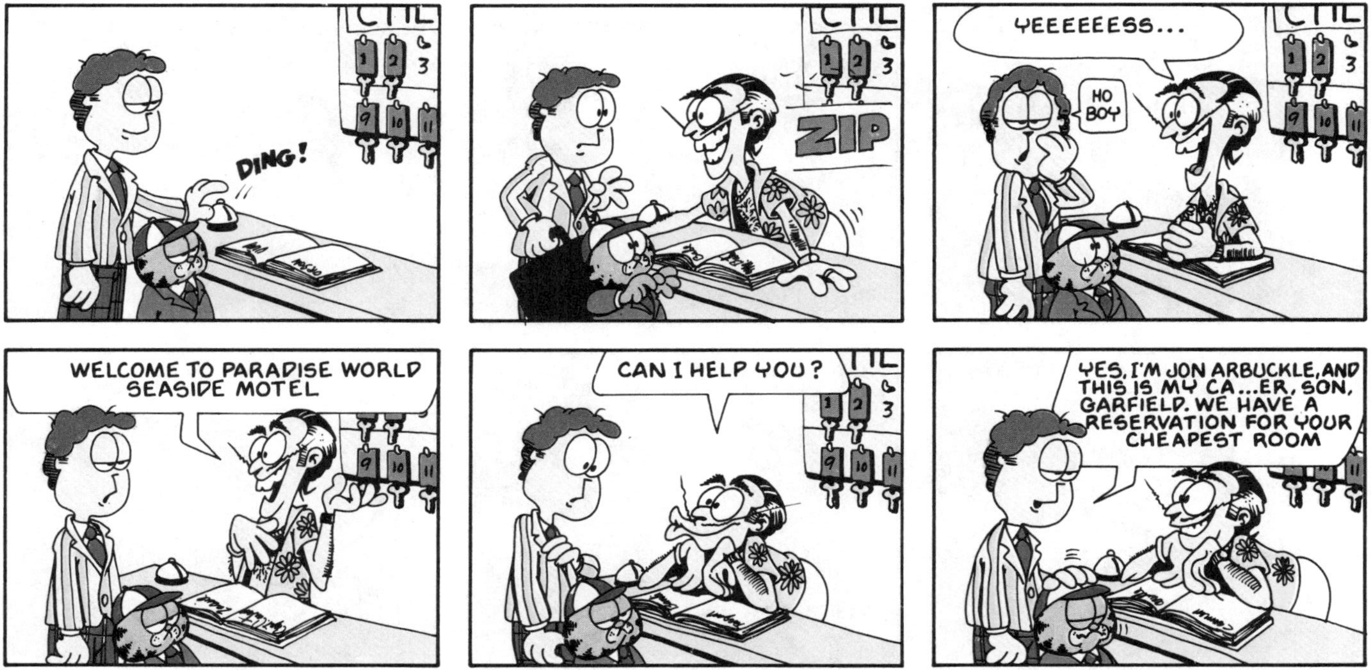
DING!
ZIP
YEEEEEESS...
HO BOY
WELCOME TO PARADISE WORLD SEASIDE MOTEL
CAN I HELP YOU?
YES, I'M JON ARBUCKLE, AND THIS IS MY CA...ER, SON, GARFIELD. WE HAVE A RESERVATION FOR YOUR CHEAPEST ROOM

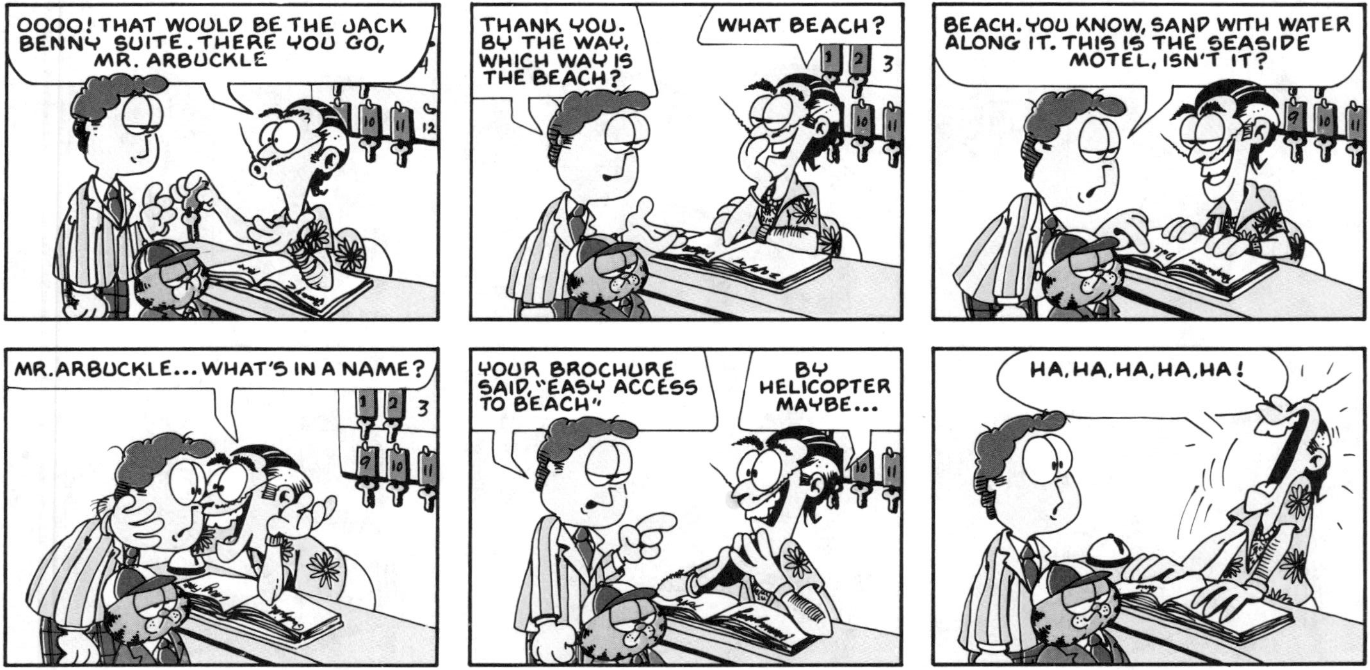
OOOO! THAT WOULD BE THE JACK BENNY SUITE. THERE YOU GO, MR. ARBUCKLE
THANK YOU. BY THE WAY, WHICH WAY IS THE BEACH?
WHAT BEACH?
BEACH. YOU KNOW, SAND WITH WATER ALONG IT. THIS IS THE SEASIDE MOTEL, ISN'T IT?
MR. ARBUCKLE... WHAT'S IN A NAME?
YOUR BROCHURE SAID, "EASY ACCESS TO BEACH"
BY HELICOPTER MAYBE...
HA, HA, HA, HA, HA!

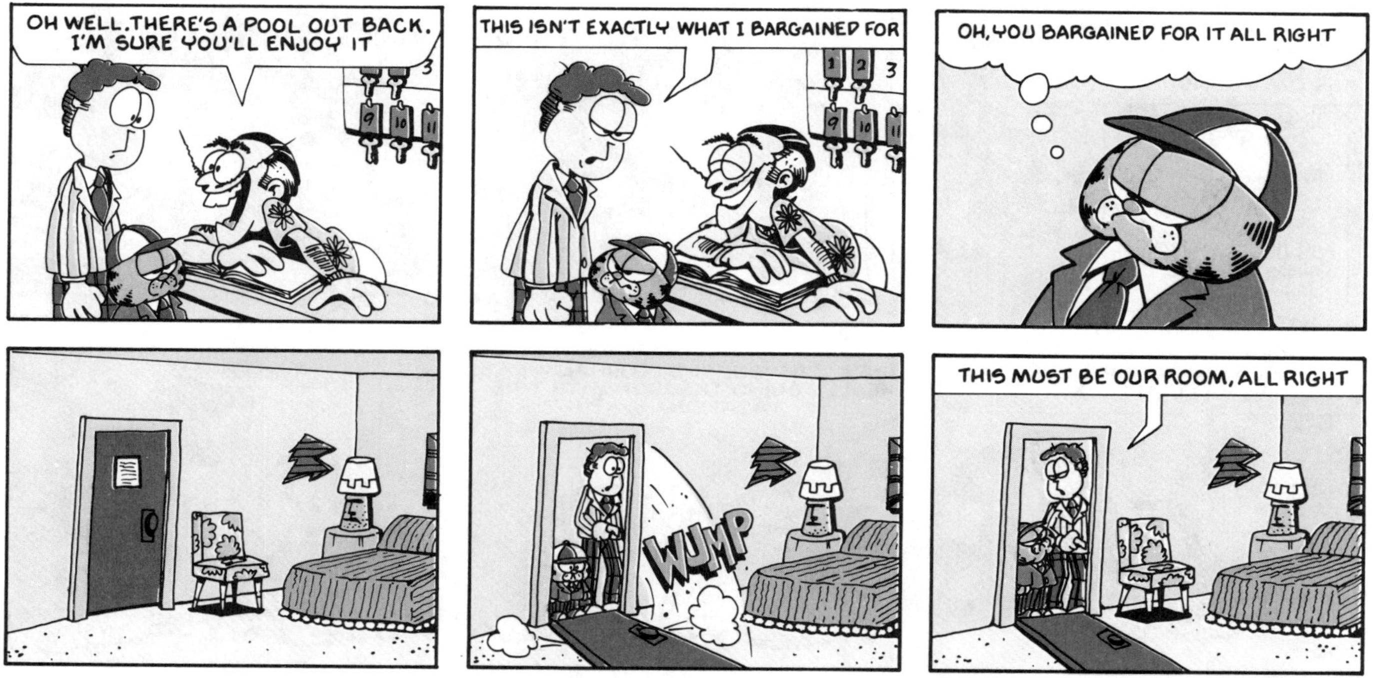
OH WELL. THERE'S A POOL OUT BACK. I'M SURE YOU'LL ENJOY IT
THIS ISN'T EXACTLY WHAT I BARGAINED FOR
OH, YOU BARGAINED FOR IT ALL RIGHT
WUMP
THIS MUST BE OUR ROOM, ALL RIGHT

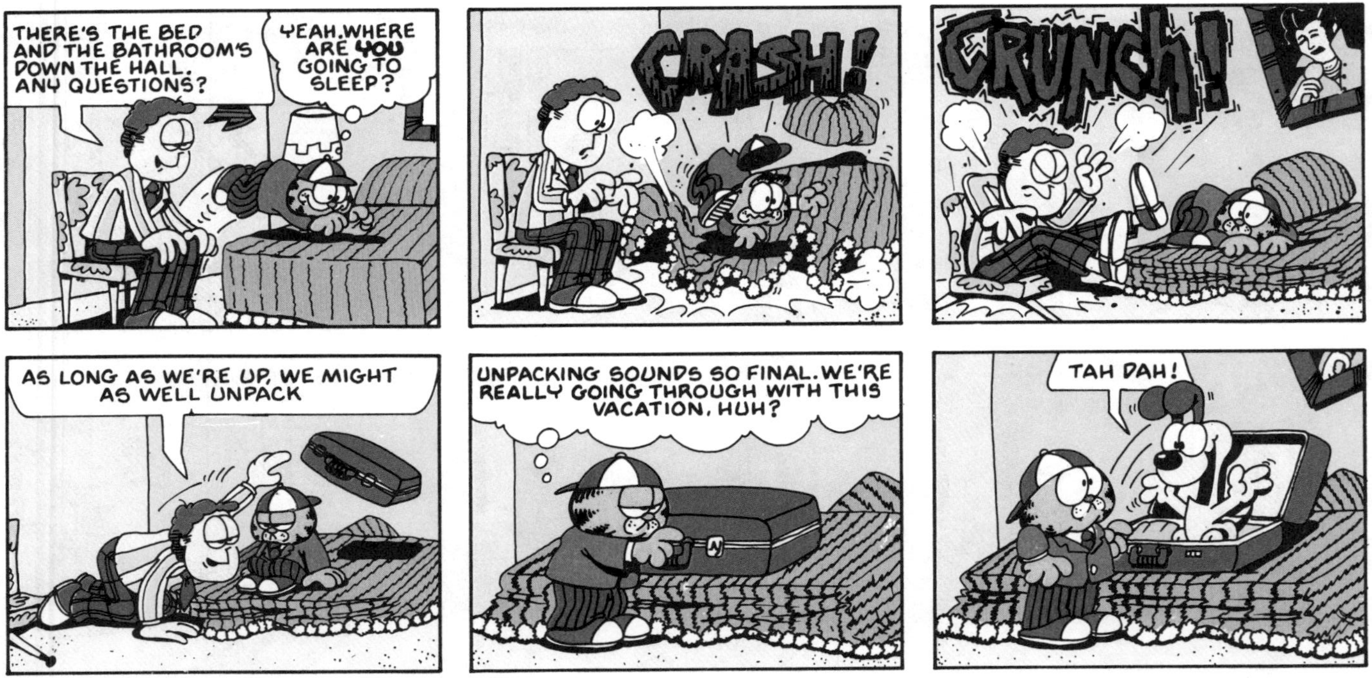
THERE'S THE BED AND THE BATHROOM'S DOWN THE HALL. ANY QUESTIONS?
YEAH. WHERE ARE YOU GOING TO SLEEP?
CRASH!
CRUNCH!
AS LONG AS WE'RE UP, WE MIGHT AS WELL UNPACK
UNPACKING SOUNDS SO FINAL. WE'RE REALLY GOING THROUGH WITH THIS VACATION, HUH?
TAH DAH!

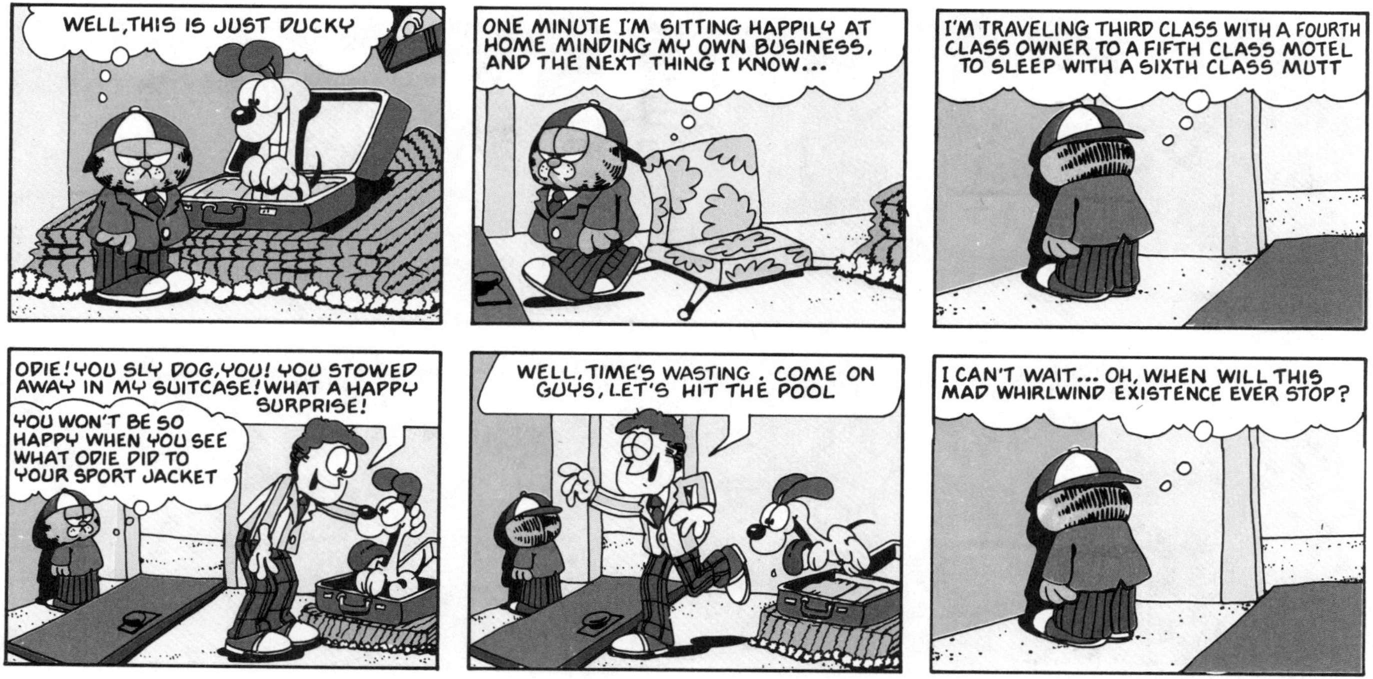
WELL,THIS IS JUST DUCKY
ONE MINUTE I'M SITTING HAPPILY AT HOME MINDING MY OWN BUSINESS, AND THE NEXT THING I KNOW...
I'M TRAVELING THIRD CLASS WITH A FOURTH CLASS OWNER TO A FIFTH CLASS MOTEL TO SLEEP WITH A SIXTH CLASS MUTT
ODIE! YOU SLY DOG,YOU! YOU STOWED AWAY IN MY SUITCASE! WHAT A HAPPY SURPRISE!
YOU WON'T BE SO HAPPY WHEN YOU SEE WHAT ODIE DID TO YOUR SPORT JACKET
WELL, TIME'S WASTING . COME ON GUYS, LET'S HIT THE POOL
I CAN'T WAIT... OH, WHEN WILL THIS MAD WHIRLWIND EXISTENCE EVER STOP?

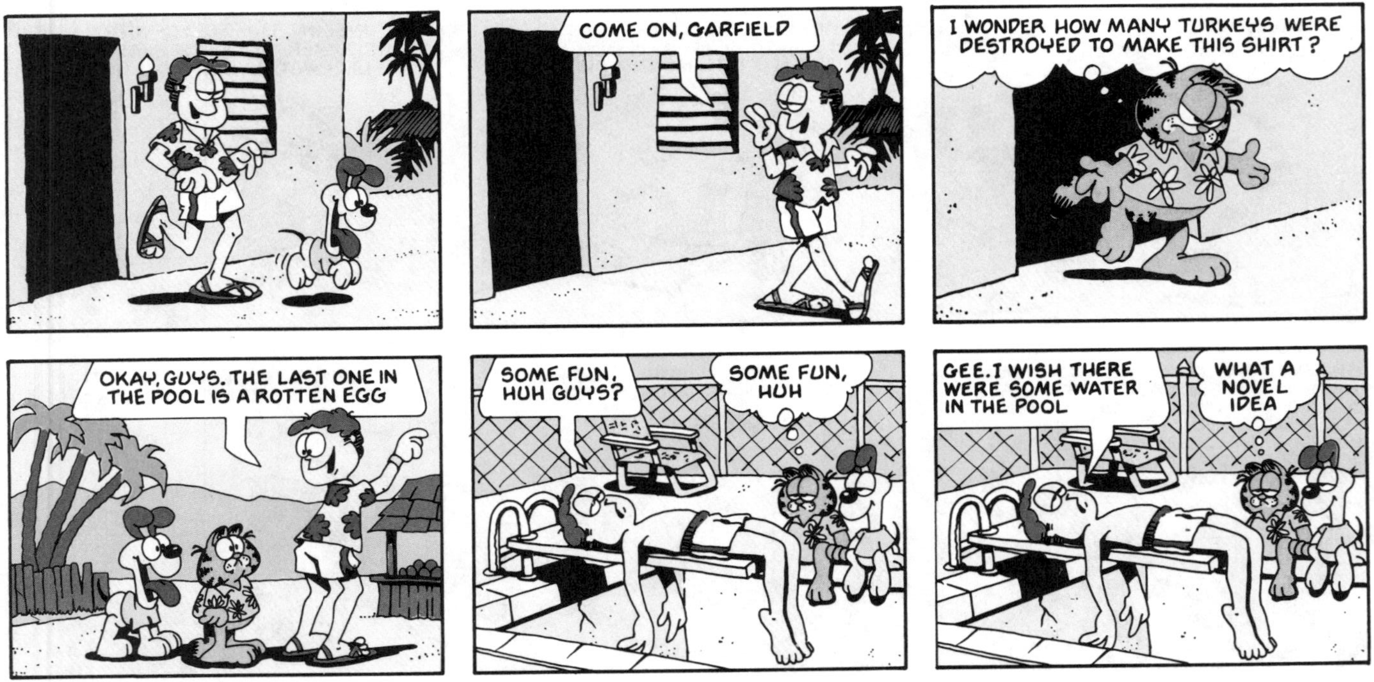
COME ON, GARFIELD
I WONDER HOW MANY TURKEYS WERE DESTROYED TO MAKE THIS SHIRT ?
OKAY, GUYS. THE LAST ONE IN THE POOL IS A ROTTEN EGG
SOME FUN, HUH GUYS?
SOME FUN, HUH
GEE. I WISH THERE WERE SOME WATER IN THE POOL
WHAT A NOVEL IDEA

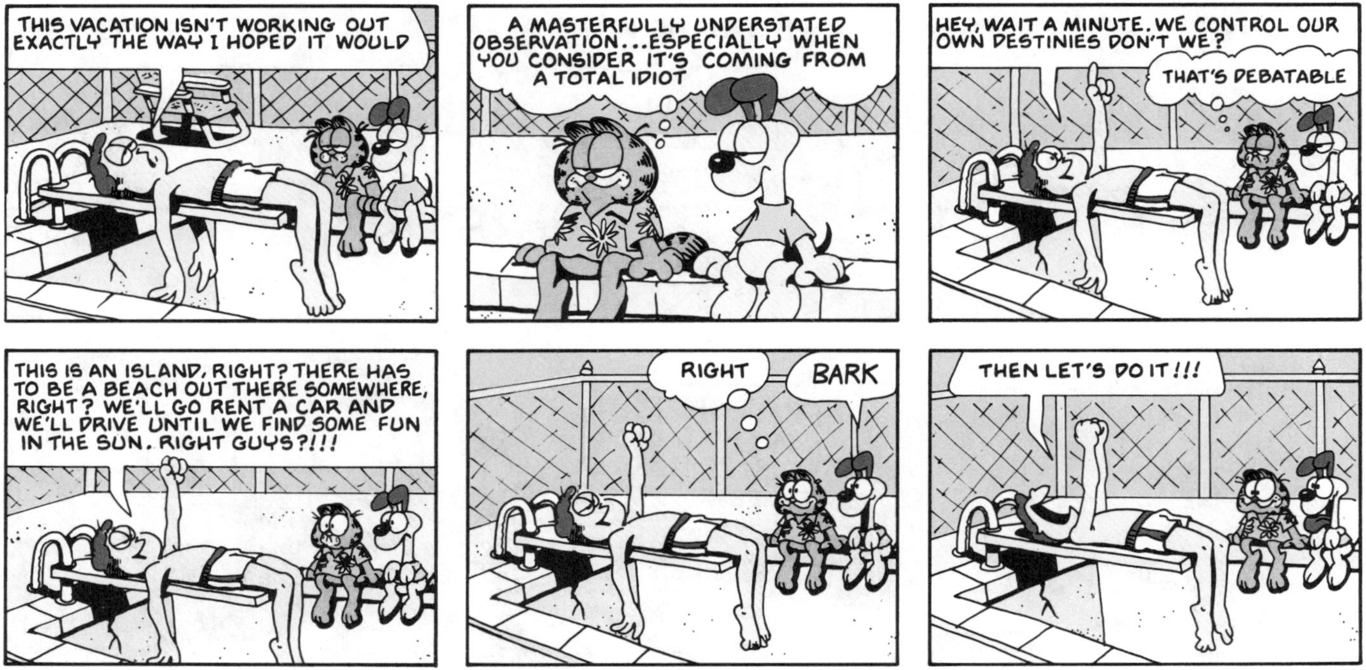
THIS VACATION ISN'T WORKING OUT EXACTLY THE WAY I HOPED IT WOULD
A MASTERFULLY UNDERSTATED OBSERVATION...ESPECIALLY WHEN YOU CONSIDER IT'S COMING FROM A TOTAL IDIOT
HEY, WAIT A MINUTE. WE CONTROL OUR OWN DESTINIES DON'T WE?
THAT'S DEBATABLE
THIS IS AN ISLAND, RIGHT? THERE HAS TO BE A BEACH OUT THERE SOMEWHERE, RIGHT? WE'LL GO RENT A CAR AND WE'LL DRIVE UNTIL WE FIND SOME FUN IN THE SUN. RIGHT GUYS?!!!
RIGHT
BARK
THEN LET'S DO IT!!!

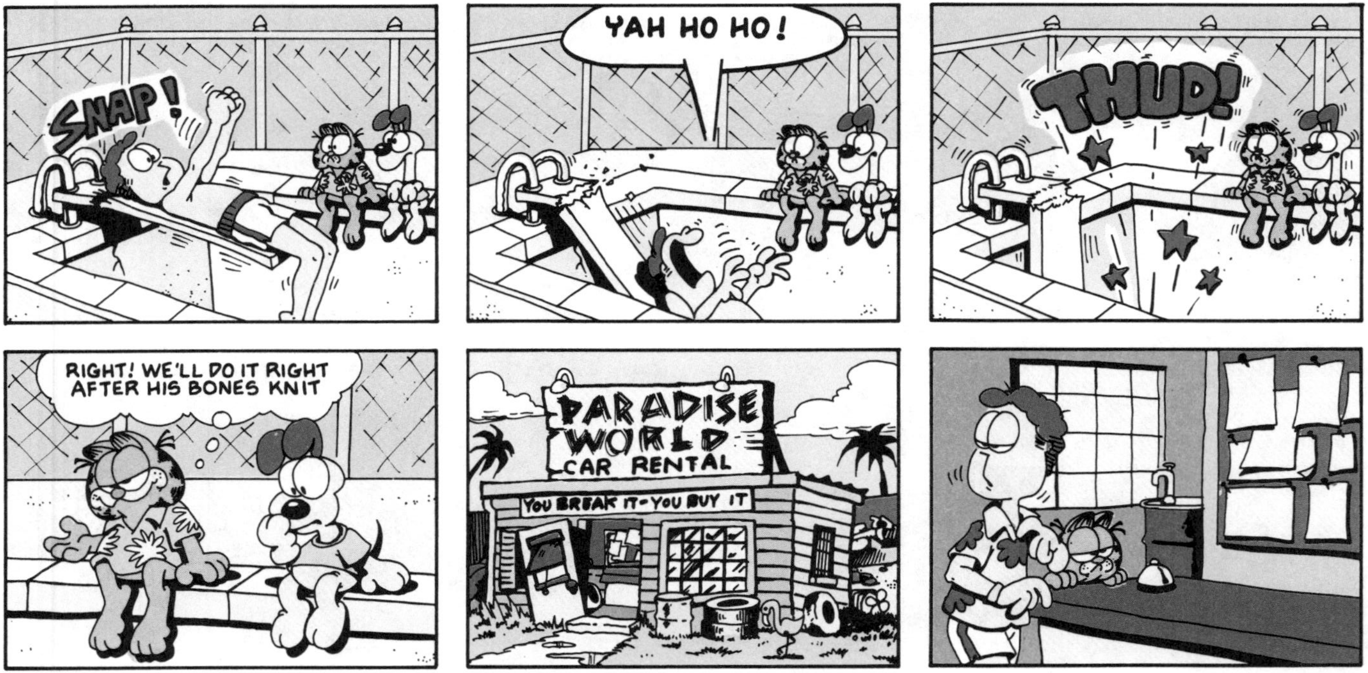
SNAP!
YAH HO HO!
THUD!
RIGHT! WE'LL DO IT RIGHT AFTER HIS BONES KNIT
PARADISE WORLD CAR RENTAL
YOU BREAK IT-YOU BUY IT

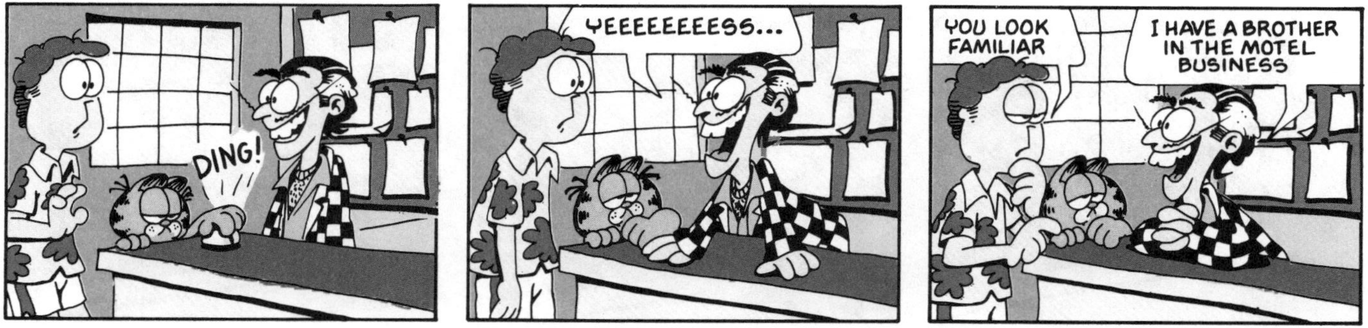
DING!
YEEEEEEEESS...
YOU LOOK FAMILIAR
I HAVE A BROTHER IN THE MOTEL BUSINESS

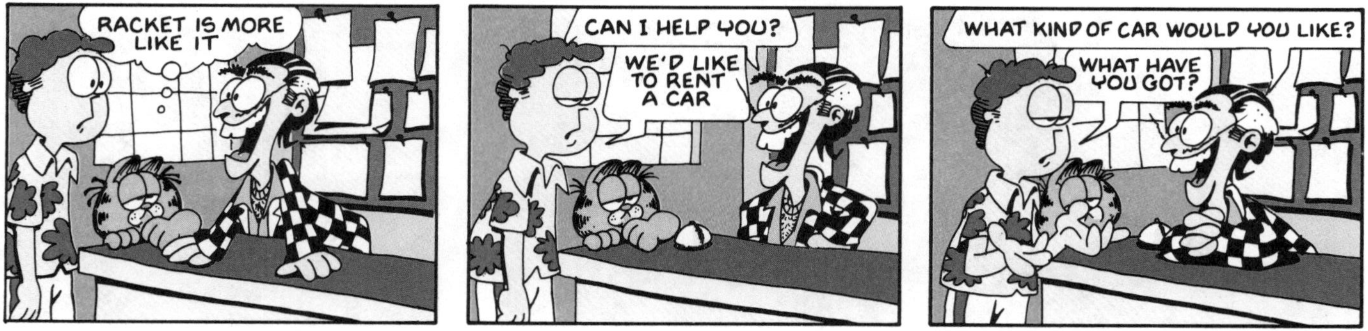
RACKET IS MORE LIKE IT
CAN I HELP YOU?
WE'D LIKE TO RENT A CAR
WHAT KIND OF CAR WOULD YOU LIKE?
WHAT HAVE YOU GOT?

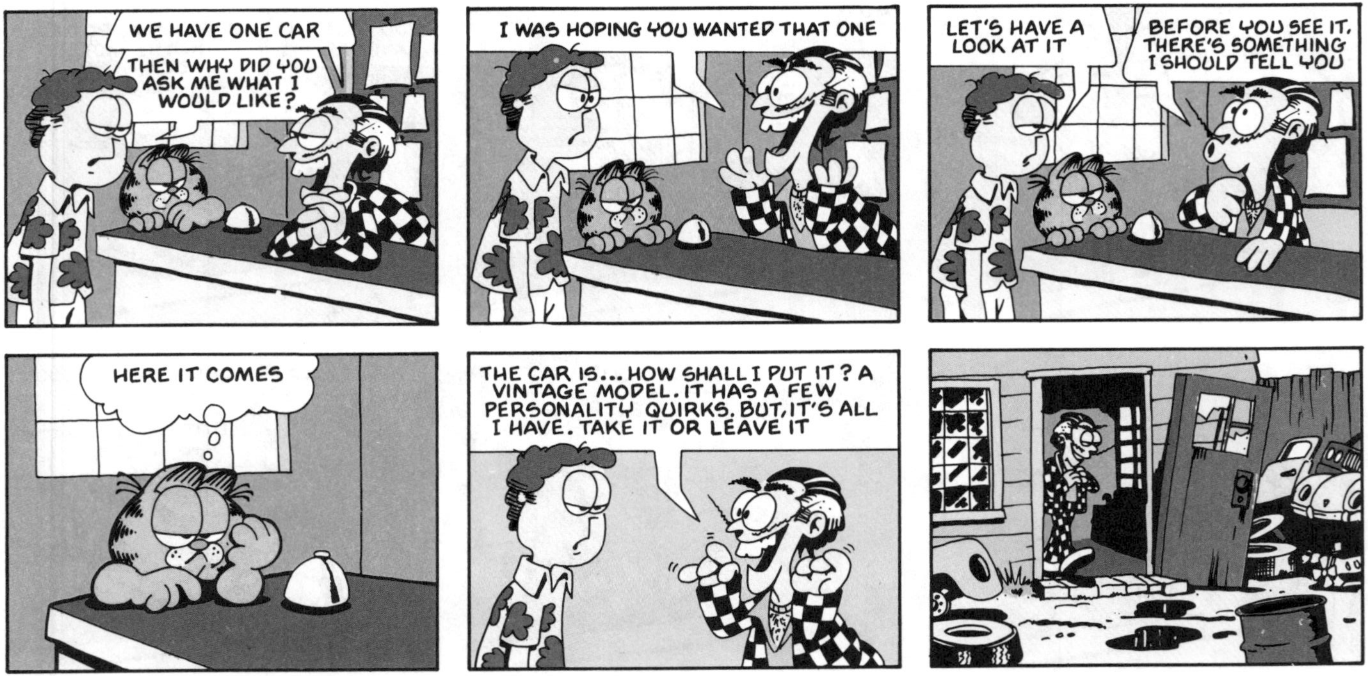
WE HAVE ONE CAR
THEN WHY DID YOU ASK ME WHAT I WOULD LIKE?
I WAS HOPING YOU WANTED THAT ONE
LET'S HAVE A LOOK AT IT
BEFORE YOU SEE IT, THERE'S SOMETHING I SHOULD TELL YOU
HERE IT COMES
THE CAR IS... HOW SHALL I PUT IT? A VINTAGE MODEL. IT HAS A FEW PERSONALITY QUIRKS. BUT, IT'S ALL I HAVE. TAKE IT OR LEAVE IT

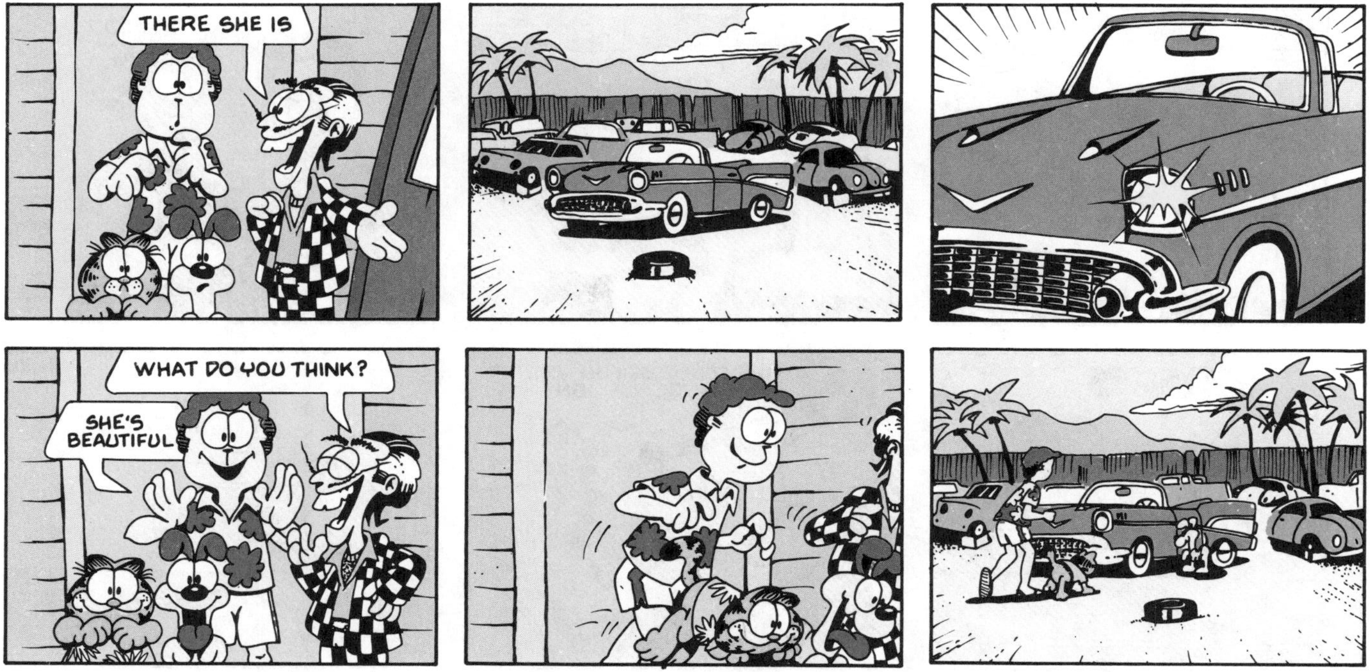
THERE SHE IS
WHAT DO YOU THINK?
SHE'S BEAUTIFUL

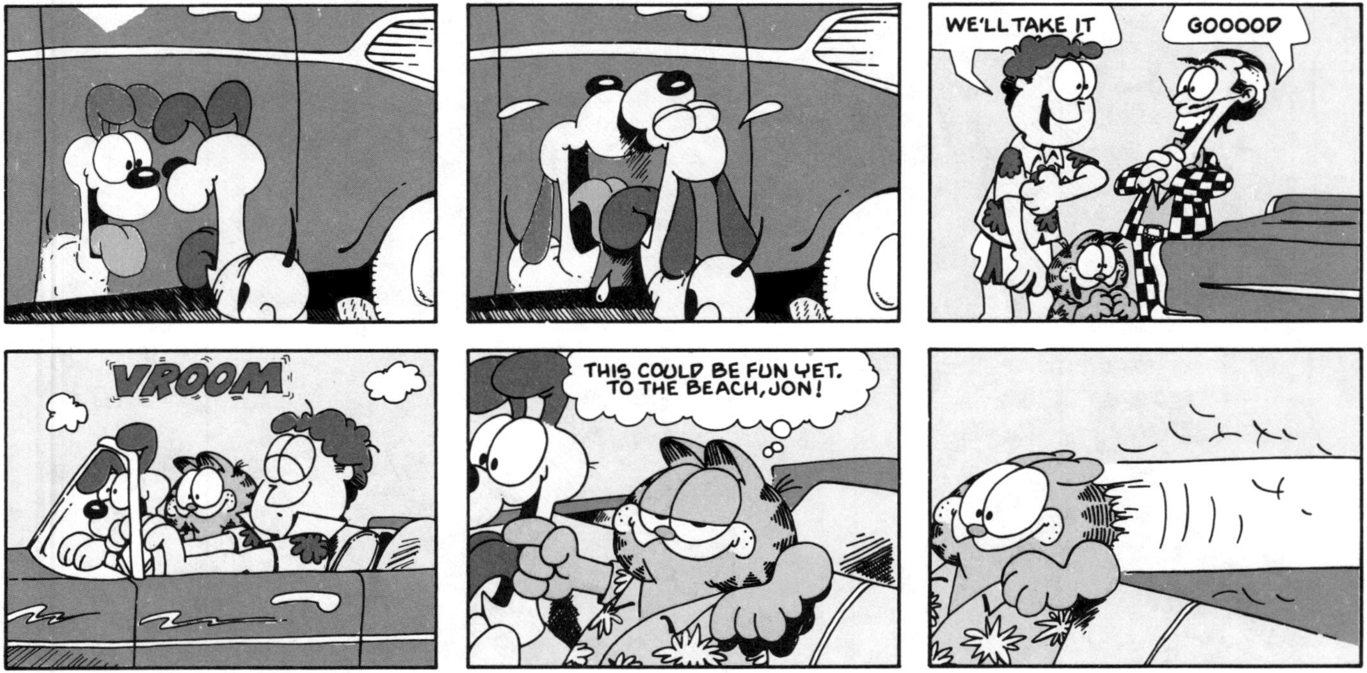
WE'LL TAKE IT
GOOOOD
VROOM
THIS COULD BE FUN YET. TO THE BEACH, JON!

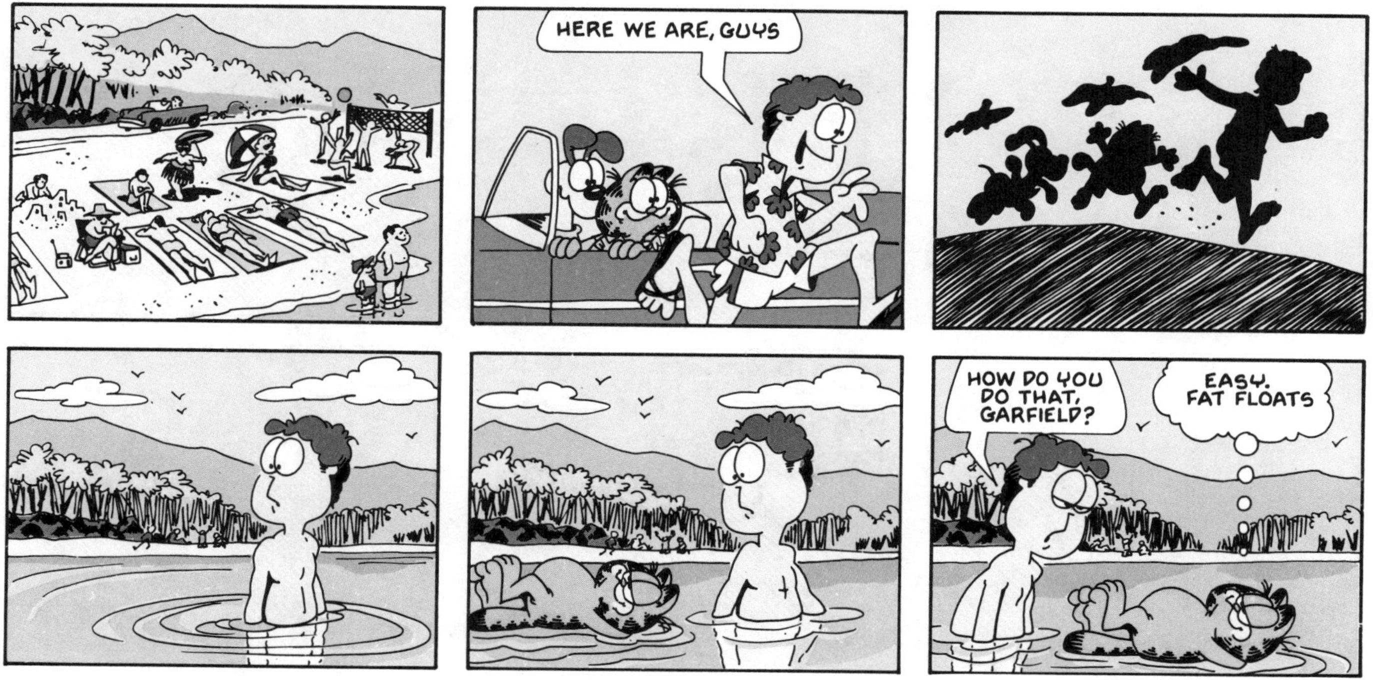
HERE WE ARE, GUYS
HOW DO YOU DO THAT, GARFIELD?
EASY. FAT FLOATS

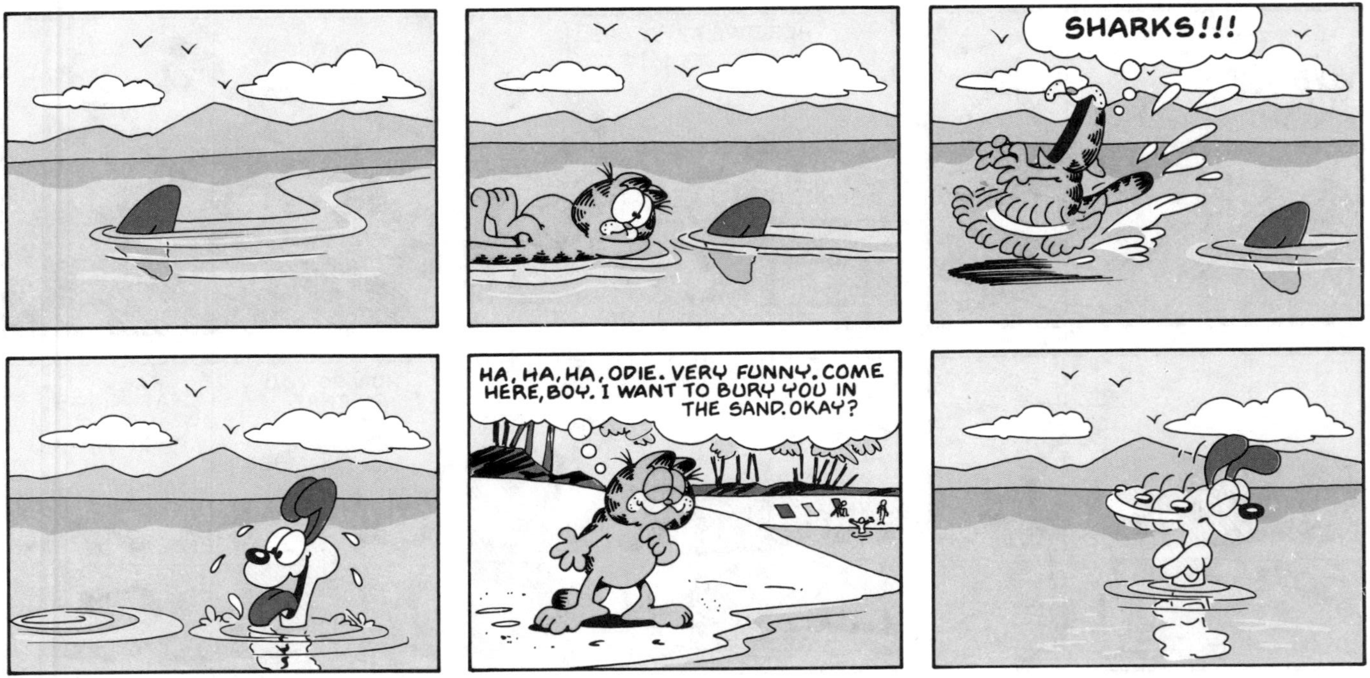
SHARKS!!!
HA, HA, HA, ODIE. VERY FUNNY. COME HERE, BOY. I WANT TO BURY YOU IN THE SAND. OKAY?

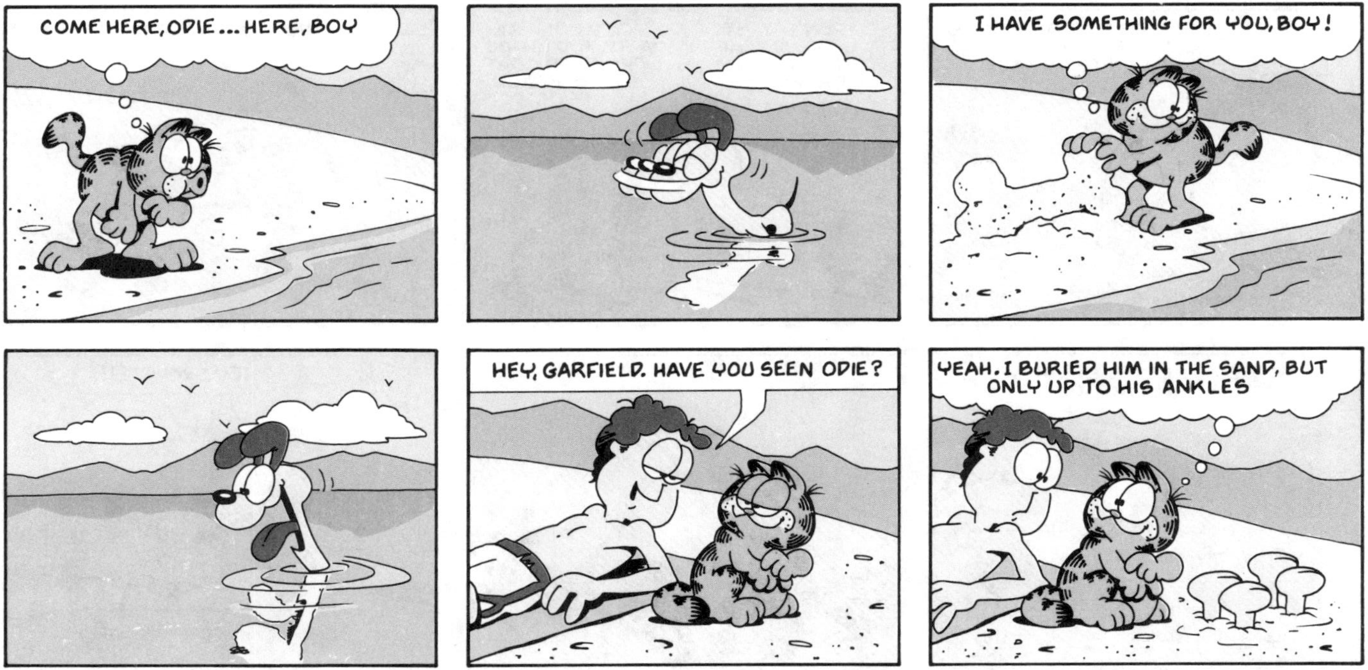
COME HERE, ODIE... HERE, BOY
I HAVE SOMETHING FOR YOU, BOY!
HEY, GARFIELD. HAVE YOU SEEN ODIE?
YEAH. I BURIED HIM IN THE SAND, BUT ONLY UP TO HIS ANKLES

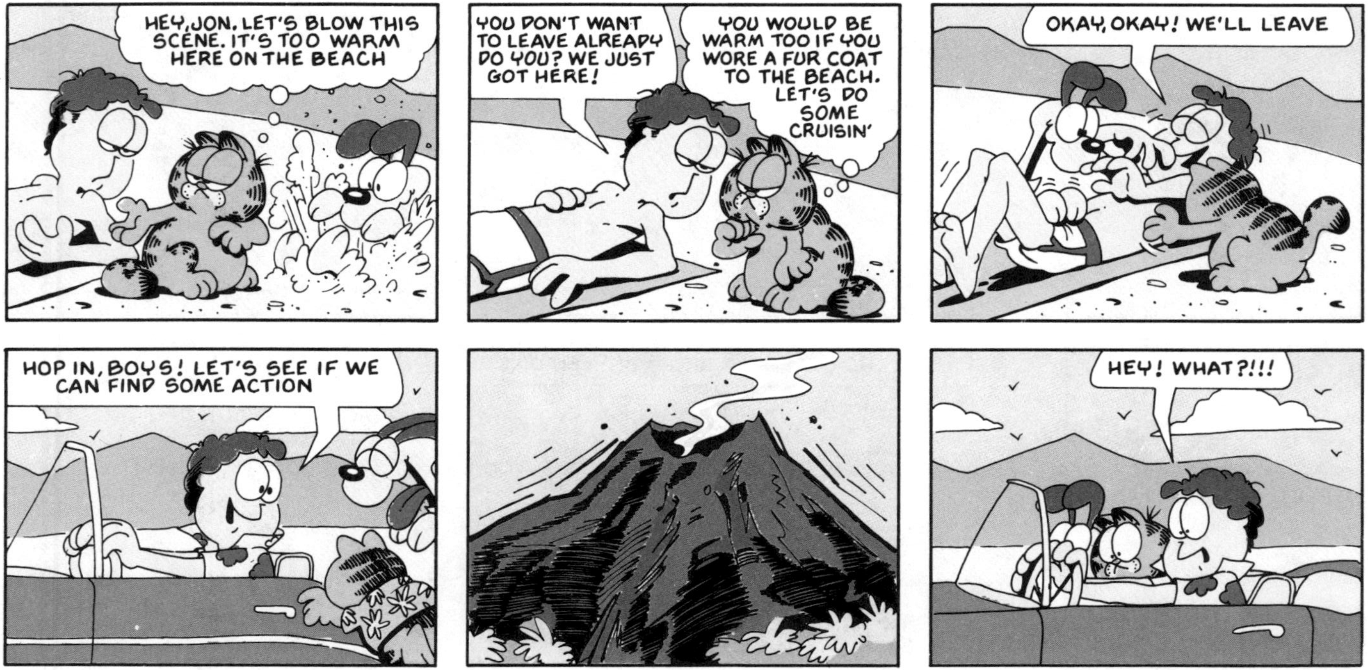
HEY, JON. LET'S BLOW THIS SCENE. IT'S TOO WARM HERE ON THE BEACH
YOU DON'T WANT TO LEAVE ALREADY DO YOU? WE JUST GOT HERE!
YOU WOULD BE WARM TOO IF YOU WORE A FUR COAT TO THE BEACH. LET'S DO SOME CRUISIN'
OKAY, OKAY! WE'LL LEAVE
HOP IN, BOYS! LET'S SEE IF WE CAN FIND SOME ACTION
HEY! WHAT?!!!

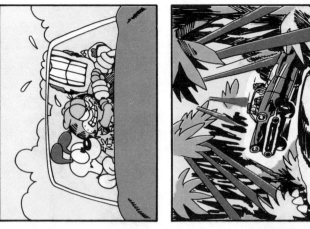

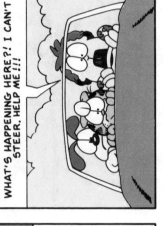

WHAT'S HAPPENING HERE?! I CAN'T STEER. HELP ME!!!

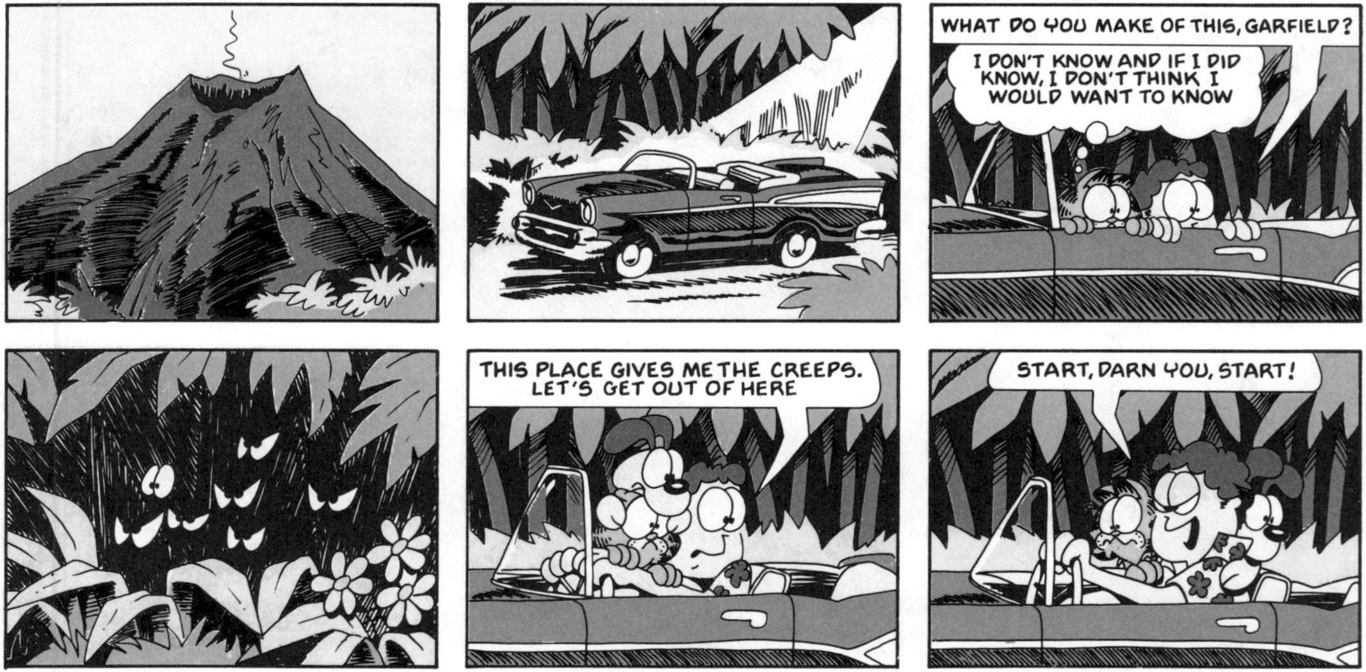
WHAT DO YOU MAKE OF THIS, GARFIELD?
I DON'T KNOW AND IF I DID KNOW, I DON'T THINK I WOULD WANT TO KNOW
THIS PLACE GIVES ME THE CREEPS. LET'S GET OUT OF HERE
START, DARN YOU, START!

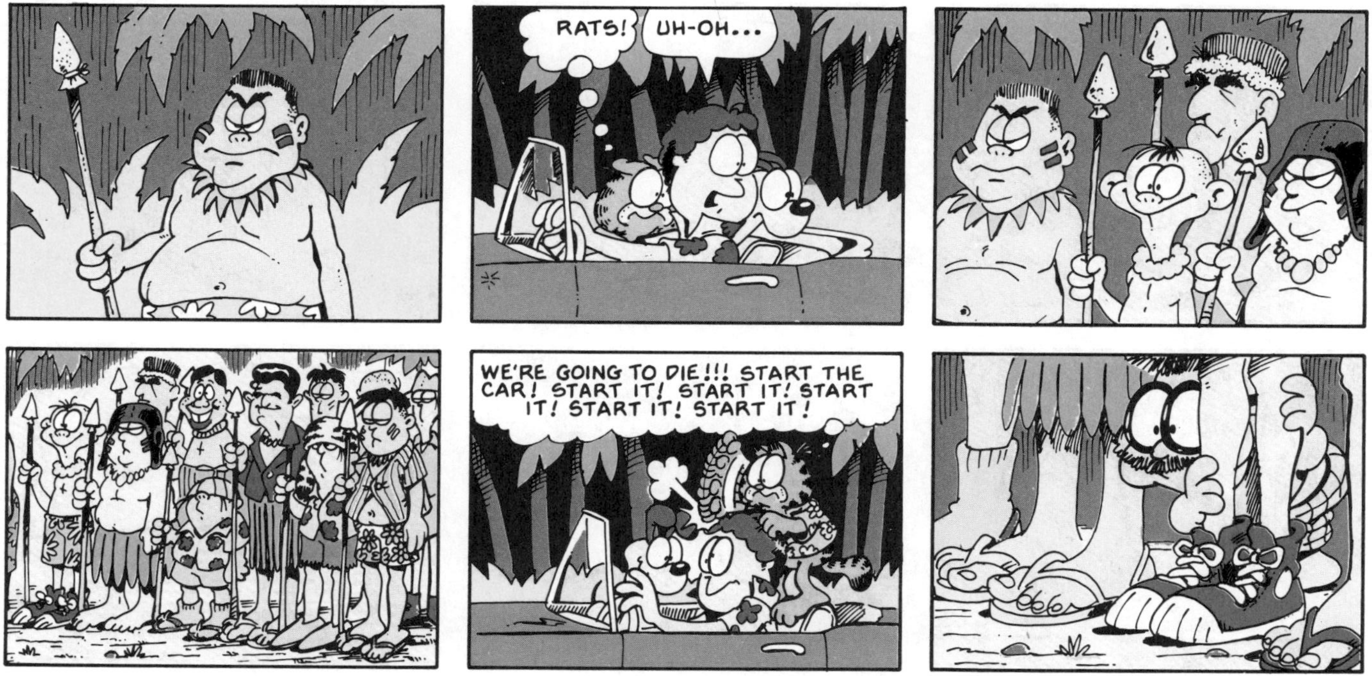
RATS!
UH-OH...
WE'RE GOING TO DIE!!! START THE CAR! START IT! START IT! START IT! START IT! START IT!

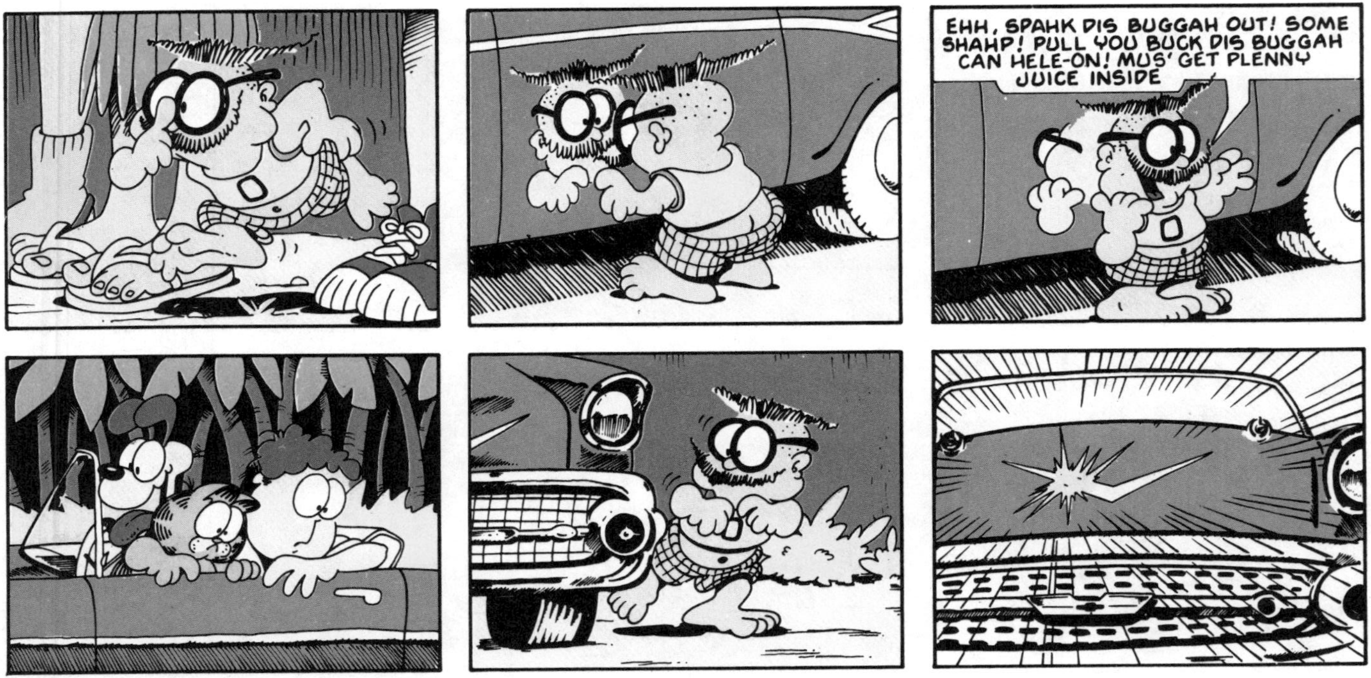
EHH, SPAHK DIS BUGGAH OUT! SOME SHAHP! PULL YOU BUCK DIS BUGGAH CAN HELE-ON! MUS' GET PLENNY JUICE INSIDE

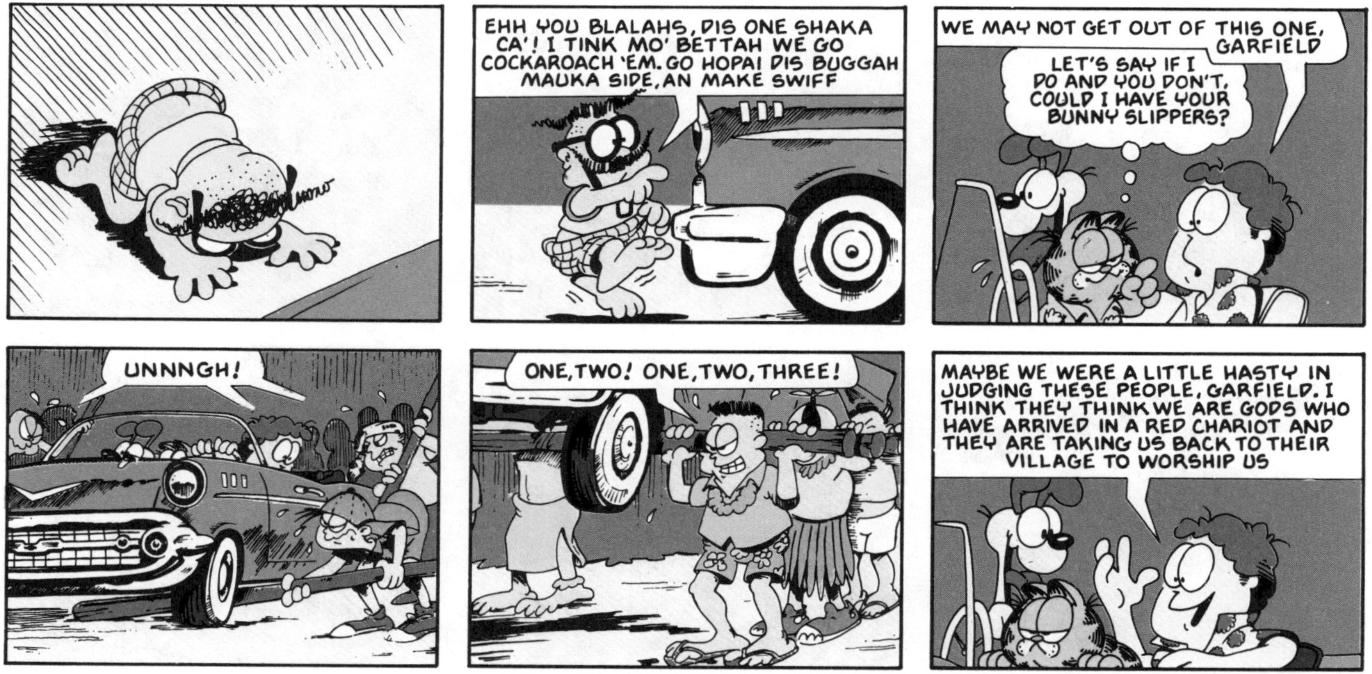
EHH YOU BLALAHS, DIS ONE SHAKA CA'! I TINK MO' BETTAH WE GO COCKAROACH 'EM. GO HOPAI DIS BUGGAH MAUKA SIDE, AN MAKE SWIFF
WE MAY NOT GET OUT OF THIS ONE, GARFIELD
LET'S SAY IF I DO AND YOU DON'T, COULD I HAVE YOUR BUNNY SLIPPERS?
UNNNGH!
ONE, TWO! ONE, TWO, THREE!
MAYBE WE WERE A LITTLE HASTY IN JUDGING THESE PEOPLE, GARFIELD. I THINK THEY THINK WE ARE GODS WHO HAVE ARRIVED IN A RED CHARIOT AND THEY ARE TAKING US BACK TO THEIR VILLAGE TO WORSHIP US

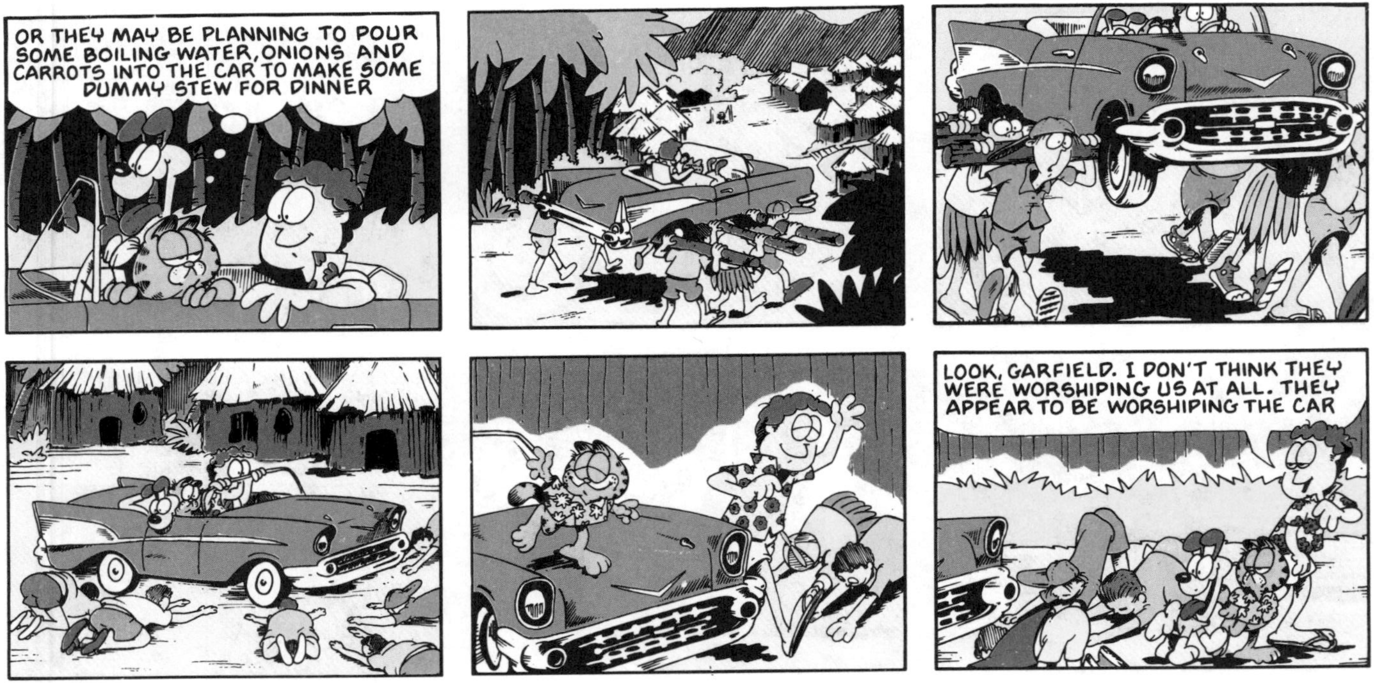
OR THEY MAY BE PLANNING TO POUR SOME BOILING WATER, ONIONS AND CARROTS INTO THE CAR TO MAKE SOME DUMMY STEW FOR DINNER
LOOK, GARFIELD. I DON'T THINK THEY WERE WORSHIPING US AT ALL. THEY APPEAR TO BE WORSHIPING THE CAR

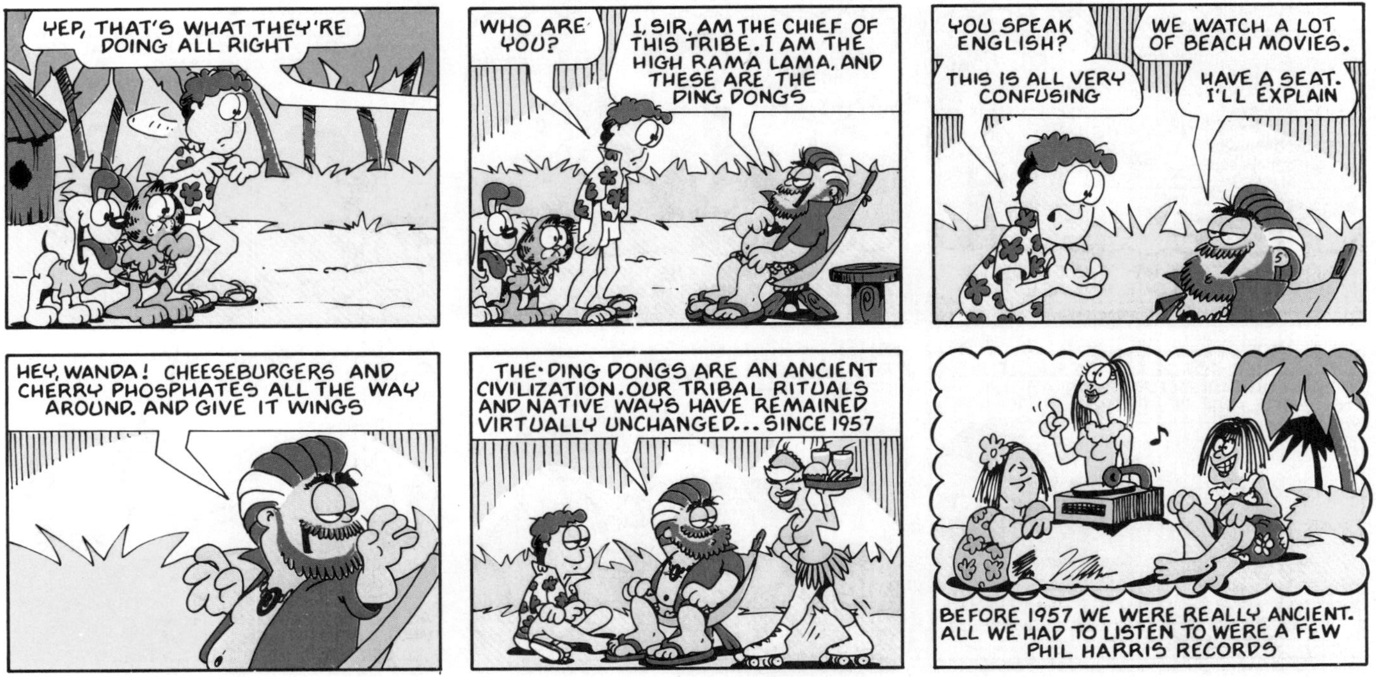
YEP, THAT'S WHAT THEY'RE DOING ALL RIGHT
WHO ARE YOU?
I, SIR, AM THE CHIEF OF THIS TRIBE. I AM THE HIGH RAMA LAMA, AND THESE ARE THE DING DONGS
YOU SPEAK ENGLISH?
THIS IS ALL VERY CONFUSING
WE WATCH A LOT OF BEACH MOVIES.
HAVE A SEAT. I'LL EXPLAIN
HEY, WANDA! CHEESEBURGERS AND CHERRY PHOSPHATES ALL THE WAY AROUND. AND GIVE IT WINGS
THE DING DONGS ARE AN ANCIENT CIVILIZATION. OUR TRIBAL RITUALS AND NATIVE WAYS HAVE REMAINED VIRTUALLY UNCHANGED... SINCE 1957
BEFORE 1957 WE WERE REALLY ANCIENT. ALL WE HAD TO LISTEN TO WERE A FEW PHIL HARRIS RECORDS

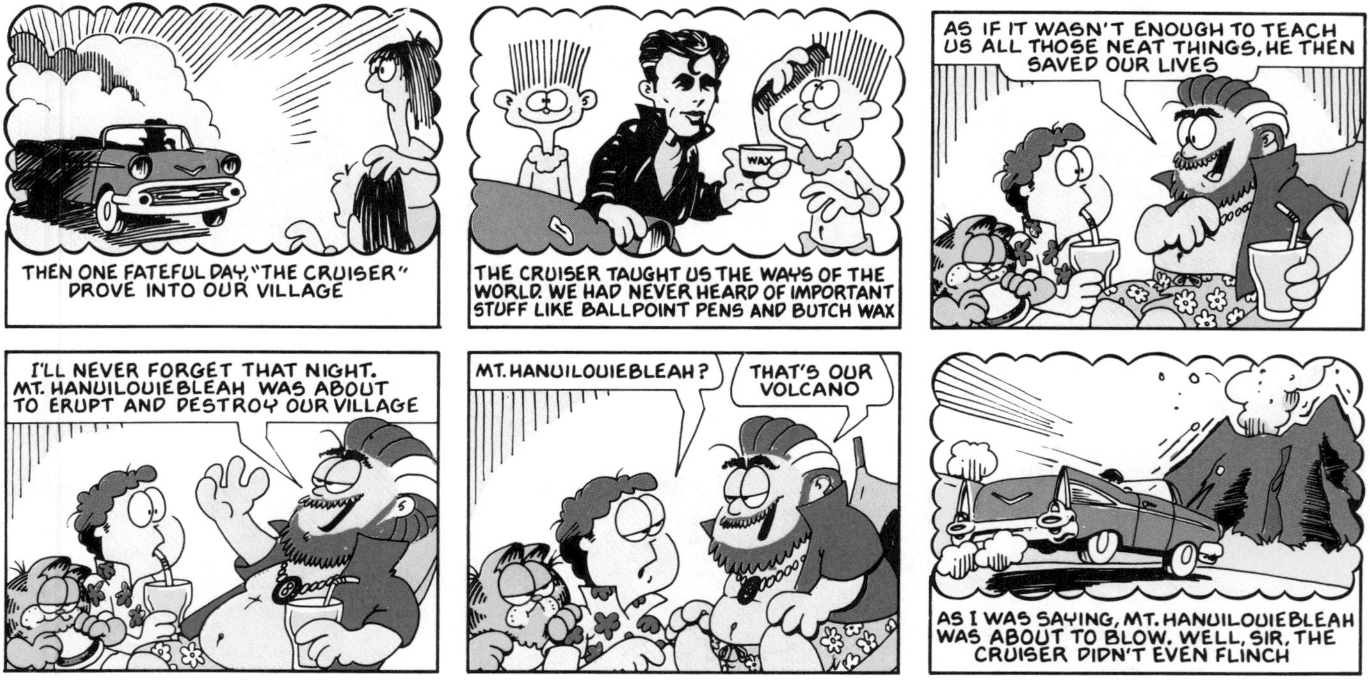
THEN ONE FATEFUL DAY, "THE CRUISER" DROVE INTO OUR VILLAGE
THE CRUISER TAUGHT US THE WAYS OF THE WORLD. WE HAD NEVER HEARD OF IMPORTANT STUFF LIKE BALLPOINT PENS AND BUTCH WAX
WAX
AS IF IT WASN'T ENOUGH TO TEACH US ALL THOSE NEAT THINGS, HE THEN SAVED OUR LIVES
I'LL NEVER FORGET THAT NIGHT. MT. HANUILOUIEBLEAH WAS ABOUT TO ERUPT AND DESTROY OUR VILLAGE
MT. HANUILOUIEBLEAH?
THAT'S OUR VOLCANO
AS I WAS SAYING, MT. HANUILOUIEBLEAH WAS ABOUT TO BLOW. WELL, SIR, THE CRUISER DIDN'T EVEN FLINCH

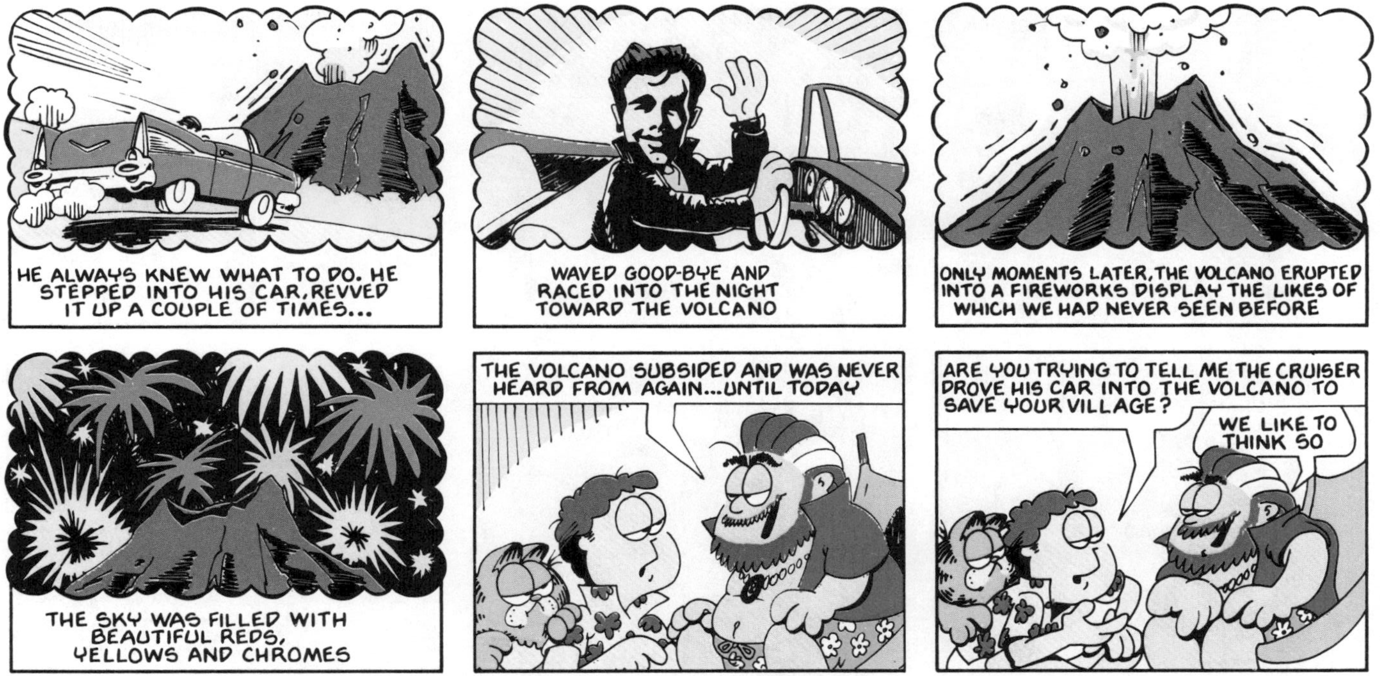
HE ALWAYS KNEW WHAT TO DO. HE STEPPED INTO HIS CAR, REVVED IT UP A COUPLE OF TIMES...
WAVED GOOD-BYE AND RACED INTO THE NIGHT TOWARD THE VOLCANO
ONLY MOMENTS LATER, THE VOLCANO ERUPTED INTO A FIREWORKS DISPLAY THE LIKES OF WHICH WE HAD NEVER SEEN BEFORE
THE SKY WAS FILLED WITH BEAUTIFUL REDS, YELLOWS AND CHROMES
THE VOLCANO SUBSIDED AND WAS NEVER HEARD FROM AGAIN...UNTIL TODAY
ARE YOU TRYING TO TELL ME THE CRUISER DROVE HIS CAR INTO THE VOLCANO TO SAVE YOUR VILLAGE?
WE LIKE TO THINK SO

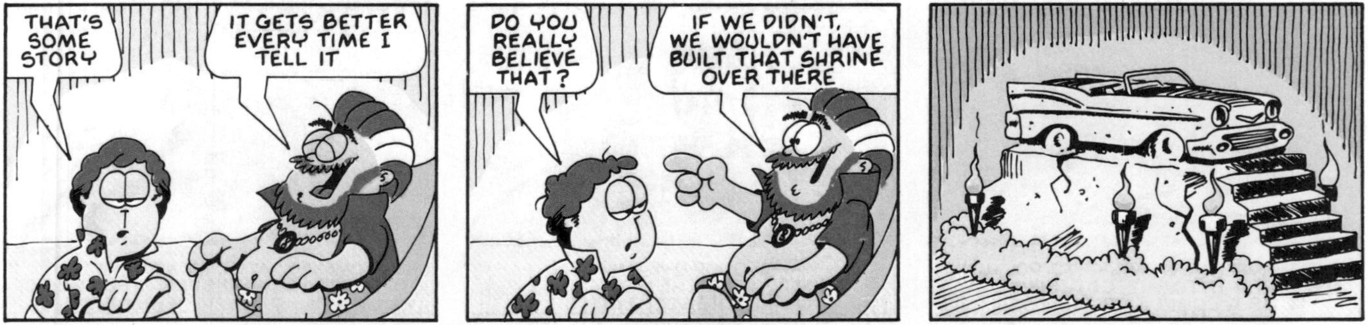
THAT'S SOME STORY
IT GETS BETTER EVERY TIME I TELL IT
DO YOU REALLY BELIEVE THAT?
IF WE DIDN'T, WE WOULDN'T HAVE BUILT THAT SHRINE OVER THERE

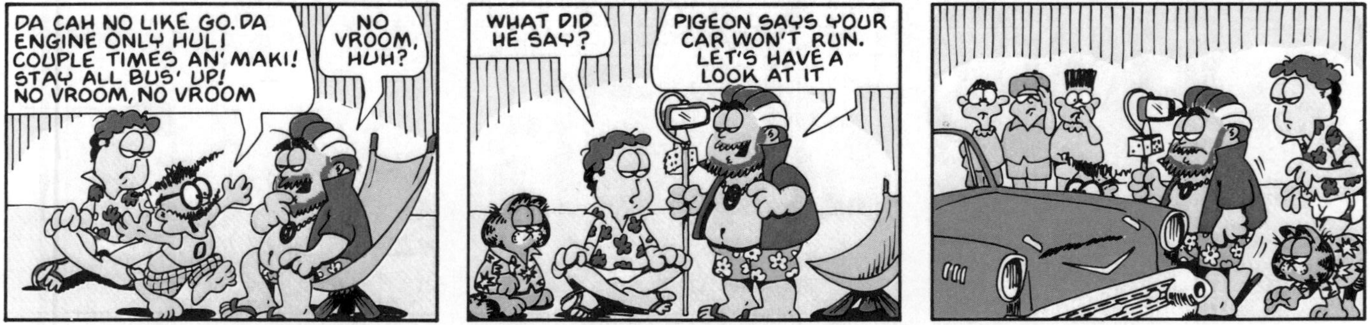
DA CAH NO LIKE GO. DA ENGINE ONLY HULI COUPLE TIMES AN' MAKI! STAY ALL BUS' UP! NO VROOM, NO VROOM
NO VROOM, HUH?
WHAT DID HE SAY?
PIGEON SAYS YOUR CAR WON'T RUN. LET'S HAVE A LOOK AT IT

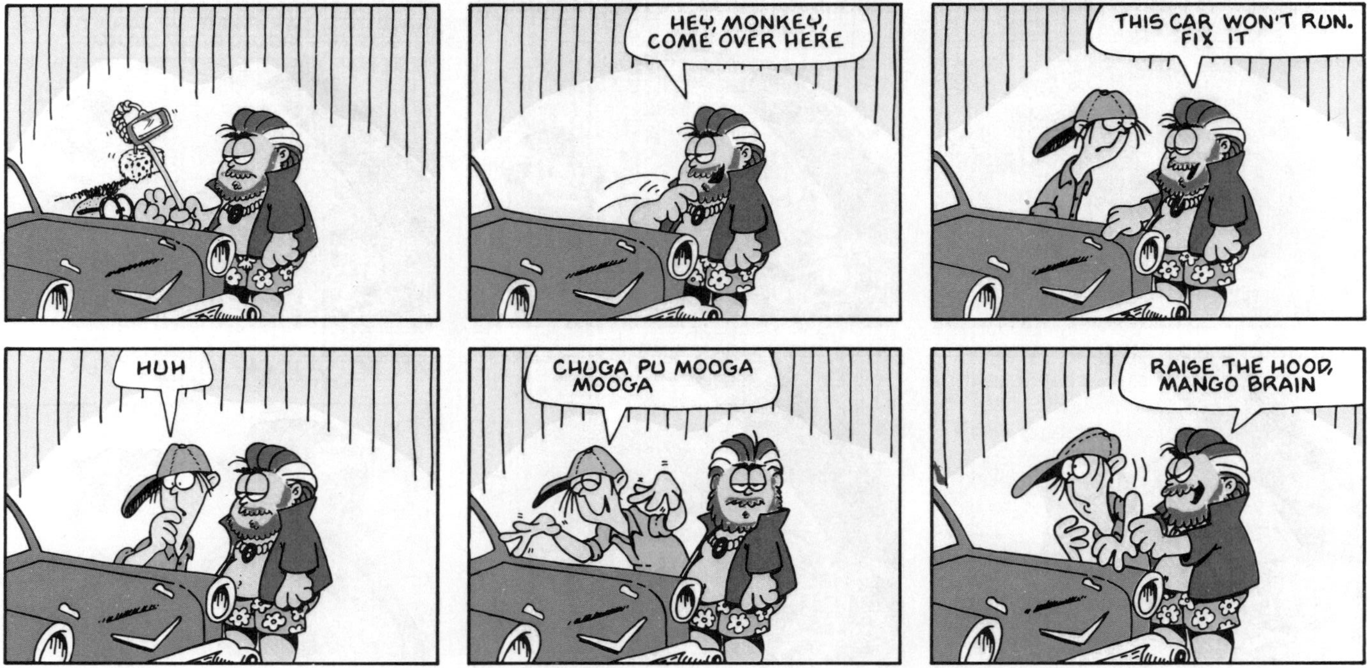
HEY, MONKEY, COME OVER HERE
THIS CAR WON'T RUN. FIX IT
HUH
CHUGA PU MOOGA MOOGA
RAISE THE HOOD, MANGO BRAIN

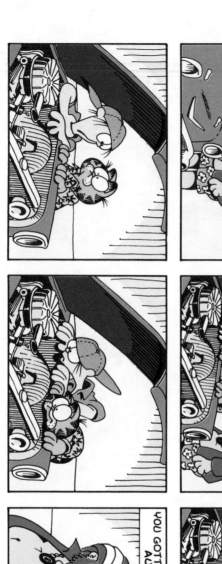

OH, YEAH

HAVE THIS CAR FIXED BY DARK, OR I'LL CUT OFF YOUR HEAD, OKAY!

YOU GOTTA KNOW HOW TO TALK TO AUTO MECHANICS

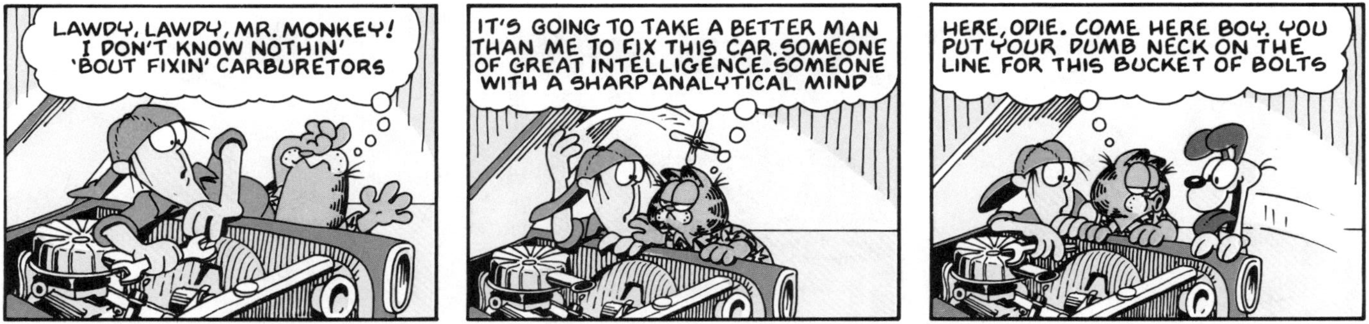
LAWDY, LAWDY, MR. MONKEY! I DON'T KNOW NOTHIN' 'BOUT FIXIN' CARBURETORS
IT'S GOING TO TAKE A BETTER MAN THAN ME TO FIX THIS CAR. SOMEONE OF GREAT INTELLIGENCE. SOMEONE WITH A SHARP ANALYTICAL MIND
HERE, ODIE. COME HERE BOY. YOU PUT YOUR DUMB NECK ON THE LINE FOR THIS BUCKET OF BOLTS

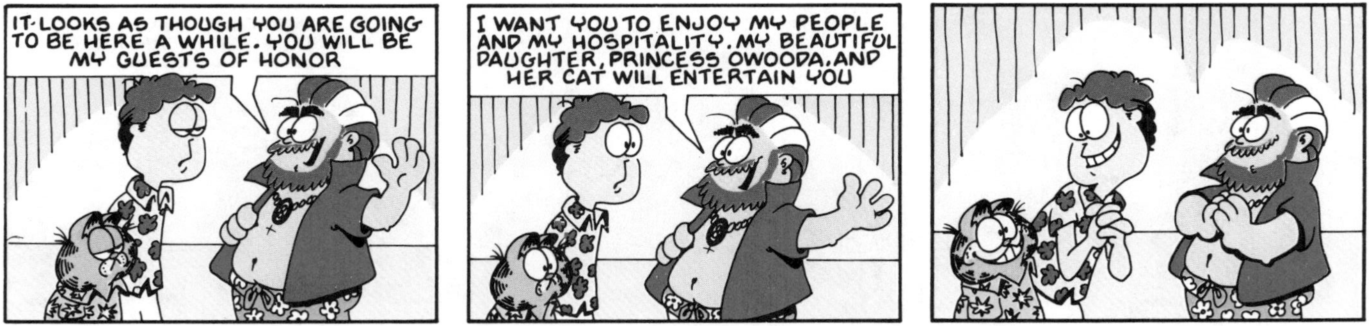
IT LOOKS AS THOUGH YOU ARE GOING TO BE HERE A WHILE. YOU WILL BE MY GUESTS OF HONOR
I WANT YOU TO ENJOY MY PEOPLE AND MY HOSPITALITY. MY BEAUTIFUL DAUGHTER, PRINCESS OWOODA, AND HER CAT WILL ENTERTAIN YOU

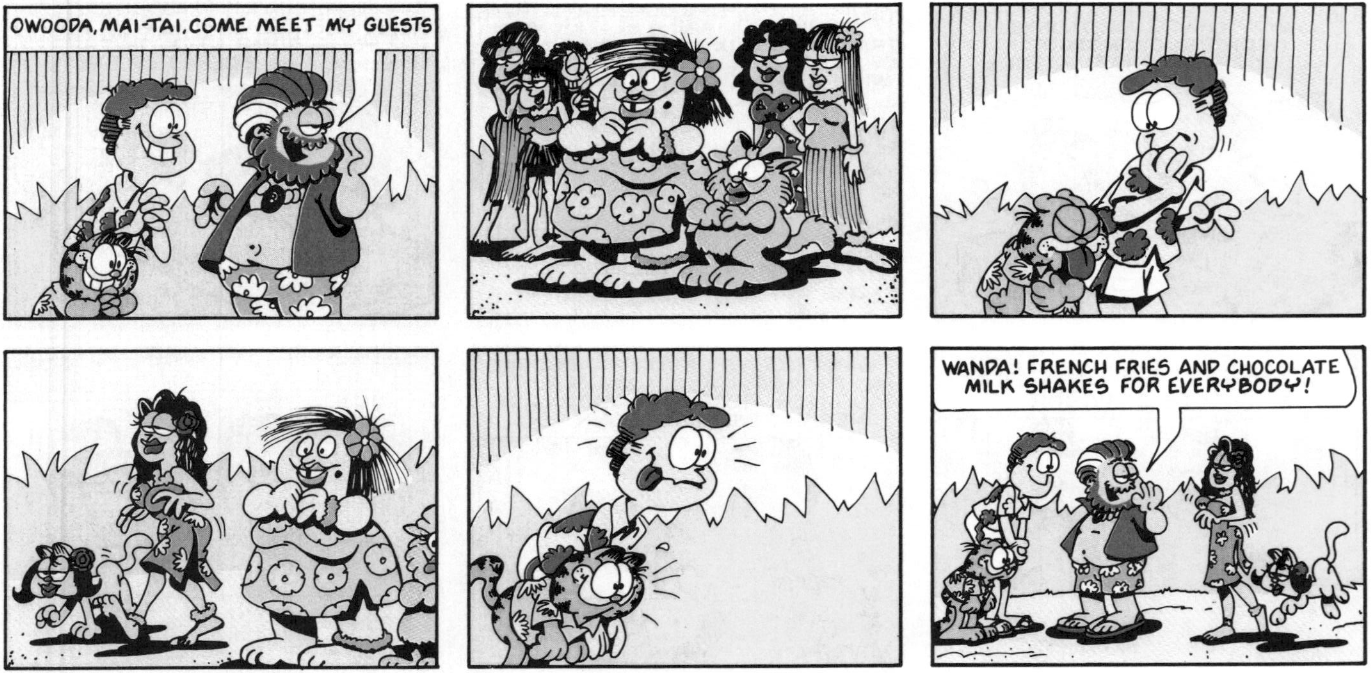
OWOODA, MAI-TAI, COME MEET MY GUESTS
WANDA! FRENCH FRIES AND CHOCOLATE MILK SHAKES FOR EVERYBODY!

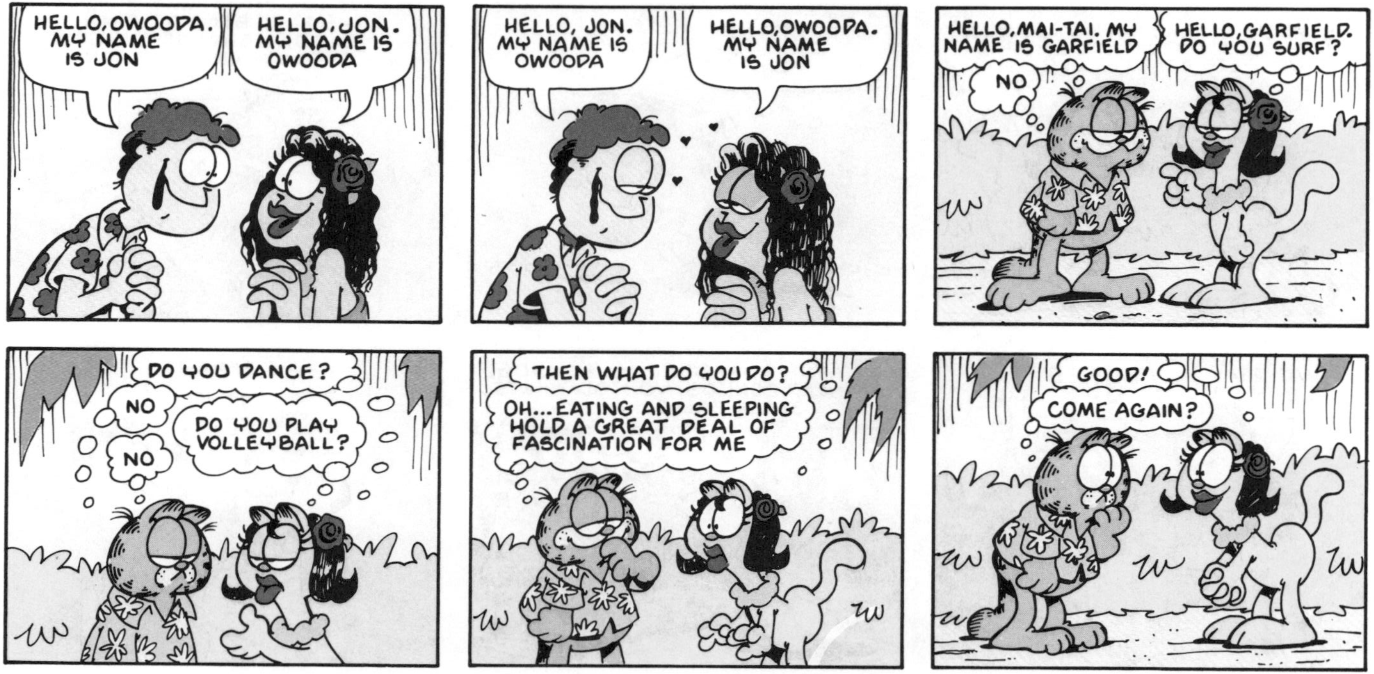
HELLO, OWOODA. MY NAME IS JON
HELLO, JON. MY NAME IS OWOODA
HELLO, JON. MY NAME IS OWOODA
HELLO, OWOODA. MY NAME IS JON
HELLO, MAI-TAI. MY NAME IS GARFIELD
HELLO, GARFIELD. DO YOU SURF?
NO
DO YOU DANCE?
NO
DO YOU PLAY VOLLEYBALL?
NO
THEN WHAT DO YOU DO?
OH... EATING AND SLEEPING HOLD A GREAT DEAL OF FASCINATION FOR ME
GOOD!
COME AGAIN?

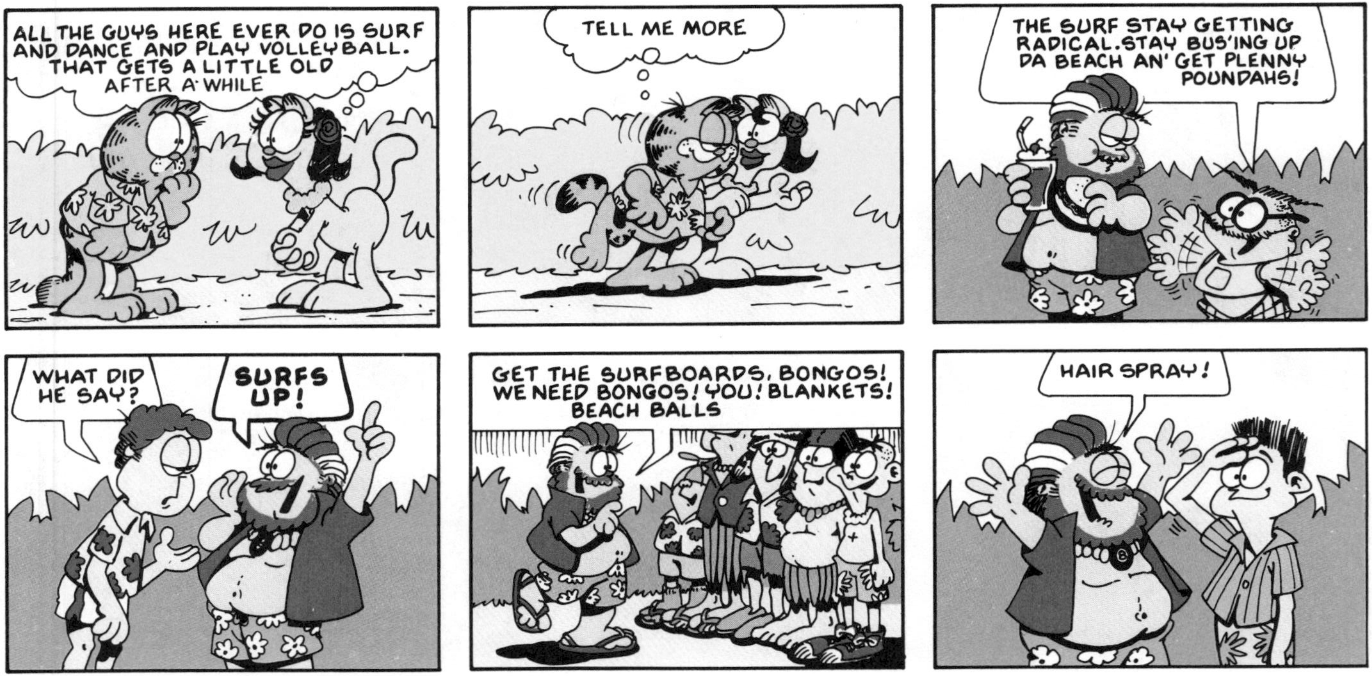
ALL THE GUYS HERE EVER DO IS SURF AND DANCE AND PLAY VOLLEYBALL. THAT GETS A LITTLE OLD AFTER A WHILE
TELL ME MORE
THE SURF STAY GETTING RADICAL. STAY BUS'ING UP DA BEACH AN' GET PLENNY POUNDAHS!
WHAT DID HE SAY?
SURFS UP!
GET THE SURFBOARDS, BONGOS! WE NEED BONGOS! YOU! BLANKETS! BEACH BALLS
HAIR SPRAY!

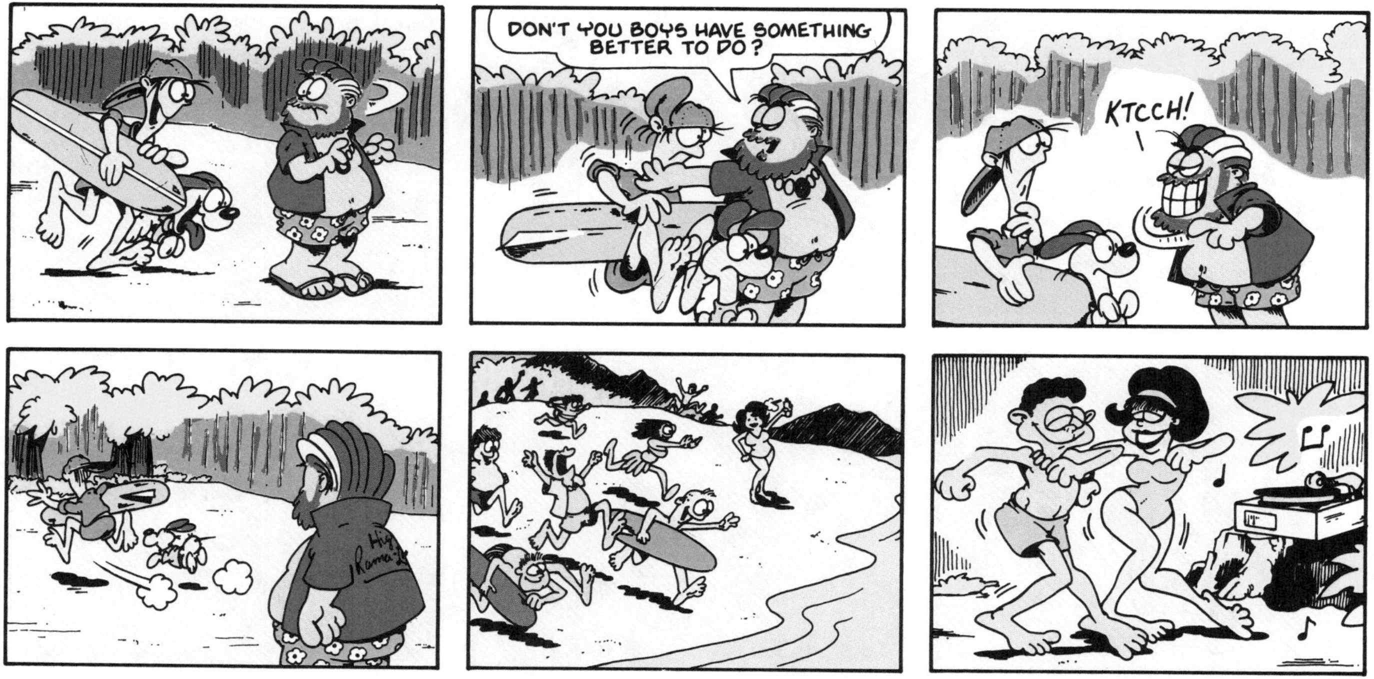
DON'T YOU BOYS HAVE SOMETHING BETTER TO DO?
KTCCH!

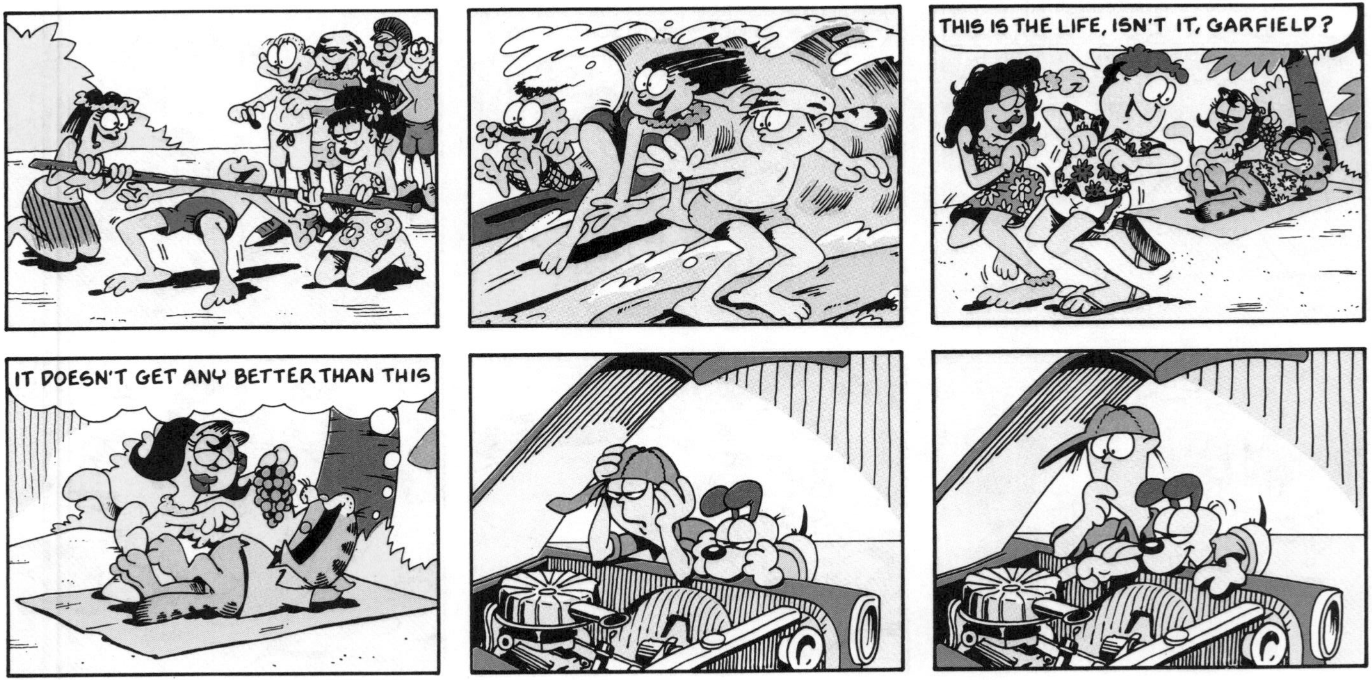

THIS IS THE LIFE, ISN'T IT, GARFIELD?
IT DOESN'T GET ANY BETTER THAN THIS

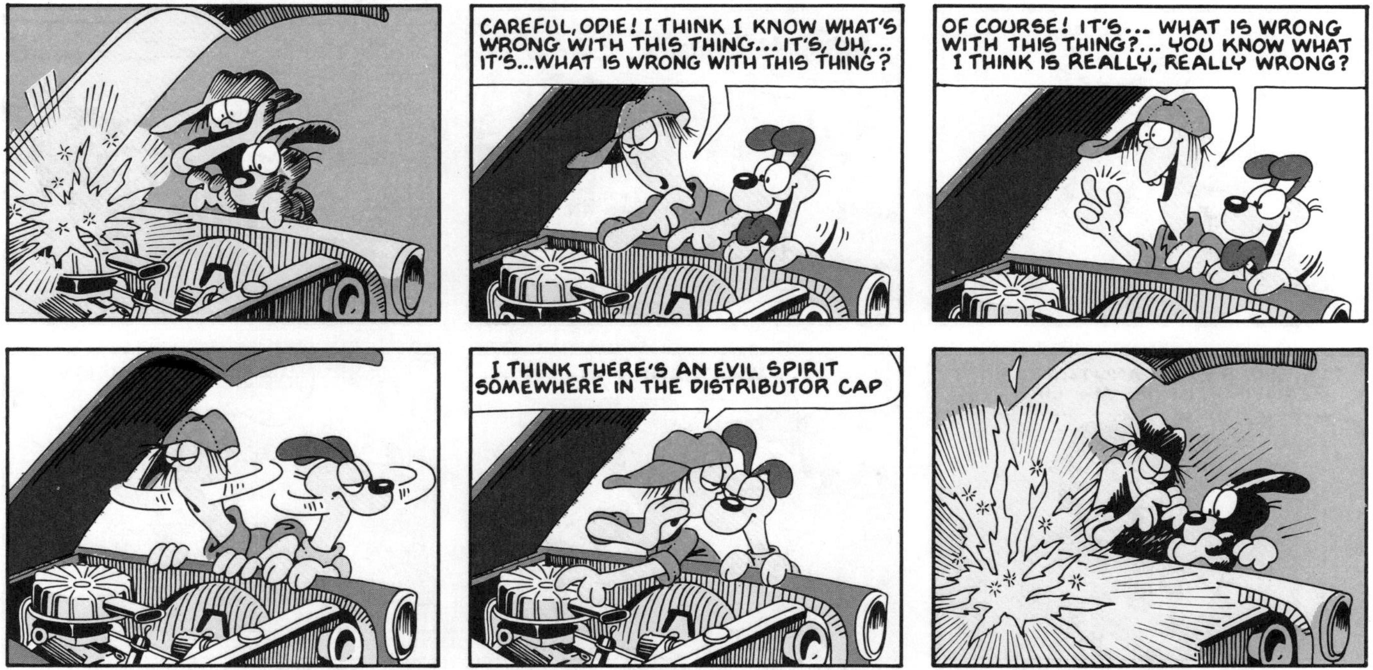
CAREFUL, ODIE! I THINK I KNOW WHAT'S WRONG WITH THIS THING... IT'S, UH,... IT'S...WHAT IS WRONG WITH THIS THING?
OF COURSE! IT'S... WHAT IS WRONG WITH THIS THING?... YOU KNOW WHAT I THINK IS REALLY, REALLY WRONG?
I THINK THERE'S AN EVIL SPIRIT SOMEWHERE IN THE DISTRIBUTOR CAP

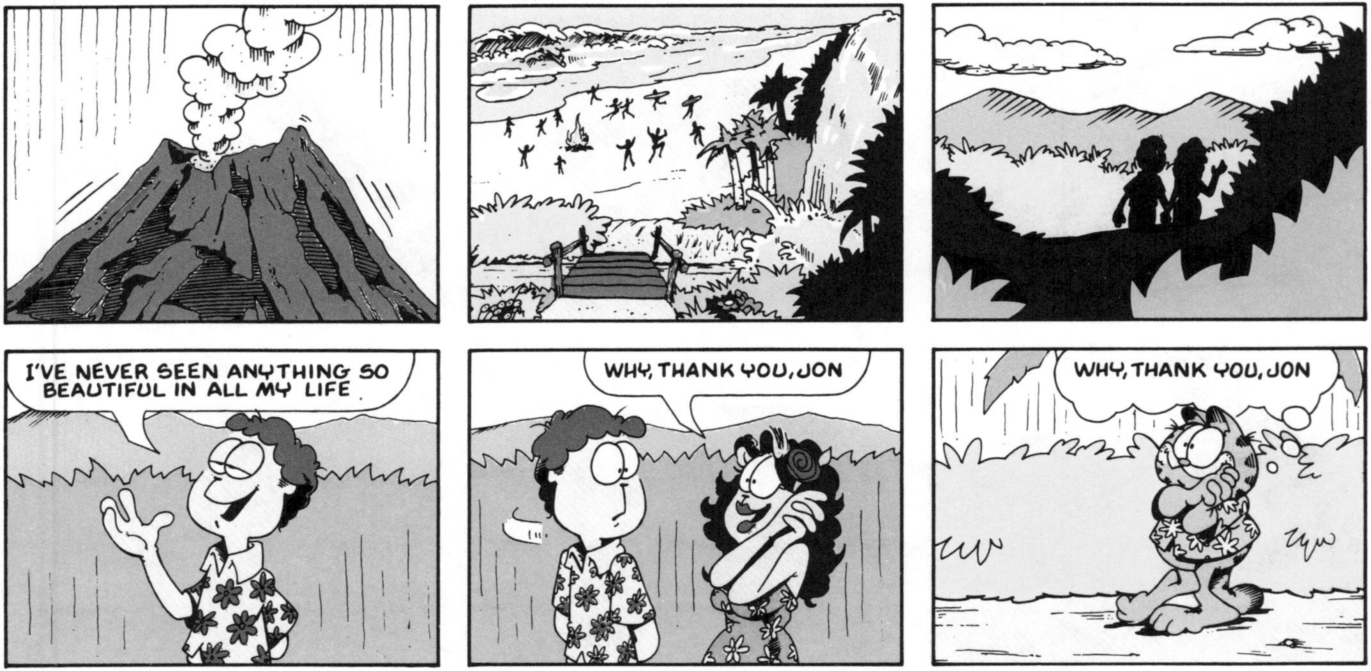
I'VE NEVER SEEN ANYTHING SO BEAUTIFUL IN ALL MY LIFE
WHY, THANK YOU, JON
WHY, THANK YOU, JON

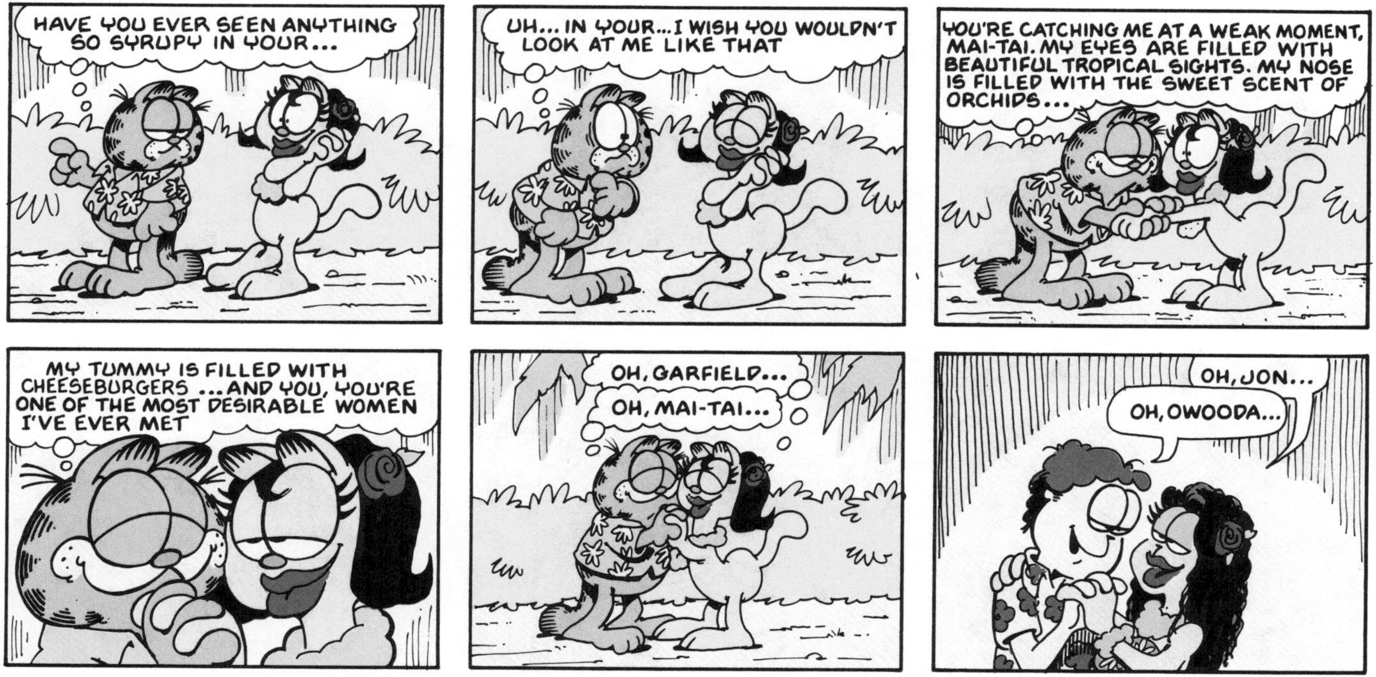
HAVE YOU EVER SEEN ANYTHING SO SYRUPY IN YOUR...
UH... IN YOUR... I WISH YOU WOULDN'T LOOK AT ME LIKE THAT
YOU'RE CATCHING ME AT A WEAK MOMENT, MAI-TAI. MY EYES ARE FILLED WITH BEAUTIFUL TROPICAL SIGHTS. MY NOSE IS FILLED WITH THE SWEET SCENT OF ORCHIDS...
MY TUMMY IS FILLED WITH CHEESEBURGERS ...AND YOU, YOU'RE ONE OF THE MOST DESIRABLE WOMEN I'VE EVER MET
OH, GARFIELD...
OH, MAI-TAI...
OH, JON...
OH, OWOODA...

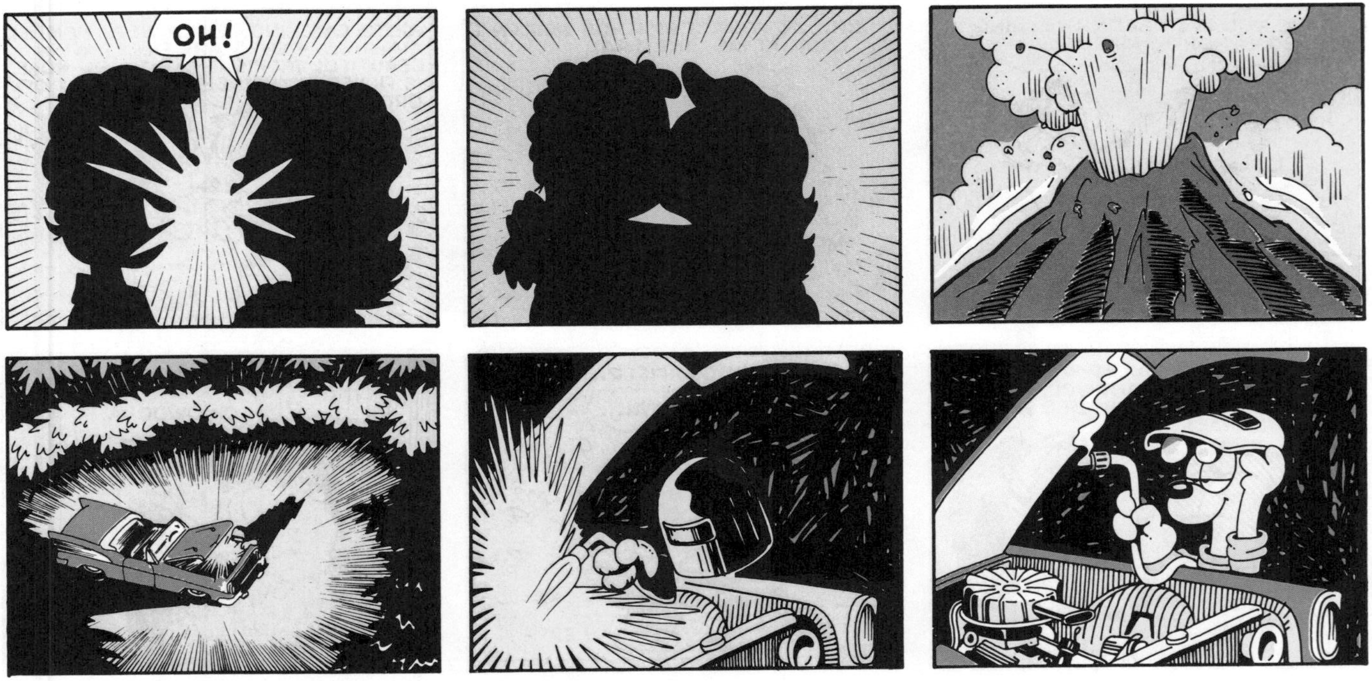
OH!

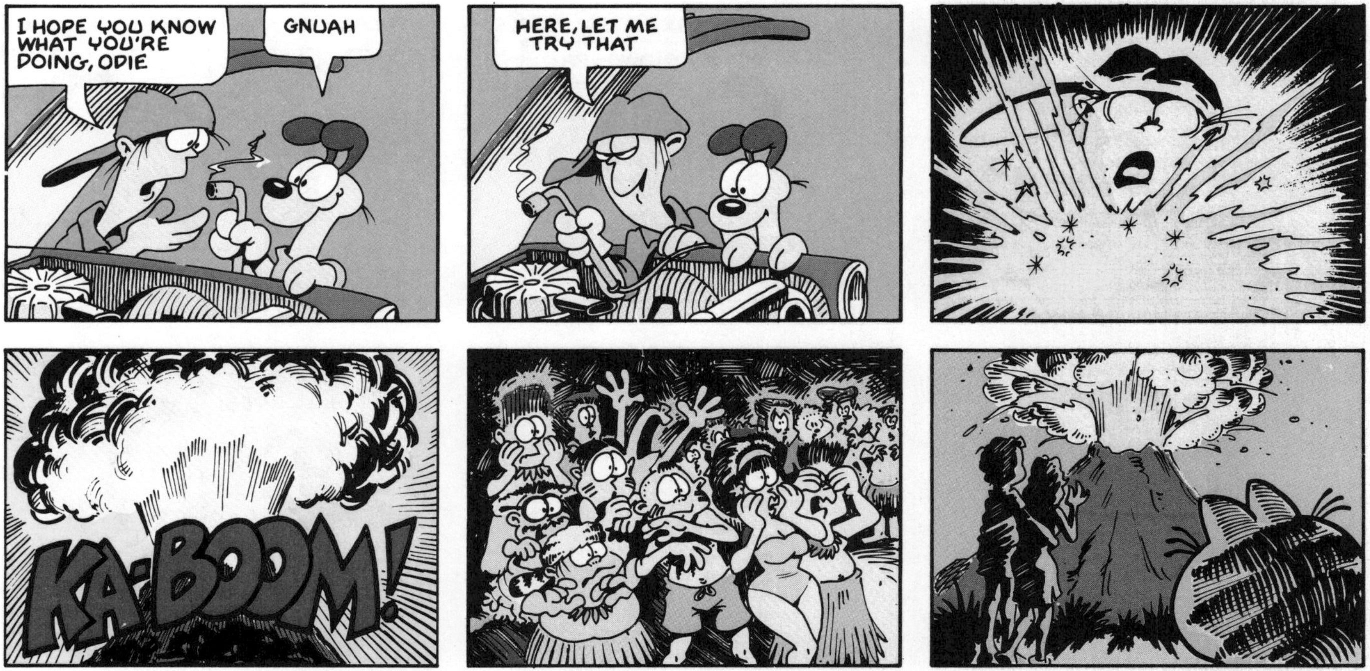
I HOPE YOU KNOW WHAT YOU'RE DOING, ODIE
GNUAH
HERE, LET ME TRY THAT
KA-BOOM!

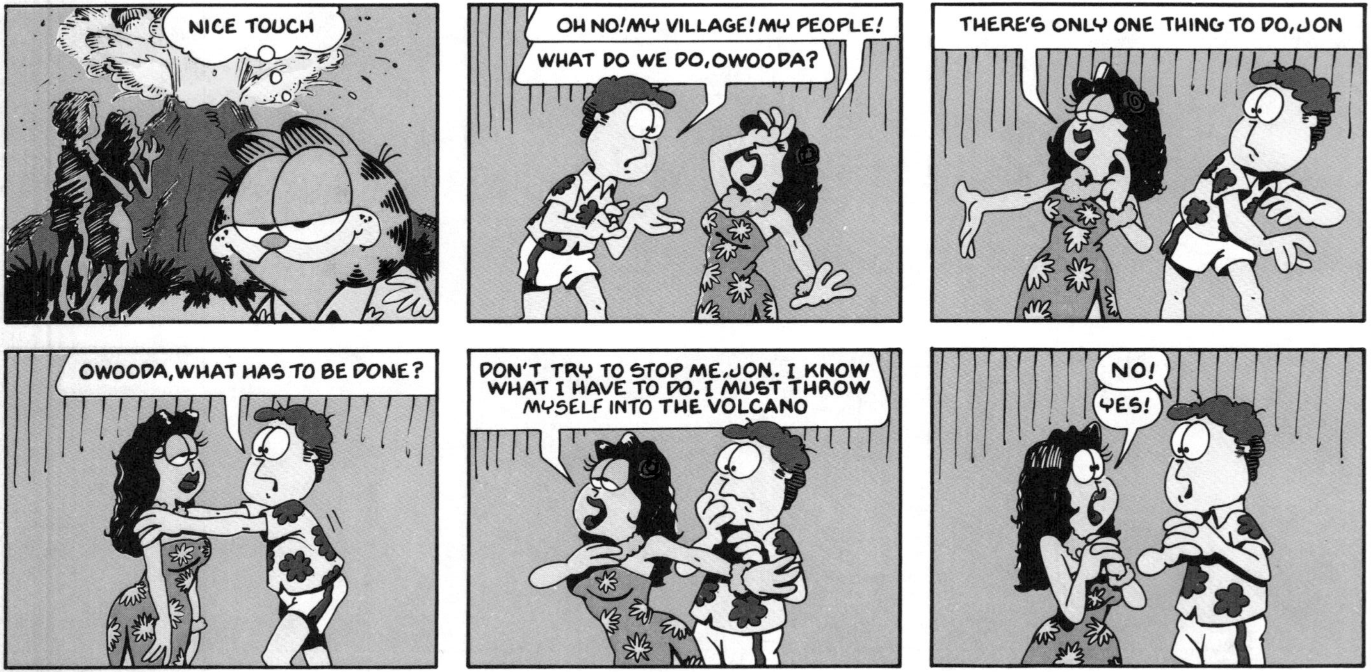
NICE TOUCH
OH NO! MY VILLAGE! MY PEOPLE!
WHAT DO WE DO, OWOODA?
THERE'S ONLY ONE THING TO DO, JON
OWOODA, WHAT HAS TO BE DONE?
DON'T TRY TO STOP ME, JON. I KNOW WHAT I HAVE TO DO. I MUST THROW MYSELF INTO THE VOLCANO
NO!
YES!

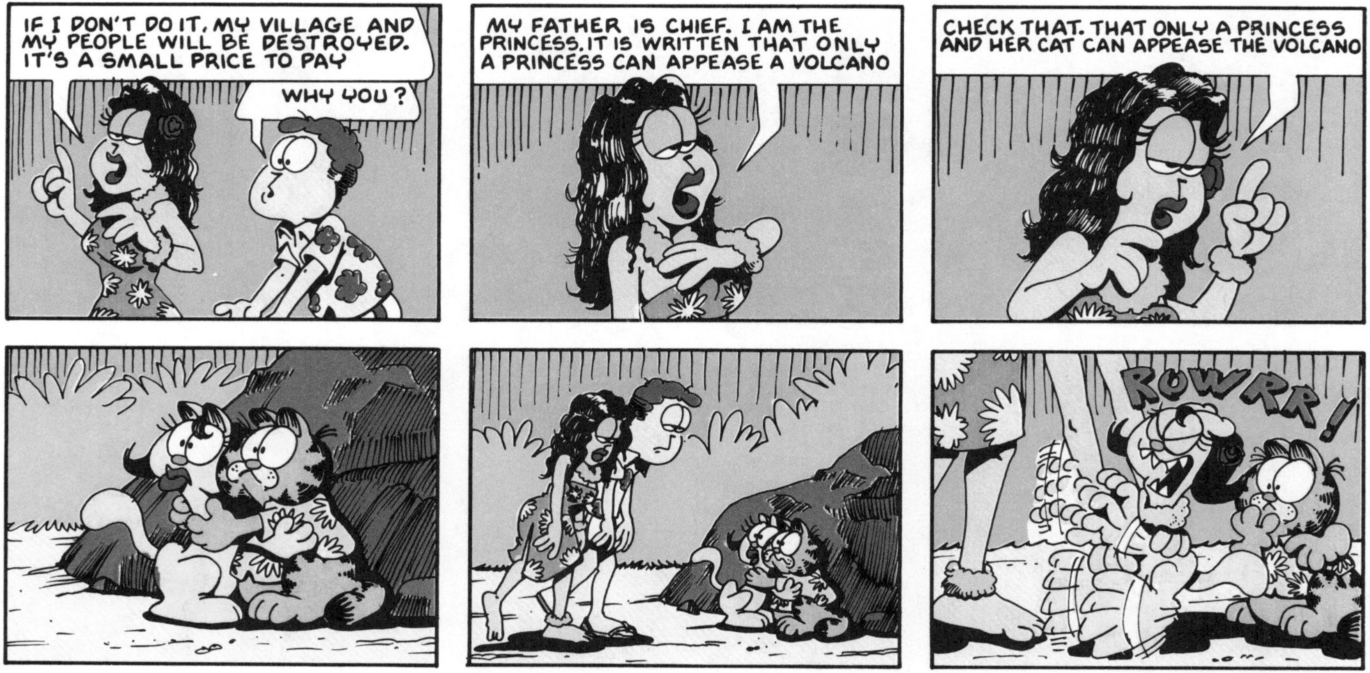
IF I DON'T DO IT, MY VILLAGE AND MY PEOPLE WILL BE DESTROYED. IT'S A SMALL PRICE TO PAY
WHY YOU?
MY FATHER IS CHIEF. I AM THE PRINCESS. IT IS WRITTEN THAT ONLY A PRINCESS CAN APPEASE A VOLCANO
CHECK THAT. THAT ONLY A PRINCESS AND HER CAT CAN APPEASE THE VOLCANO
ROWRR!

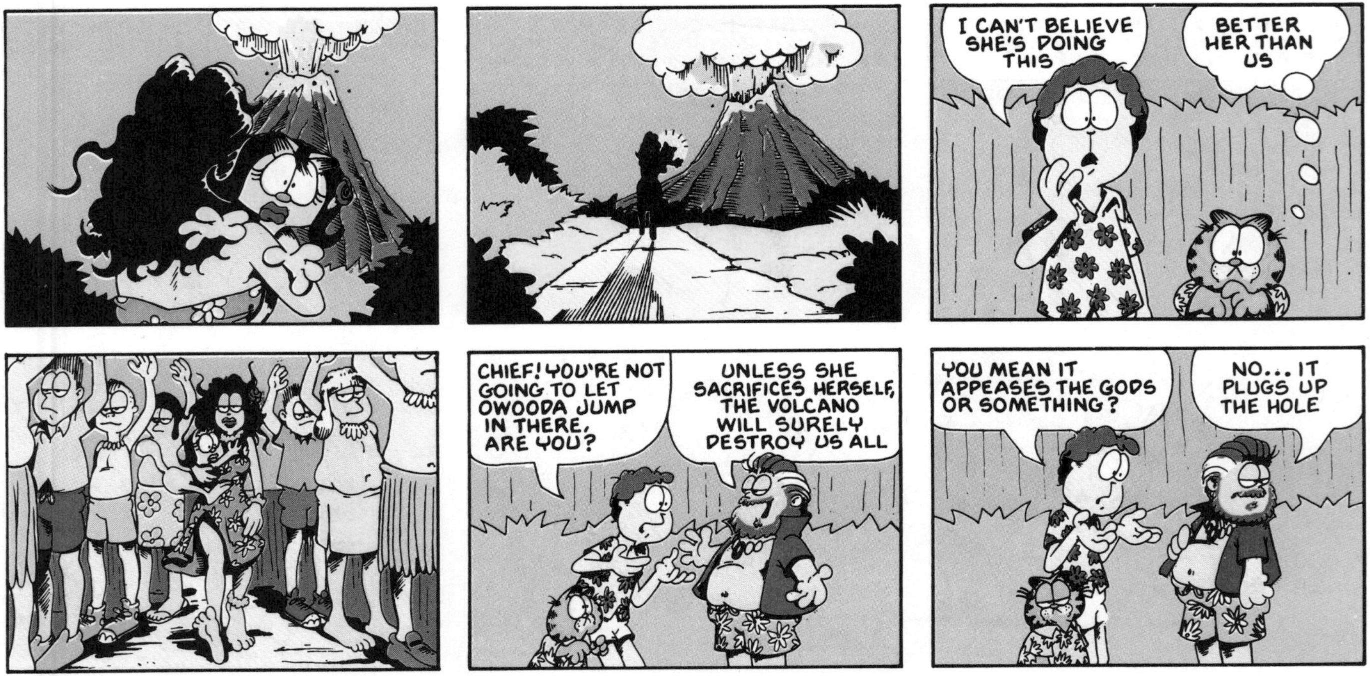
CHIEF! YOU'RE NOT GOING TO LET OWOODA JUMP IN THERE, ARE YOU?
UNLESS SHE SACRIFICES HERSELF, THE VOLCANO WILL SURELY DESTROY US ALL
YOU MEAN IT APPEASES THE GODS OR SOMETHING?
NO... IT PLUGS UP THE HOLE
I CAN'T BELIEVE SHE'S DOING THIS
BETTER HER THAN US

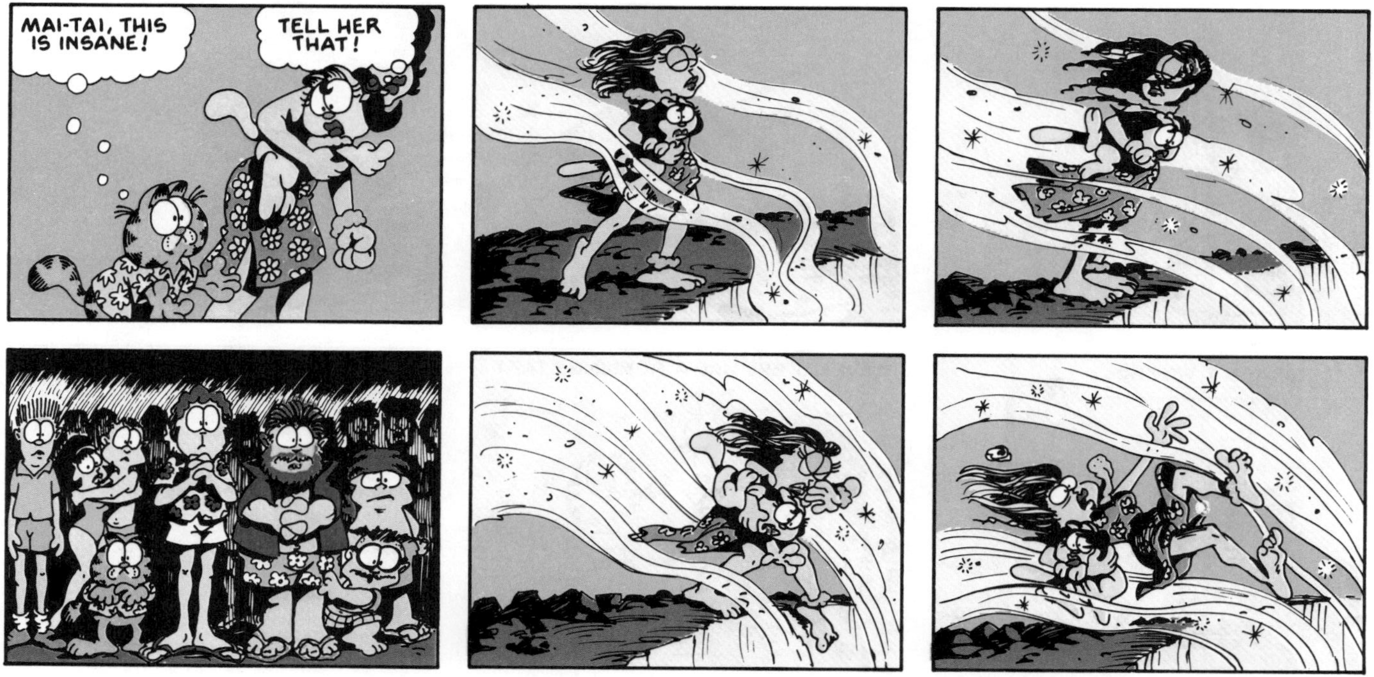
MAI-TAI, THIS IS INSANE!
TELL HER THAT!

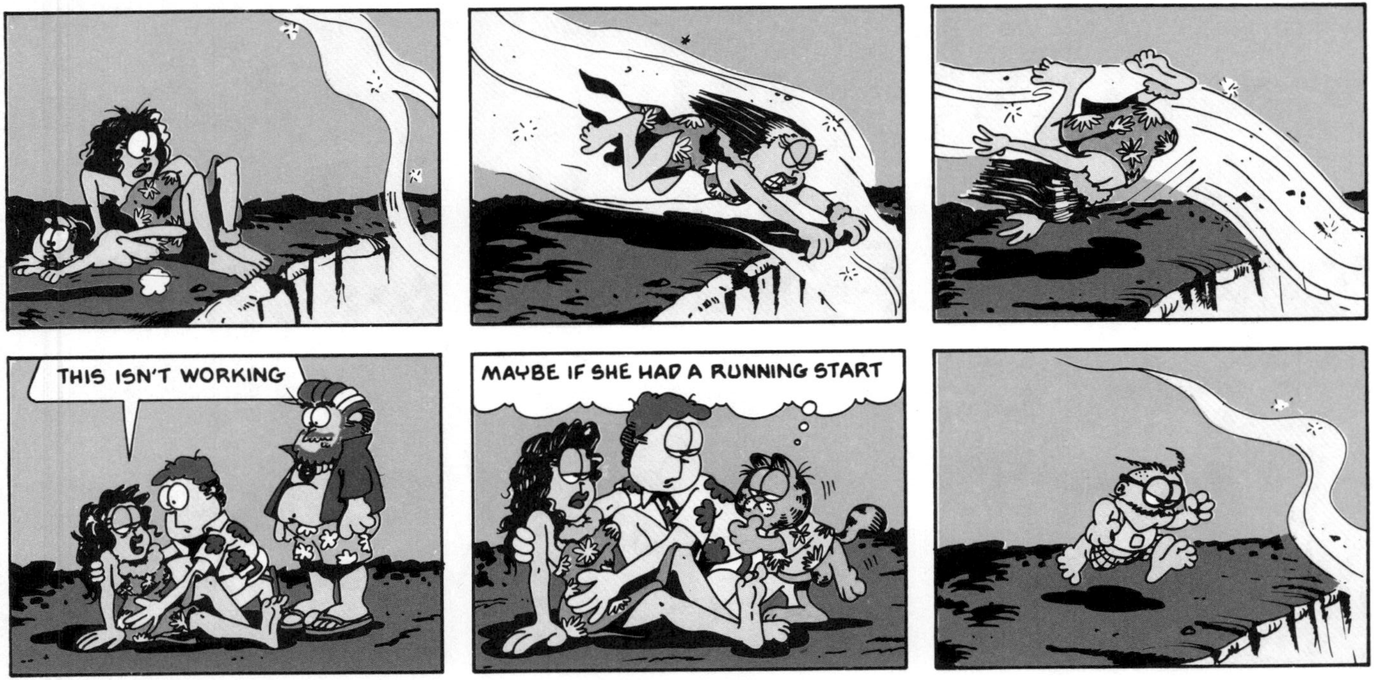
THIS ISN'T WORKING
MAYBE IF SHE HAD A RUNNING START

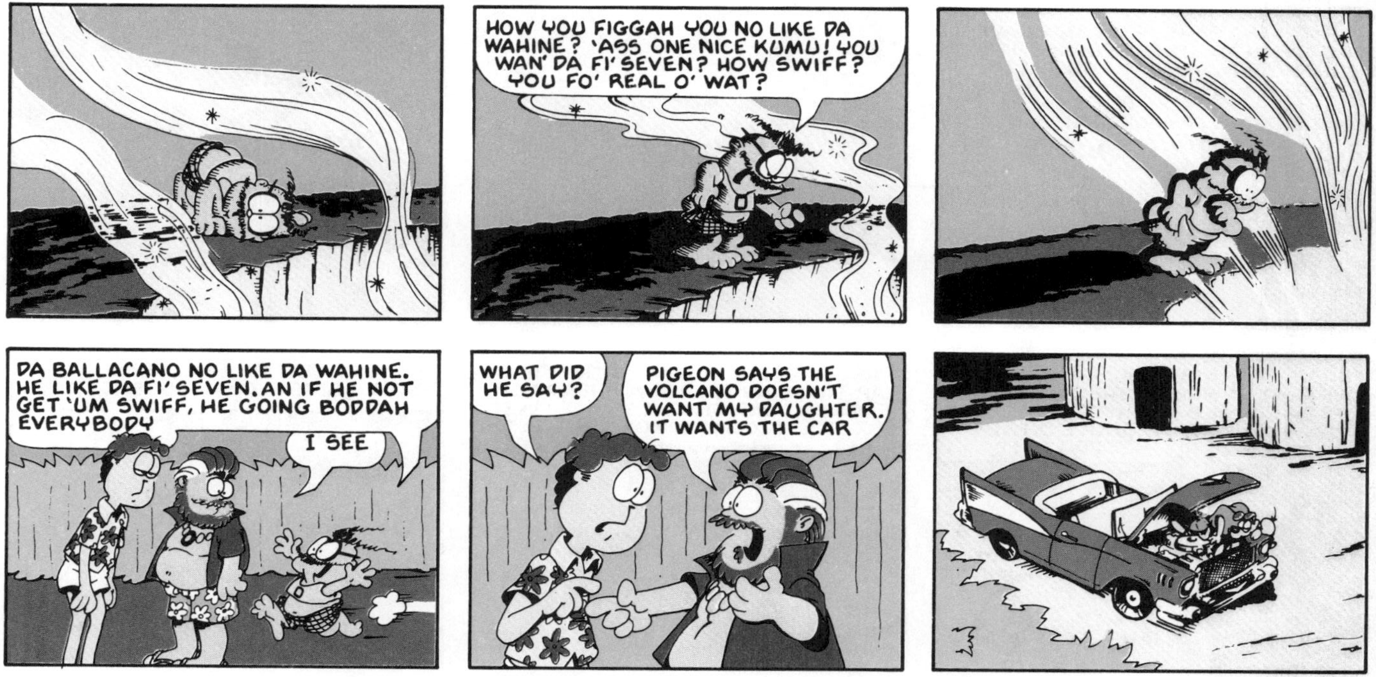
HOW YOU FIGGAH YOU NO LIKE DA WAHINE? 'ASS ONE NICE KUMU! YOU WAN' DA FI' SEVEN? HOW SWIFF? YOU FO' REAL O' WAT?
DA BALLACANO NO LIKE DA WAHINE. HE LIKE DA FI' SEVEN. AN IF HE NOT GET 'UM SWIFF, HE GOING BODDAH EVERYBODY
I SEE
WHAT DID HE SAY?
PIGEON SAYS THE VOLCANO DOESN'T WANT MY DAUGHTER. IT WANTS THE CAR

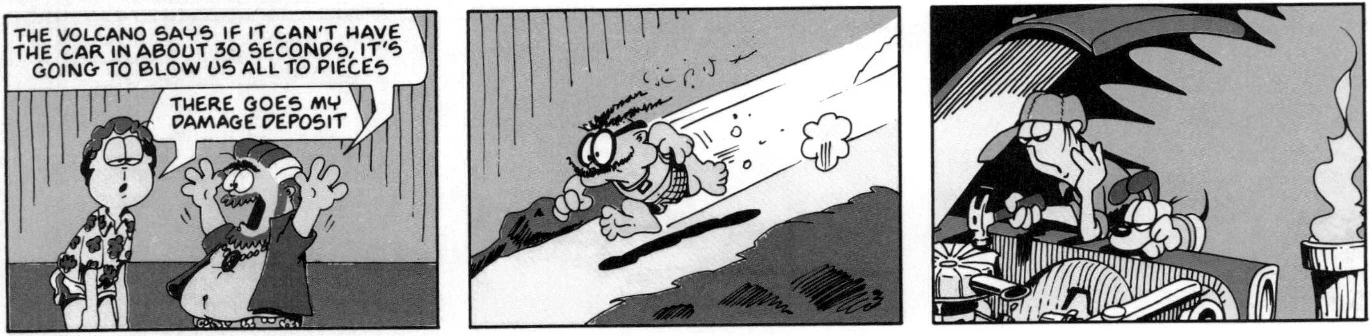
THE VOLCANO SAYS IF IT CAN'T HAVE THE CAR IN ABOUT 30 SECONDS, IT'S GOING TO BLOW US ALL TO PIECES
THERE GOES MY DAMAGE DEPOSIT

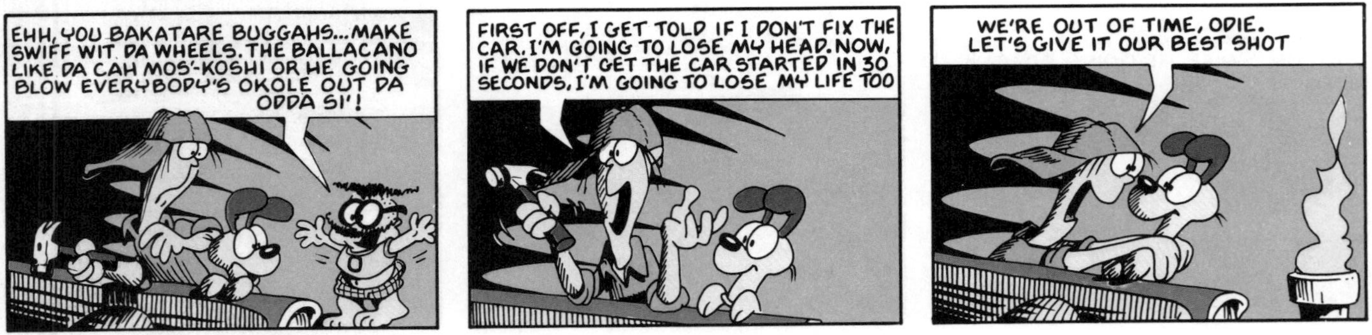
EHH, YOU BAKATARE BUGGAHS...MAKE SWIFF WIT DA WHEELS. THE BALLACANO LIKE DA CAH MOS'-KOSHI OR HE GOING BLOW EVERYBODY'S OKOLE OUT DA ODDA SI'!
FIRST OFF, I GET TOLD IF I DON'T FIX THE CAR, I'M GOING TO LOSE MY HEAD. NOW, IF WE DON'T GET THE CAR STARTED IN 30 SECONDS, I'M GOING TO LOSE MY LIFE TOO
WE'RE OUT OF TIME, ODIE. LET'S GIVE IT OUR BEST SHOT

!
PING!
PING!
VAROOM
VAROOM!
YAY!

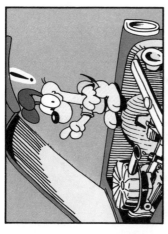

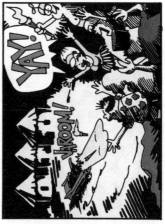

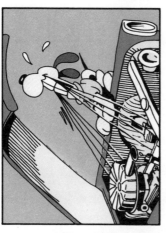

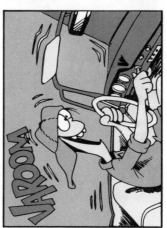

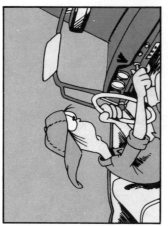

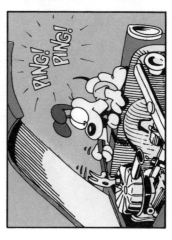

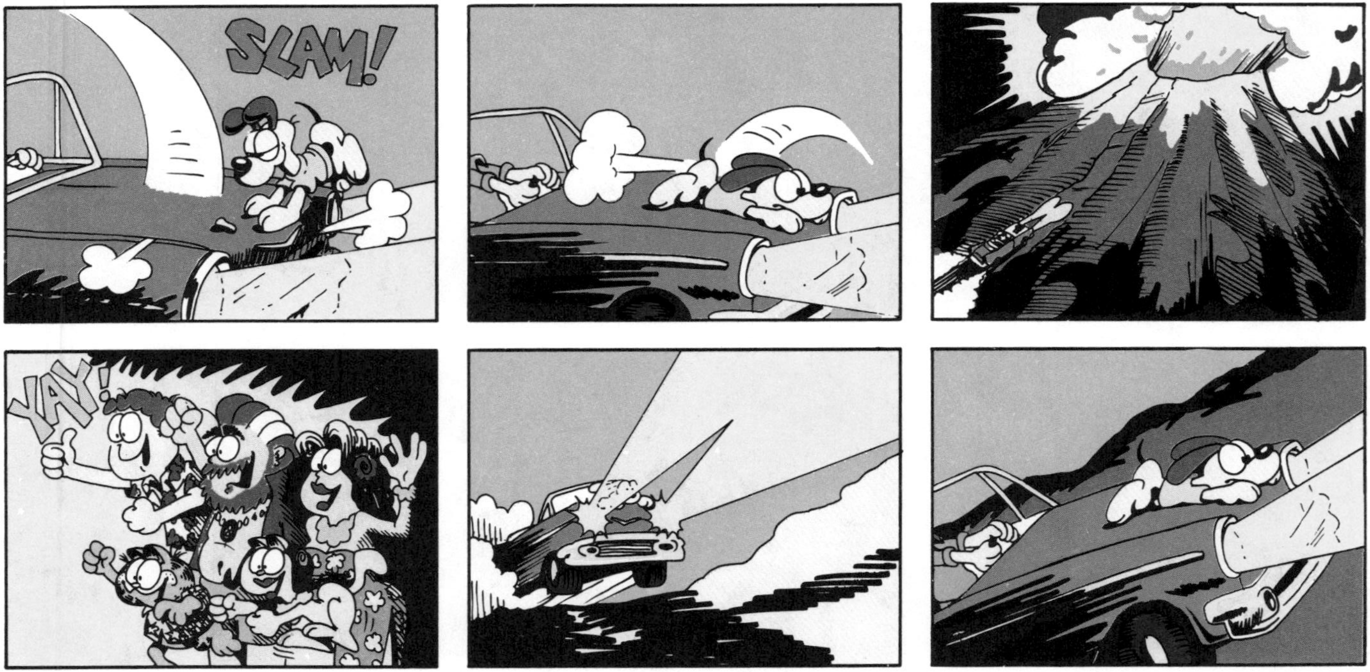
SLAM!
YAY!

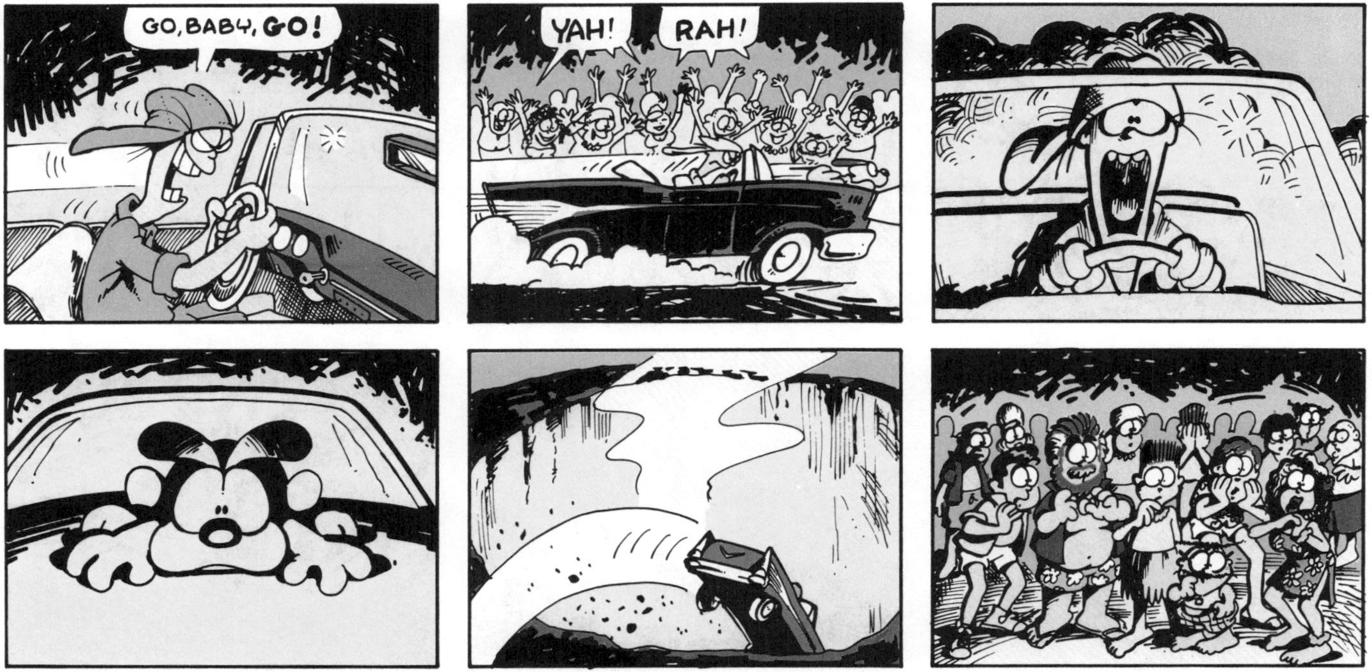
GO, BABY, GO!
YAH!
RAH!

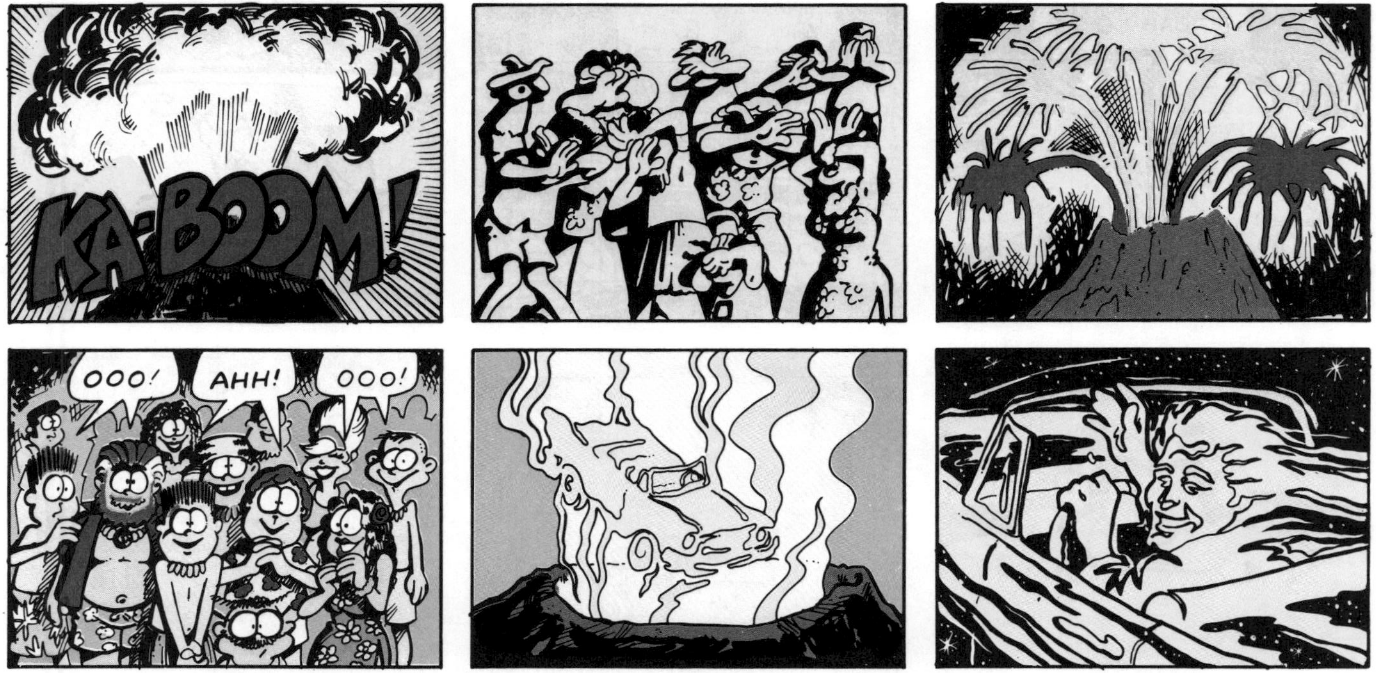
KA-BOOM!
OOO!
AHH!
OOO!

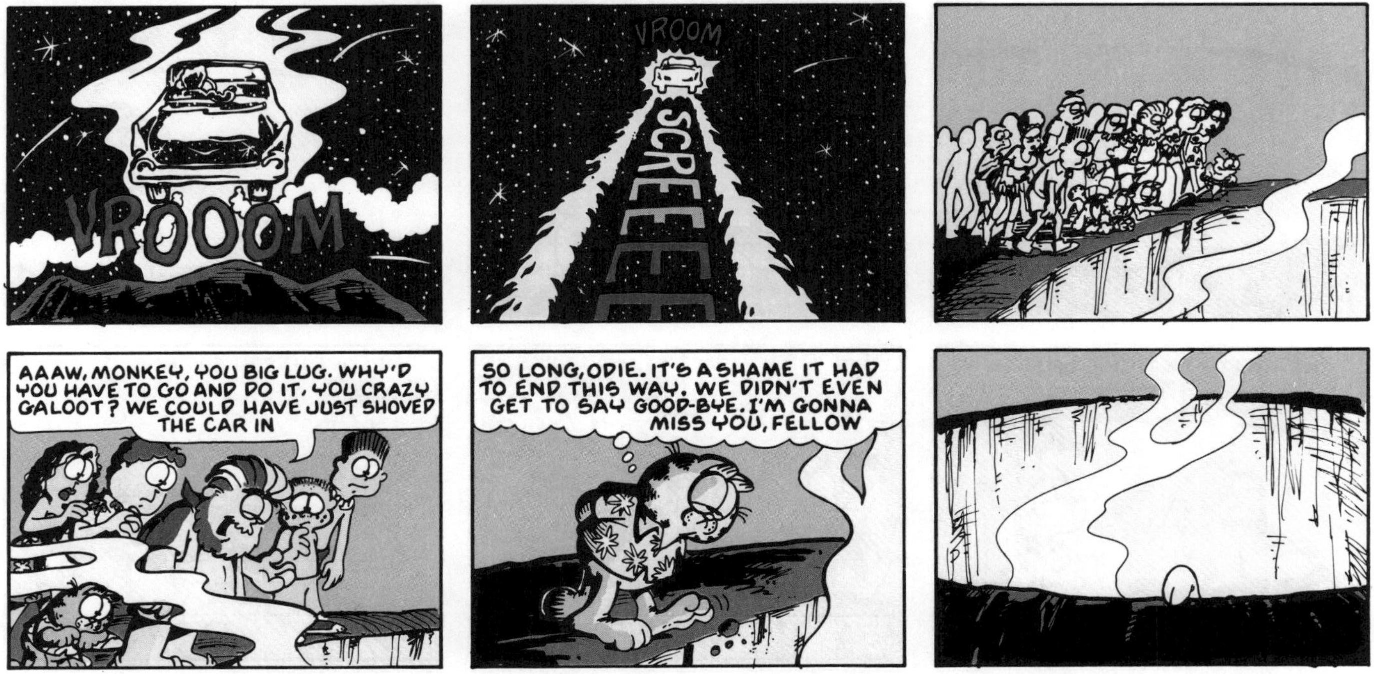
VROOOM
VROOM
SCREEE
AAAW, MONKEY, YOU BIG LUG. WHY'D YOU HAVE TO GO AND DO IT, YOU CRAZY GALOOT? WE COULD HAVE JUST SHOVED THE CAR IN
SO LONG, ODIE. IT'S A SHAME IT HAD TO END THIS WAY. WE DIDN'T EVEN GET TO SAY GOOD-BYE. I'M GONNA MISS YOU, FELLOW

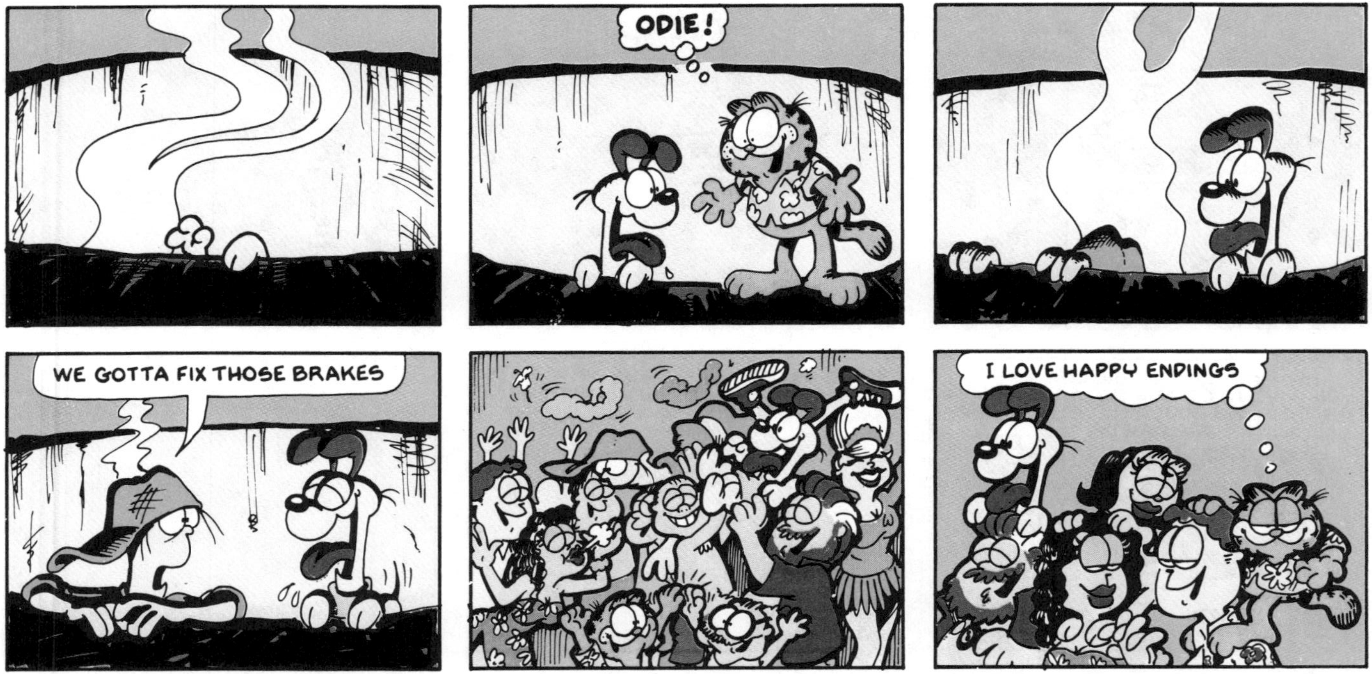
ODIE!
WE GOTTA FIX THOSE BRAKES
I LOVE HAPPY ENDINGS

Garfield Goes Hollywood

by Jim Davis

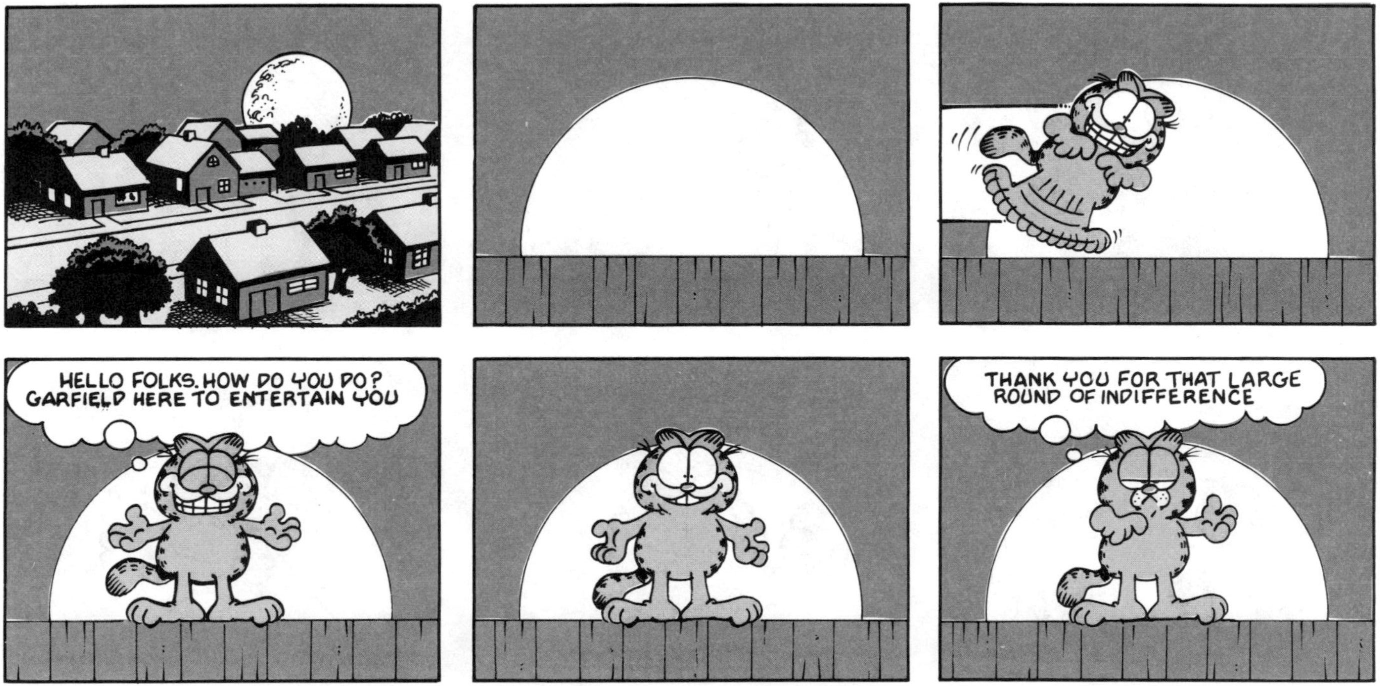
HELLO FOLKS. HOW DO YOU DO? GARFIELD HERE TO ENTERTAIN YOU
THANK YOU FOR THAT LARGE ROUND OF INDIFFERENCE

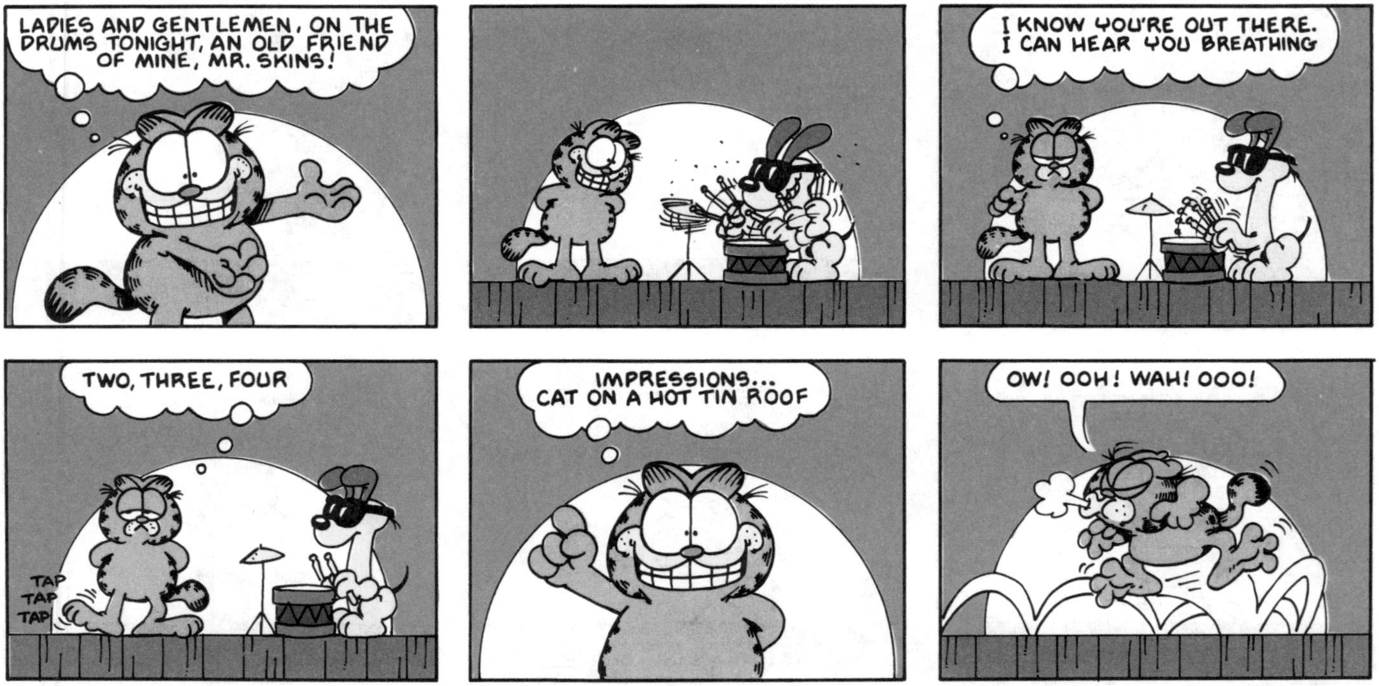
LADIES AND GENTLEMEN, ON THE DRUMS TONIGHT, AN OLD FRIEND OF MINE, MR. SKINS!
I KNOW YOU'RE OUT THERE. I CAN HEAR YOU BREATHING
TWO, THREE, FOUR
TAP TAP TAP
IMPRESSIONS... CAT ON A HOT TIN ROOF
OW! OOH! WAH! OOO!

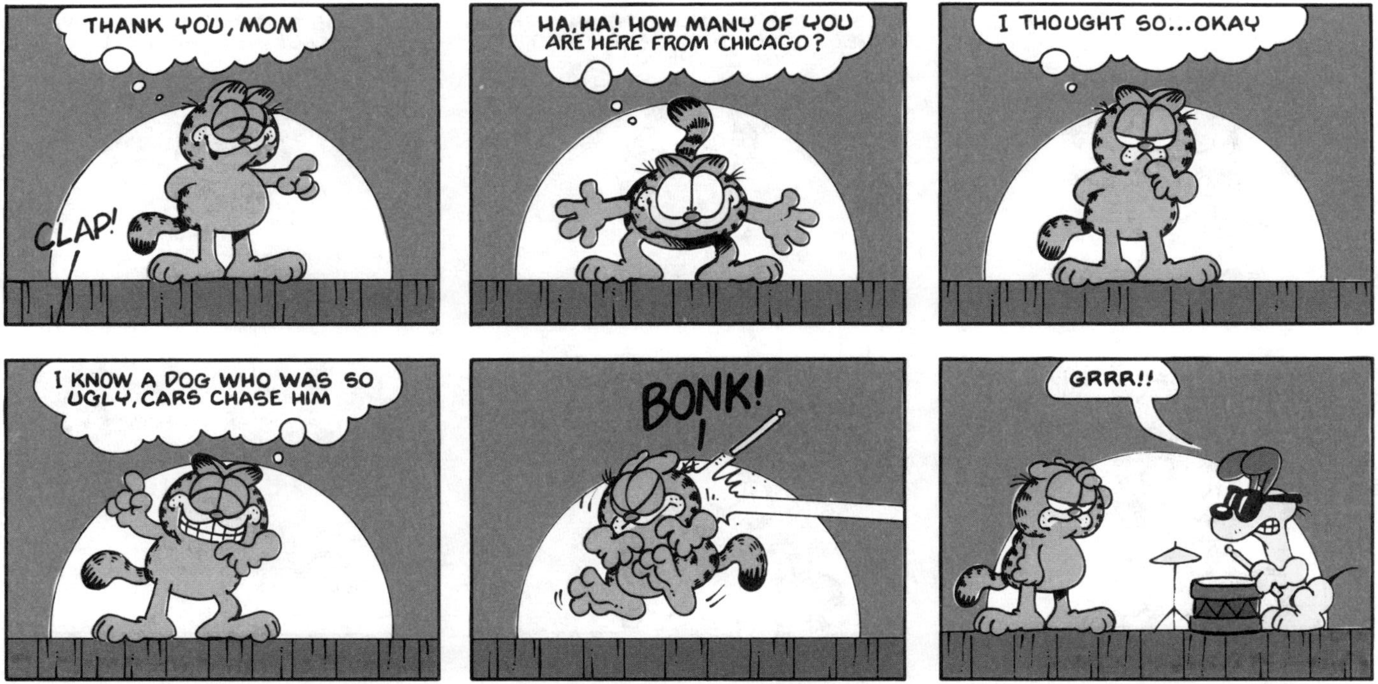
THANK YOU, MOM
CLAP!
HA, HA! HOW MANY OF YOU ARE HERE FROM CHICAGO?
I THOUGHT SO...OKAY
I KNOW A DOG WHO WAS SO UGLY, CARS CHASE HIM
BONK!
GRRR!!

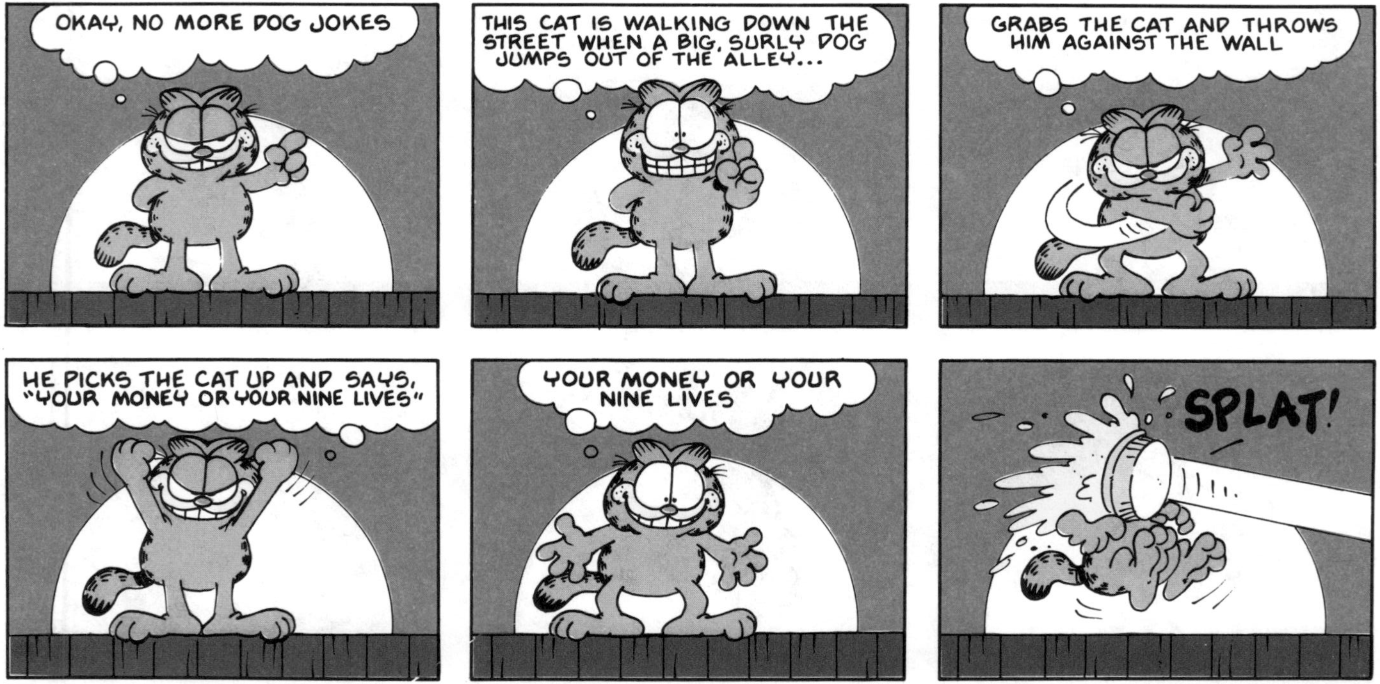
OKAY, NO MORE DOG JOKES
THIS CAT IS WALKING DOWN THE STREET WHEN A BIG, SURLY DOG JUMPS OUT OF THE ALLEY...
GRABS THE CAT AND THROWS HIM AGAINST THE WALL
HE PICKS THE CAT UP AND SAYS, "YOUR MONEY OR YOUR NINE LIVES"
YOUR MONEY OR YOUR NINE LIVES
SPLAT!

NICE TOUCH
I CAN SEE I GOTTA WARM THINGS UP HERE... ALL YOUR MOTHERS WEAR ARMY BOOTS!
BONK!
SPLAT!
THUD!
CRASH!

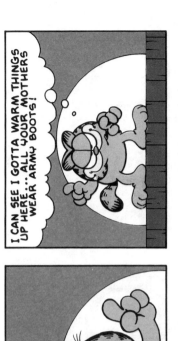

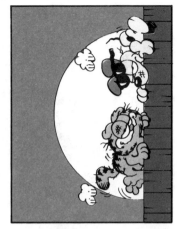

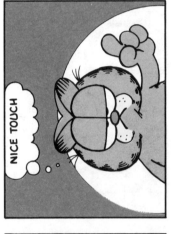

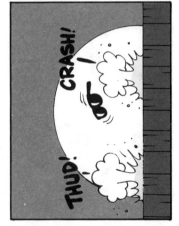

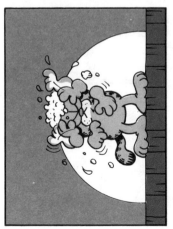

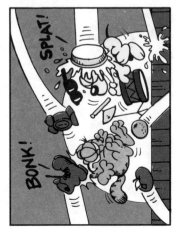

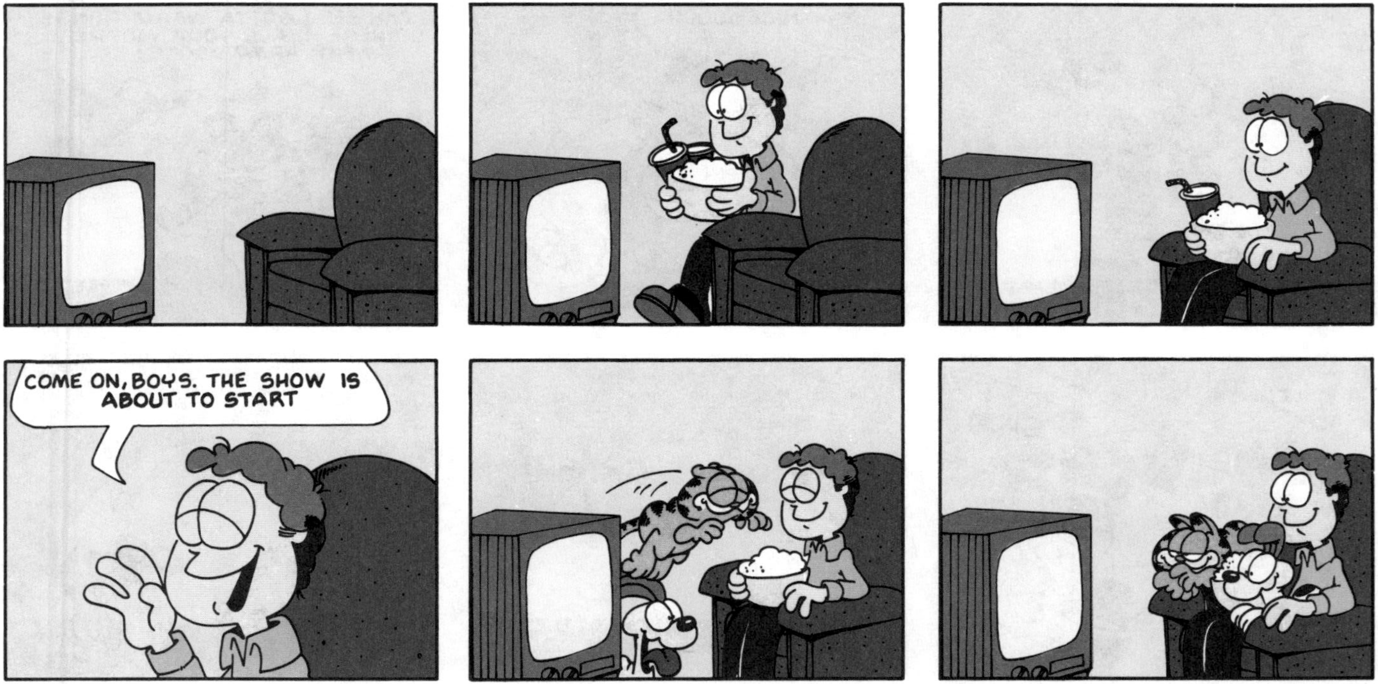
COME ON, BOYS. THE SHOW IS ABOUT TO START

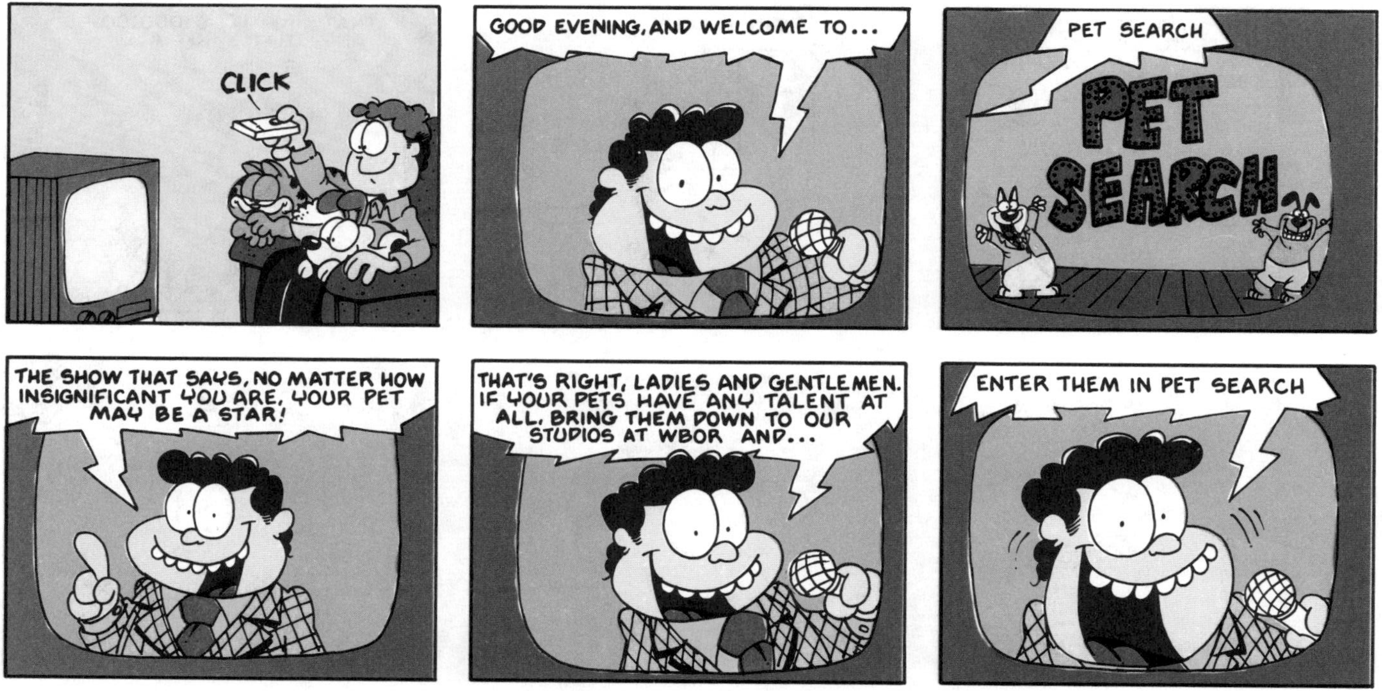
CLICK
GOOD EVENING, AND WELCOME TO...
PET SEARCH
PET SEARCH
THE SHOW THAT SAYS, NO MATTER HOW INSIGNIFICANT YOU ARE, YOUR PET MAY BE A STAR!
THAT'S RIGHT, LADIES AND GENTLEMEN. IF YOUR PETS HAVE ANY TALENT AT ALL, BRING THEM DOWN TO OUR STUDIOS AT WBOR AND...
ENTER THEM IN PET SEARCH

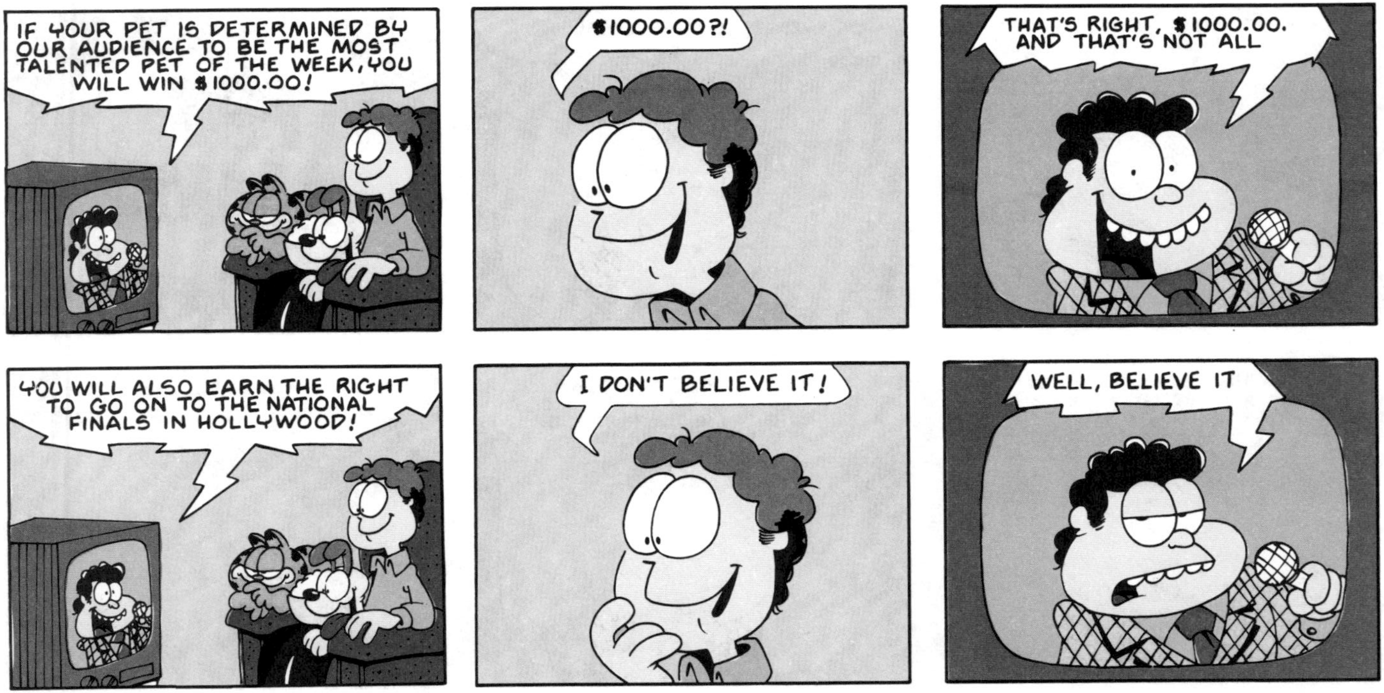
IF YOUR PET IS DETERMINED BY OUR AUDIENCE TO BE THE MOST TALENTED PET OF THE WEEK, YOU WILL WIN $1000.00!
$1000.00?!
THAT'S RIGHT, $1000.00. AND THAT'S NOT ALL
YOU WILL ALSO EARN THE RIGHT TO GO ON TO THE NATIONAL FINALS IN HOLLYWOOD!
I DON'T BELIEVE IT!
WELL, BELIEVE IT

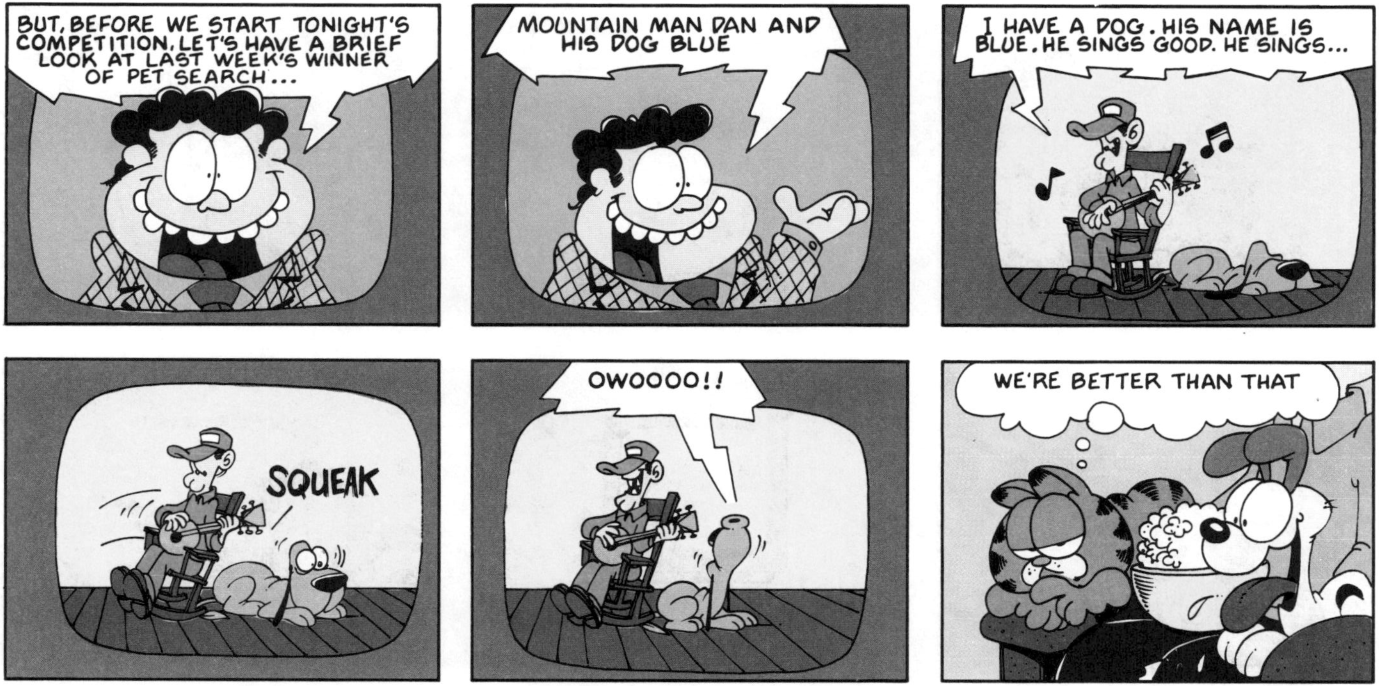
BUT, BEFORE WE START TONIGHT'S COMPETITION, LET'S HAVE A BRIEF LOOK AT LAST WEEK'S WINNER OF PET SEARCH...
MOUNTAIN MAN DAN AND HIS DOG BLUE
I HAVE A DOG. HIS NAME IS BLUE. HE SINGS GOOD. HE SINGS...
SQUEAK
OWOOOO!!
WE'RE BETTER THAN THAT

GEE, A THOUSAND DOLLARS

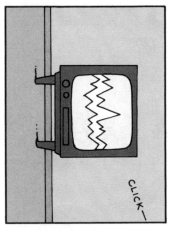

CLICK—

I WISH YOU BOYS HAD SOME TALENT.
WE COULD BE ON THAT SHOW

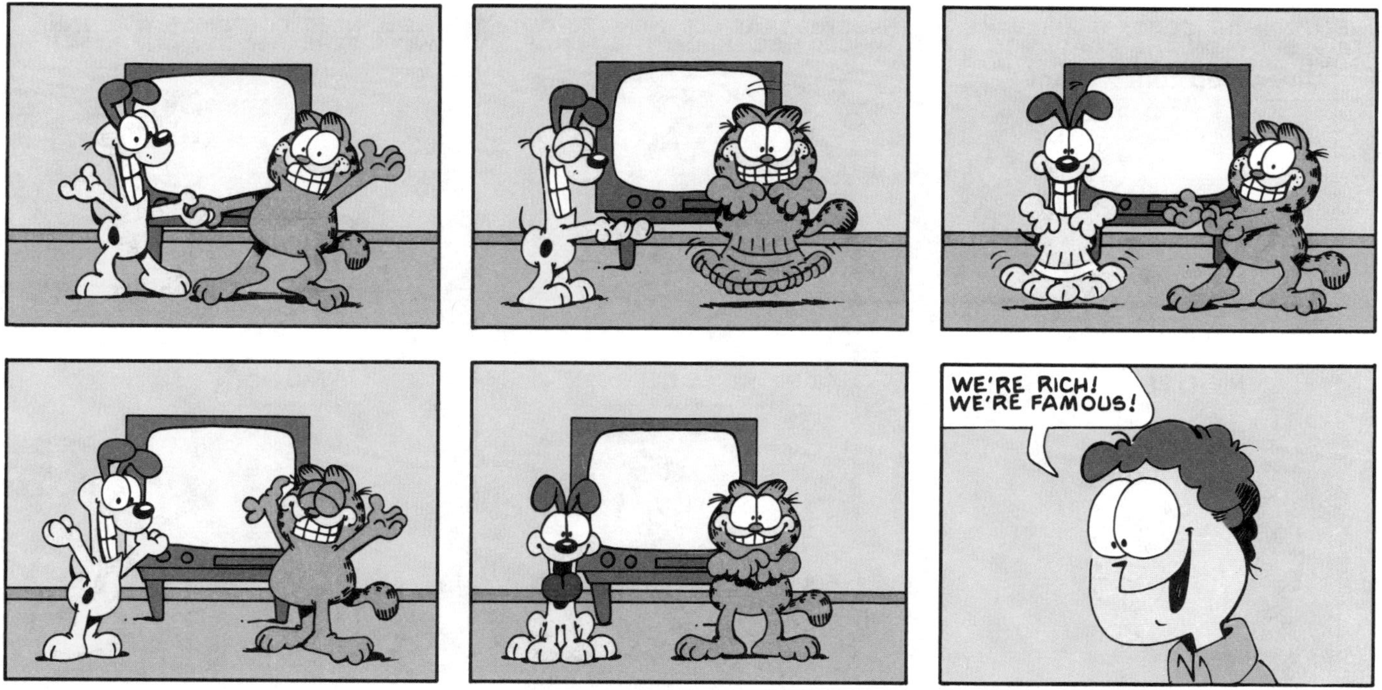
WE'RE RICH!
WE'RE FAMOUS!

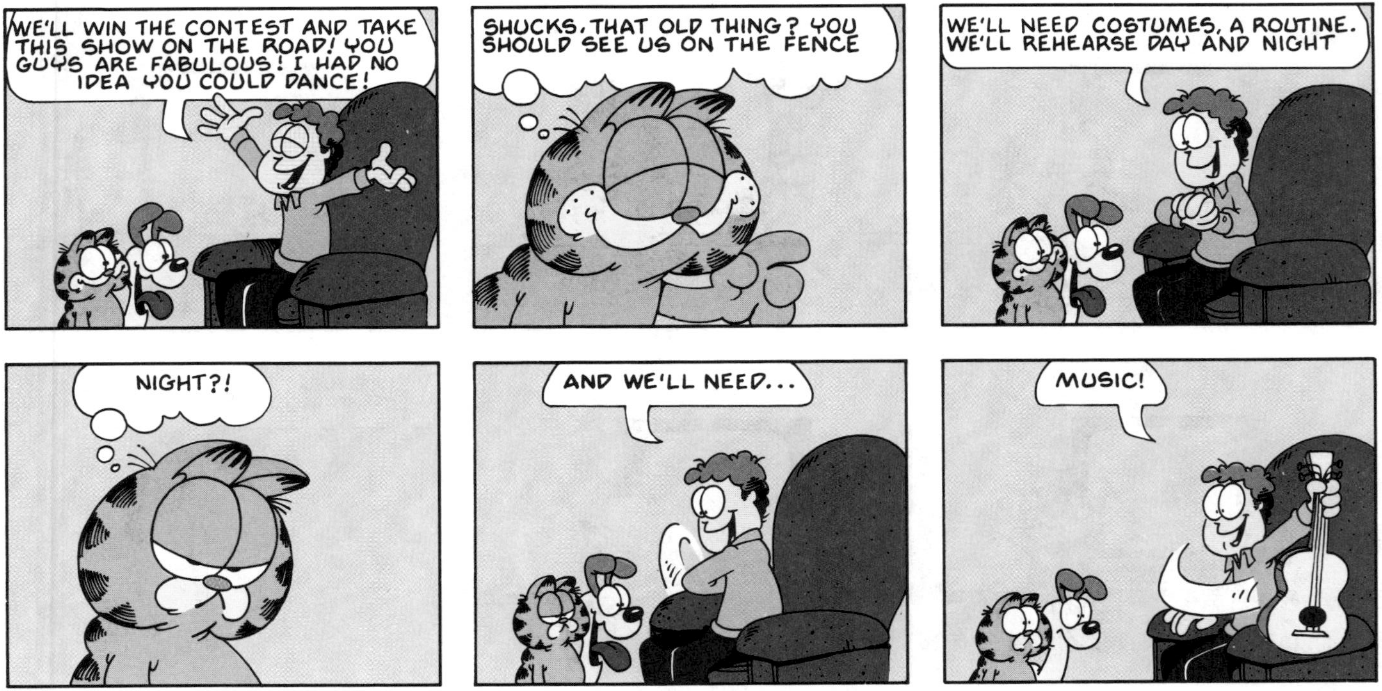
WE'LL WIN THE CONTEST AND TAKE THIS SHOW ON THE ROAD! YOU GUYS ARE FABULOUS! I HAD NO IDEA YOU COULD DANCE!
SHUCKS, THAT OLD THING? YOU SHOULD SEE US ON THE FENCE
WE'LL NEED COSTUMES, A ROUTINE. WE'LL REHEARSE DAY AND NIGHT
NIGHT?!
AND WE'LL NEED...
MUSIC!

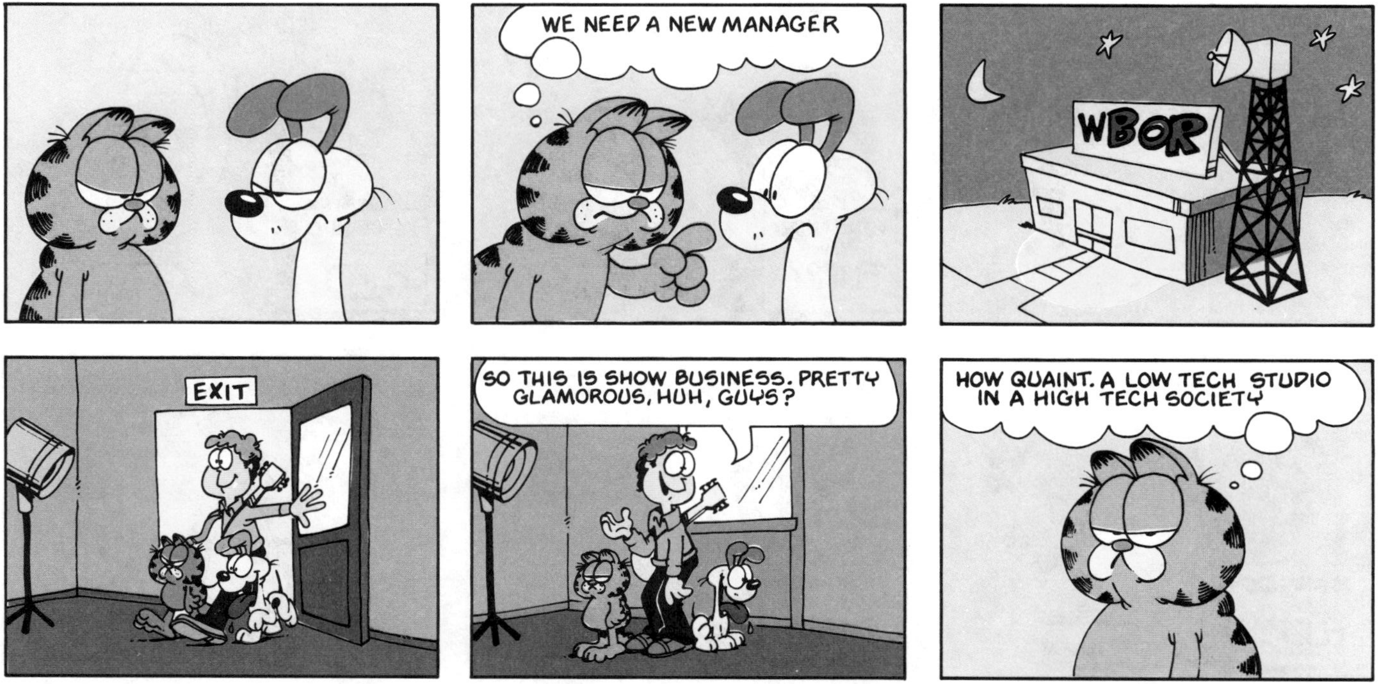
WE NEED A NEW MANAGER
WBOR
EXIT
SO THIS IS SHOW BUSINESS. PRETTY GLAMOROUS, HUH, GUYS?
HOW QUAINT. A LOW TECH STUDIO IN A HIGH TECH SOCIETY

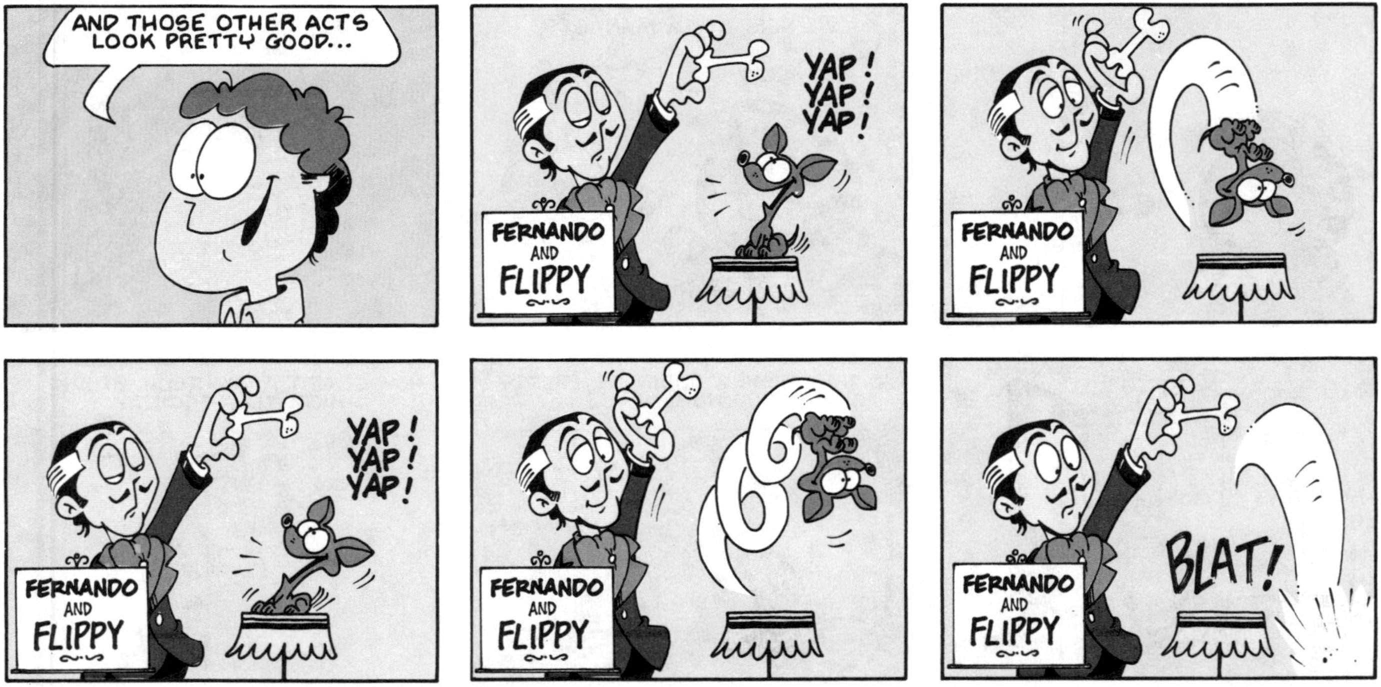
AND THOSE OTHER ACTS LOOK PRETTY GOOD...
FERNANDO AND FLIPPY
YAP! YAP! YAP!
FERNANDO AND FLIPPY
FERNANDO AND FLIPPY
YAP! YAP! YAP!
FERNANDO AND FLIPPY
FERNANDO AND FLIPPY
BLAT!

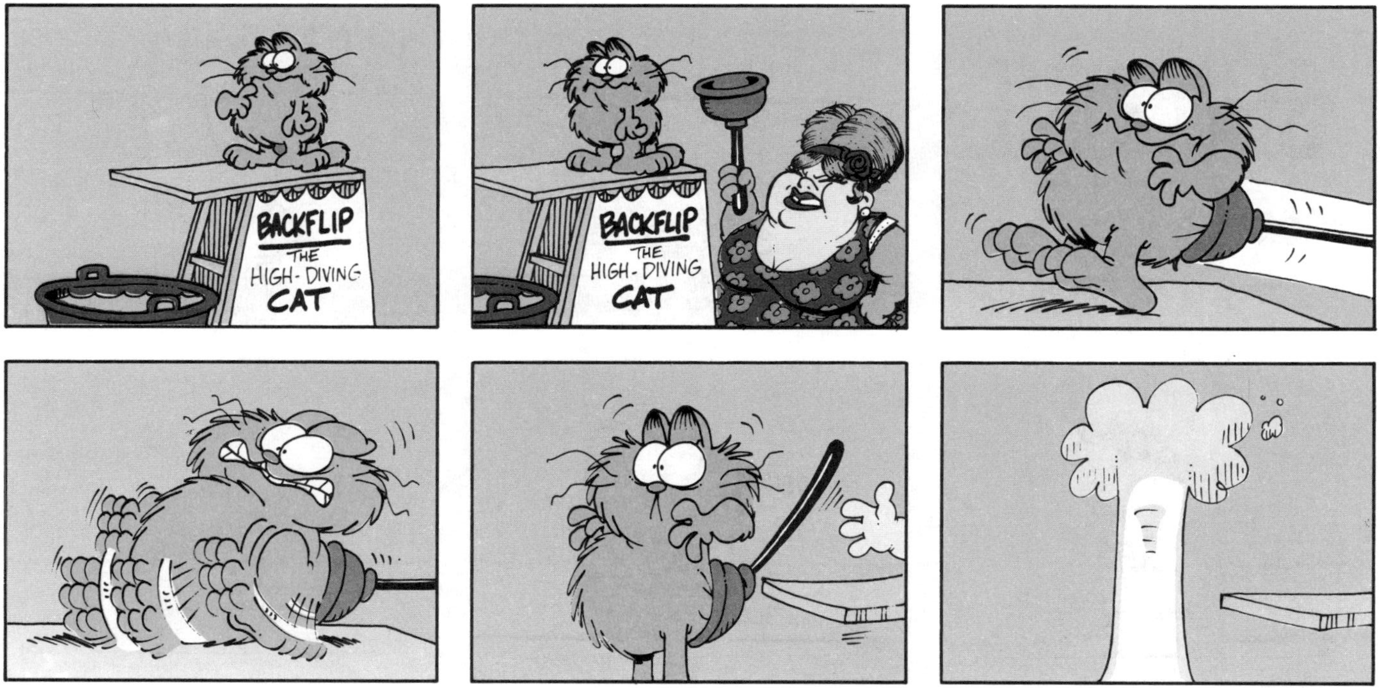
BACKFLIP
THE
HIGH-DIVING
CAT
BACKFLIP
THE
HIGH-DIVING
CAT

SPLOOSH

SPLOOSH!

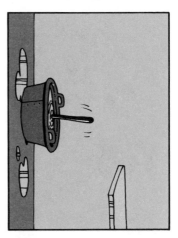

SPLOOSH!

AAAAAAACCK!

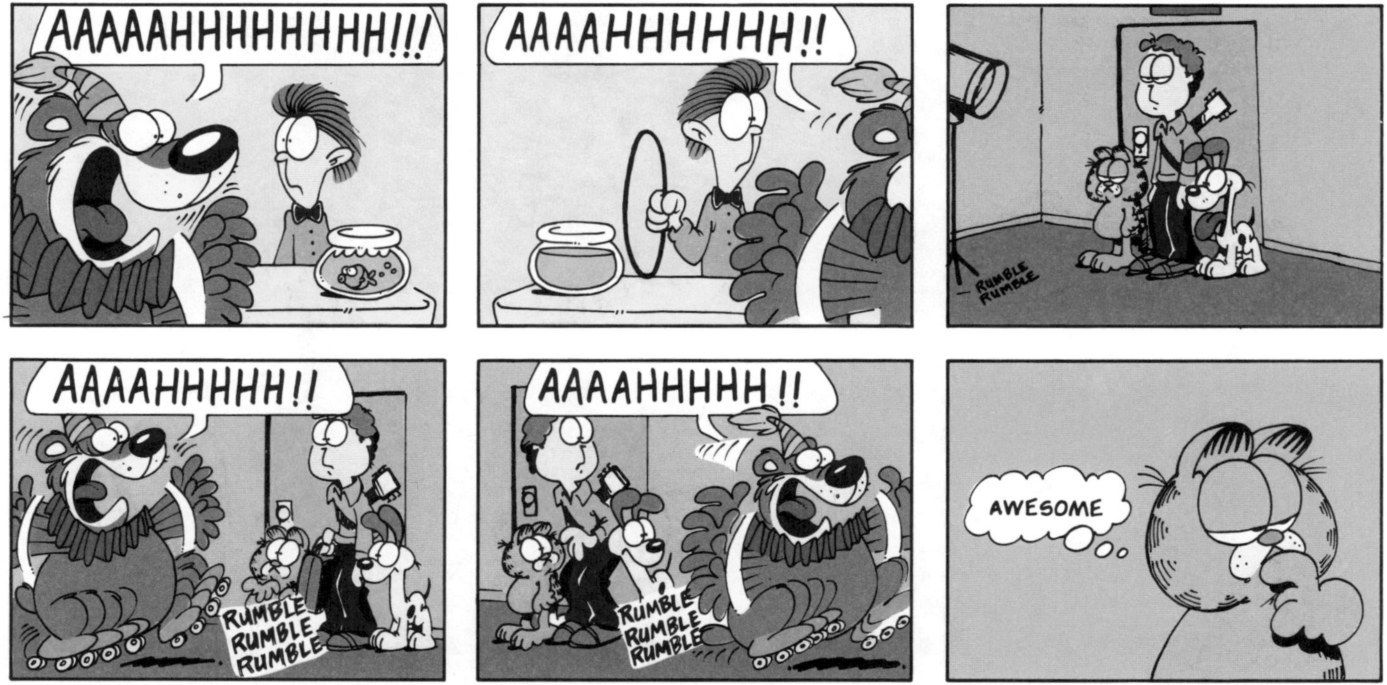
AAAAAHHHHHHHHH!!!
AAAAHHHHHHH!!
RUMBLE
RUMBLE
AAAAHHHHH!!
RUMBLE
RUMBLE
RUMBLE
AAAAHHHHH!!
RUMBLE
RUMBLE
RUMBLE
AWESOME

OKAY, BOYS, REMEMBER WHAT WE REHEARSED

LET'S GET INTO OUR COSTUMES

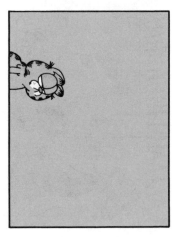

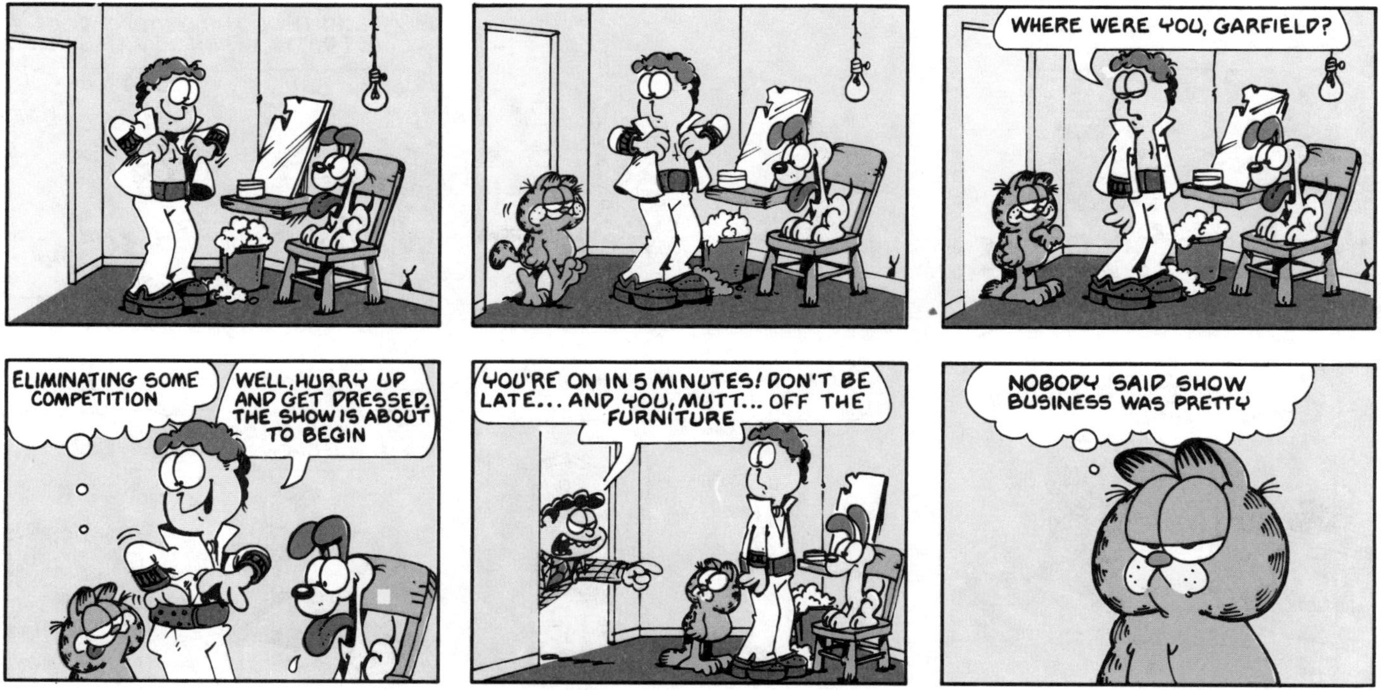
WHERE WERE YOU, GARFIELD?
WELL, HURRY UP AND GET DRESSED. THE SHOW IS ABOUT TO BEGIN
ELIMINATING SOME COMPETITION
YOU'RE ON IN 5 MINUTES! DON'T BE LATE... AND YOU, MUTT... OFF THE FURNITURE
NOBODY SAID SHOW BUSINESS WAS PRETTY

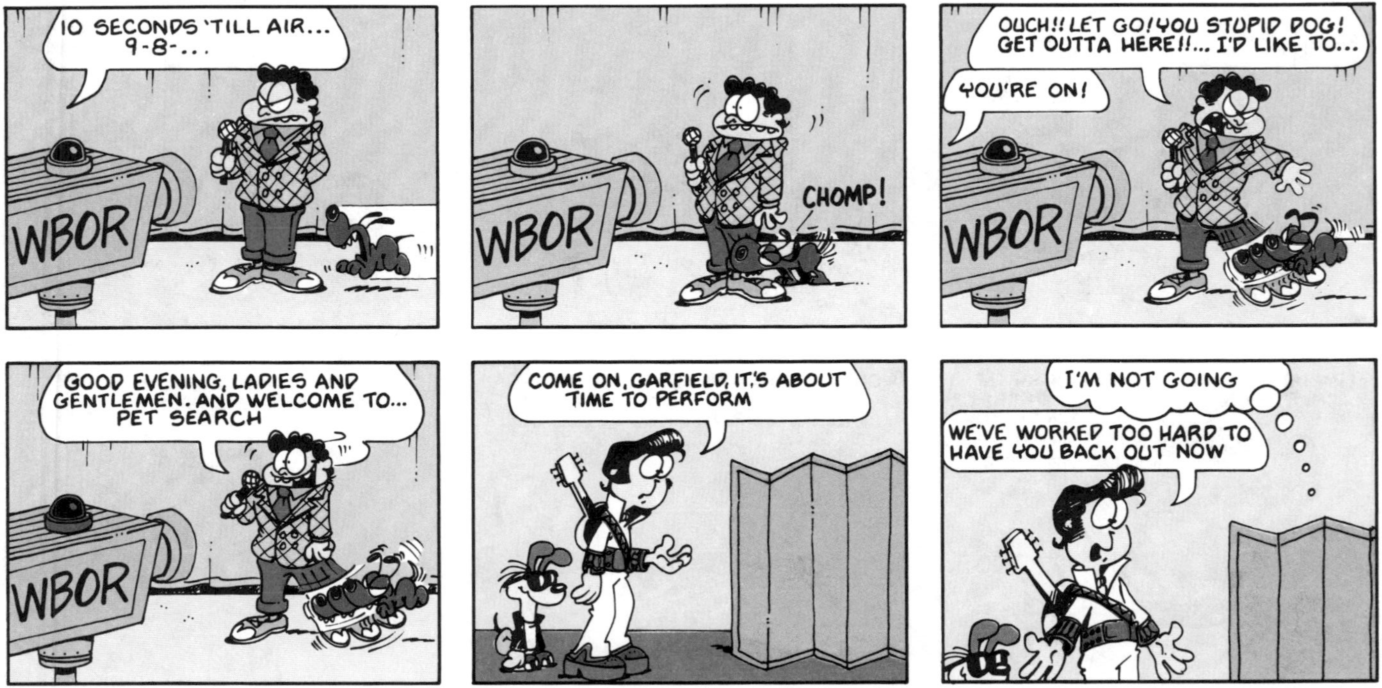
10 SECONDS 'TILL AIR... 9-8-...
WBOR
WBOR
CHOMP!
OUCH!! LET GO! YOU STUPID DOG! GET OUTTA HERE!!... I'D LIKE TO...
YOU'RE ON!
WBOR
GOOD EVENING, LADIES AND GENTLEMEN. AND WELCOME TO... PET SEARCH
WBOR
COME ON, GARFIELD, IT'S ABOUT TIME TO PERFORM
I'M NOT GOING
WE'VE WORKED TOO HARD TO HAVE YOU BACK OUT NOW

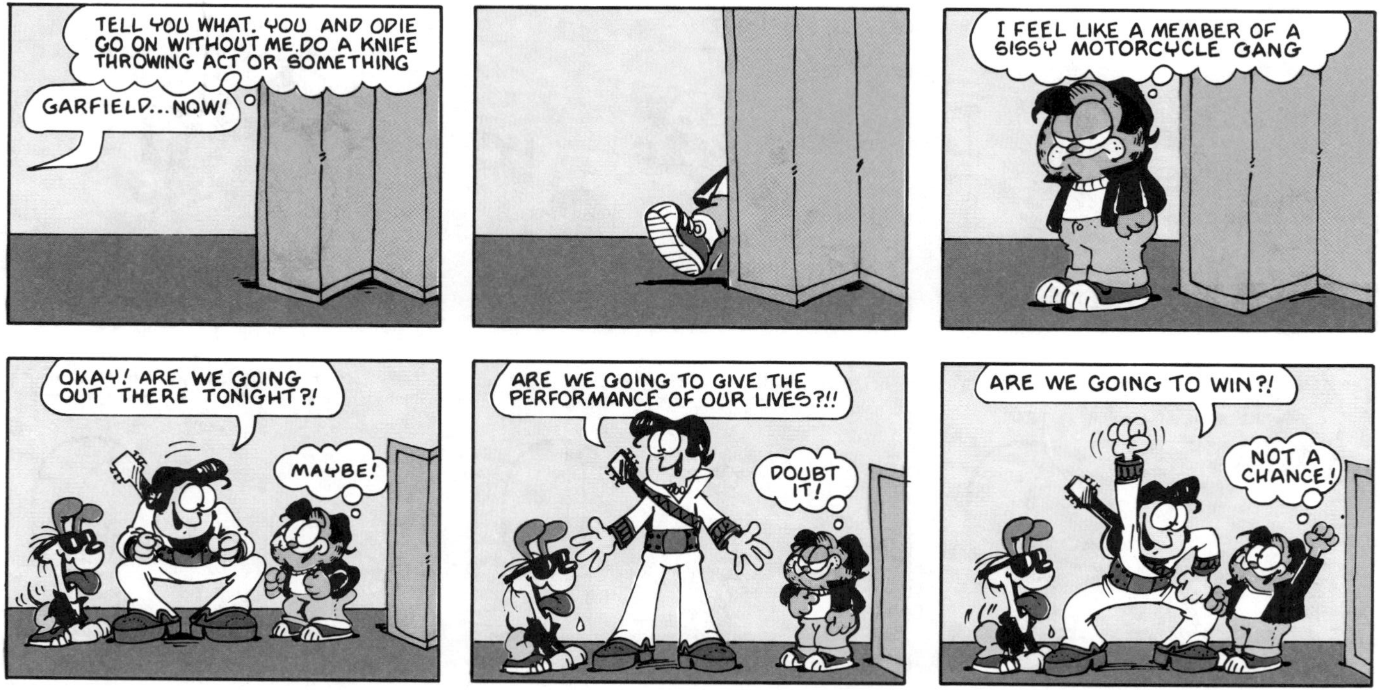
GARFIELD...NOW!
TELL YOU WHAT. YOU AND ODIE GO ON WITHOUT ME. DO A KNIFE THROWING ACT OR SOMETHING
I FEEL LIKE A MEMBER OF A SISSY MOTORCYCLE GANG
OKAY! ARE WE GOING OUT THERE TONIGHT?!
MAYBE!
ARE WE GOING TO GIVE THE PERFORMANCE OF OUR LIVES?!!
DOUBT IT!
ARE WE GOING TO WIN?!
NOT A CHANCE!

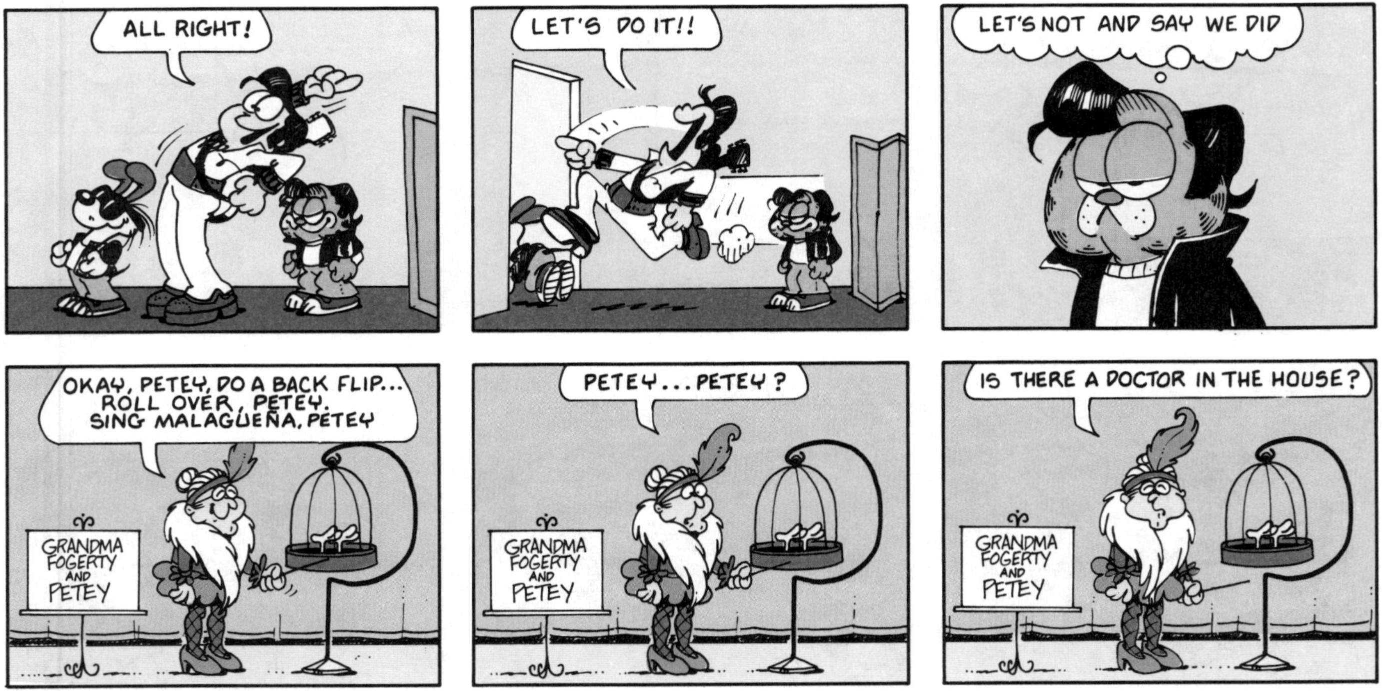
ALL RIGHT!
LET'S DO IT!!
LET'S NOT AND SAY WE DID
OKAY, PETEY, DO A BACK FLIP... ROLL OVER, PETEY. SING MALAGUEÑA, PETEY
GRANDMA FOGERTY AND PETEY
PETEY... PETEY?
GRANDMA FOGERTY AND PETEY
IS THERE A DOCTOR IN THE HOUSE?
GRANDMA FOGERTY AND PETEY

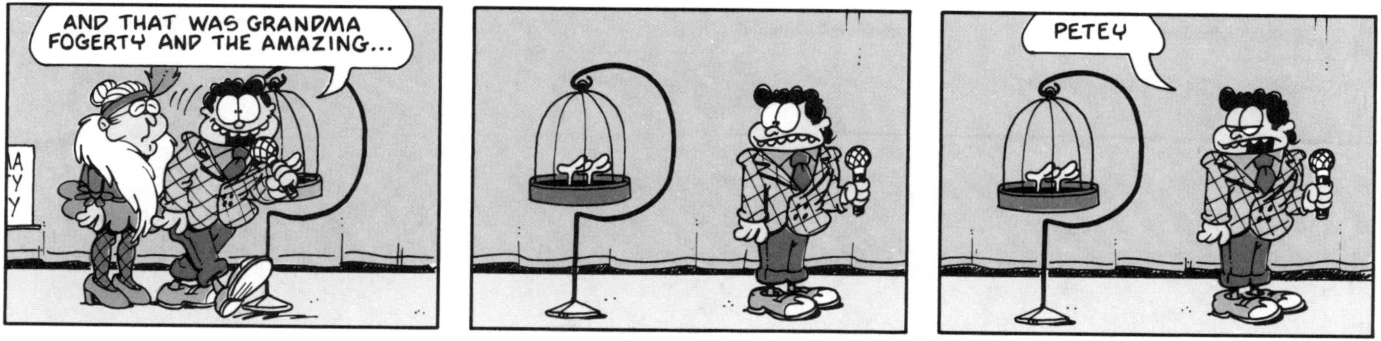
AND THAT WAS GRANDMA FOGERTY AND THE AMAZING...
PETEY

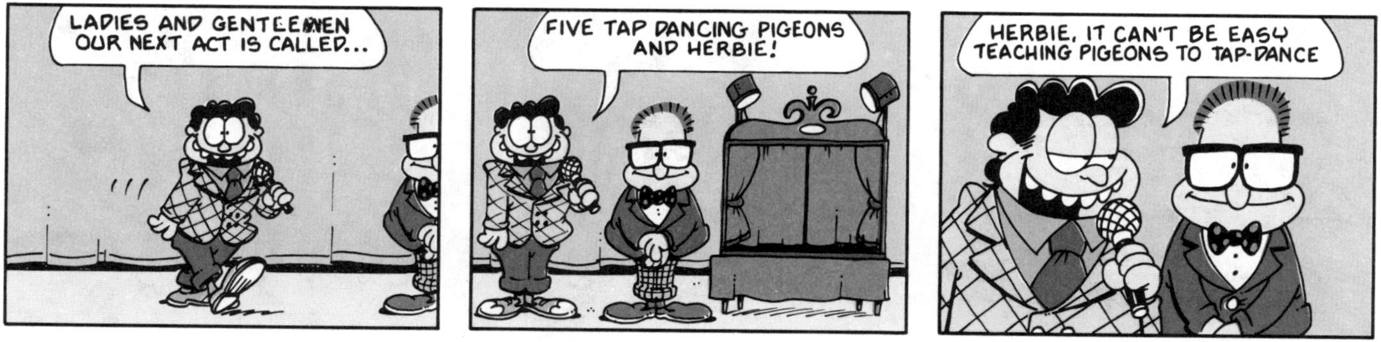
LADIES AND GENTLEMEN OUR NEXT ACT IS CALLED...
FIVE TAP DANCING PIGEONS AND HERBIE!
HERBIE, IT CAN'T BE EASY TEACHING PIGEONS TO TAP-DANCE

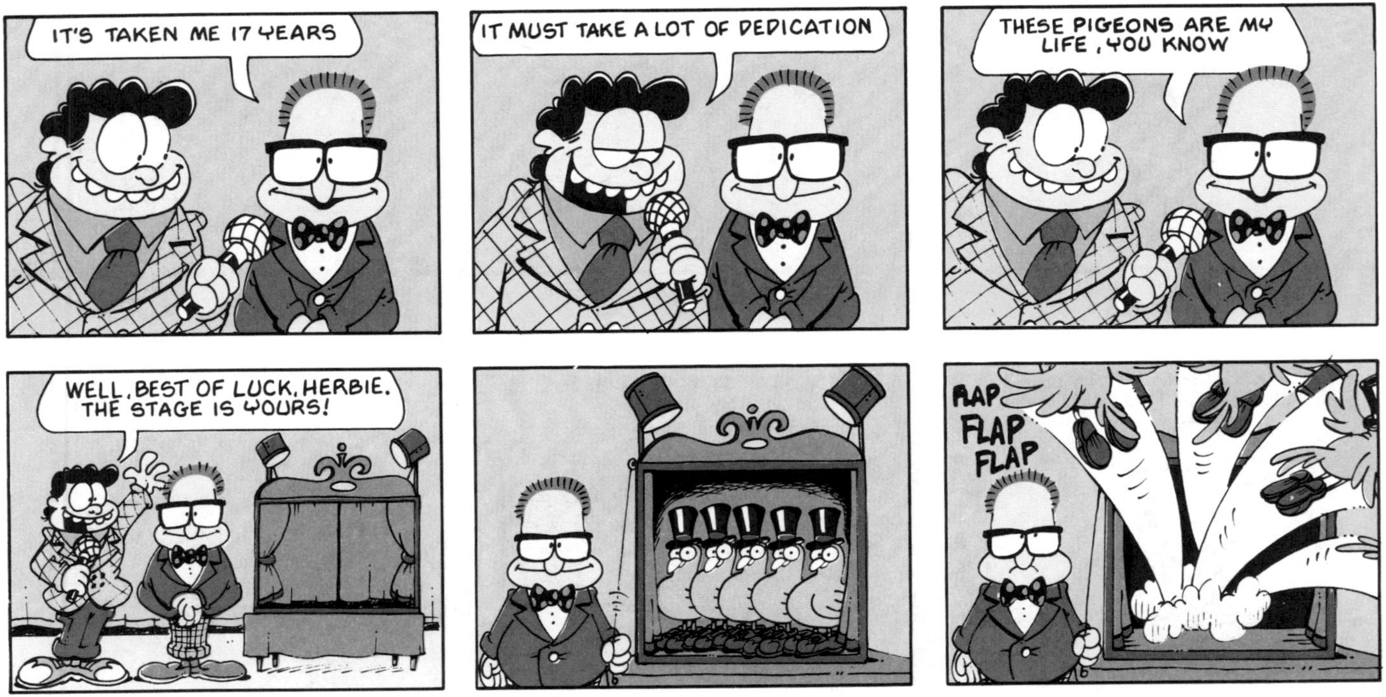
IT'S TAKEN ME 17 YEARS
IT MUST TAKE A LOT OF DEDICATION
THESE PIGEONS ARE MY LIFE, YOU KNOW
WELL, BEST OF LUCK, HERBIE. THE STAGE IS YOURS!
FLAP
FLAP
FLAP

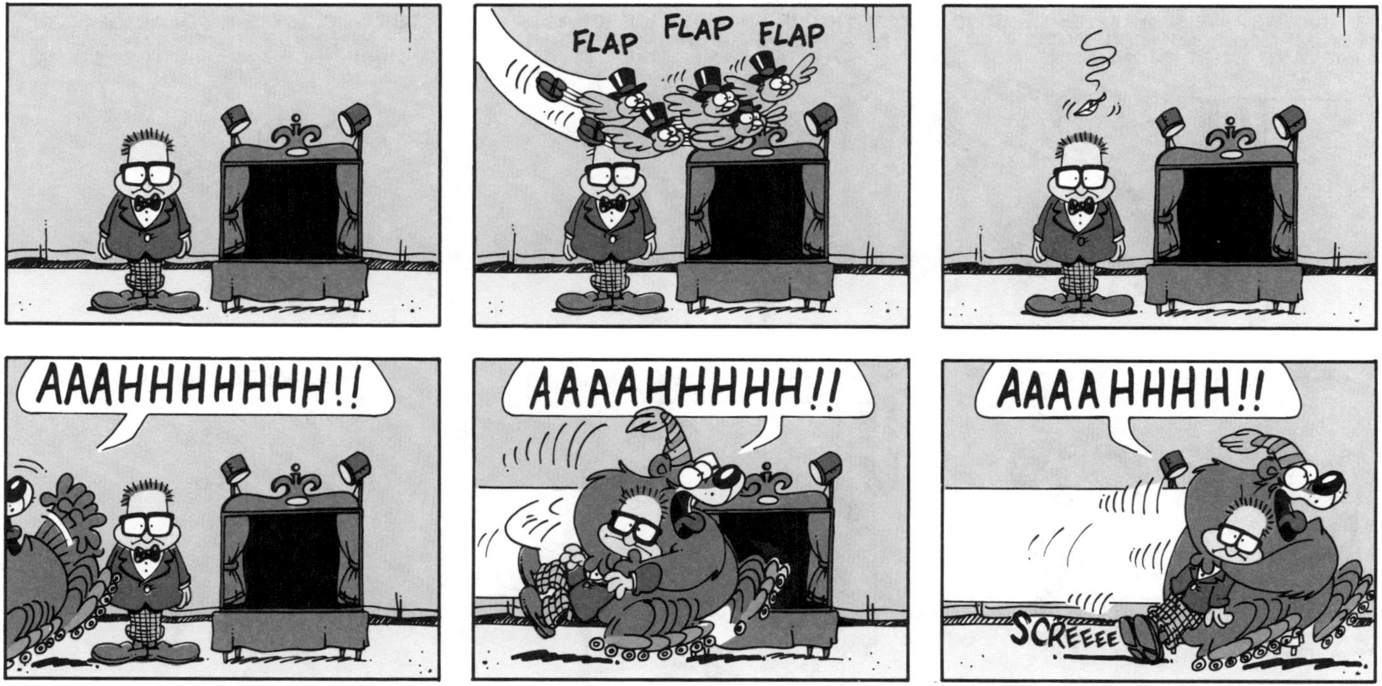
FLAP
FLAP
FLAP
AAAHHHHHHH!!
AAAAHHHHHH!!
AAAAHHHH!!
SCREEEEE

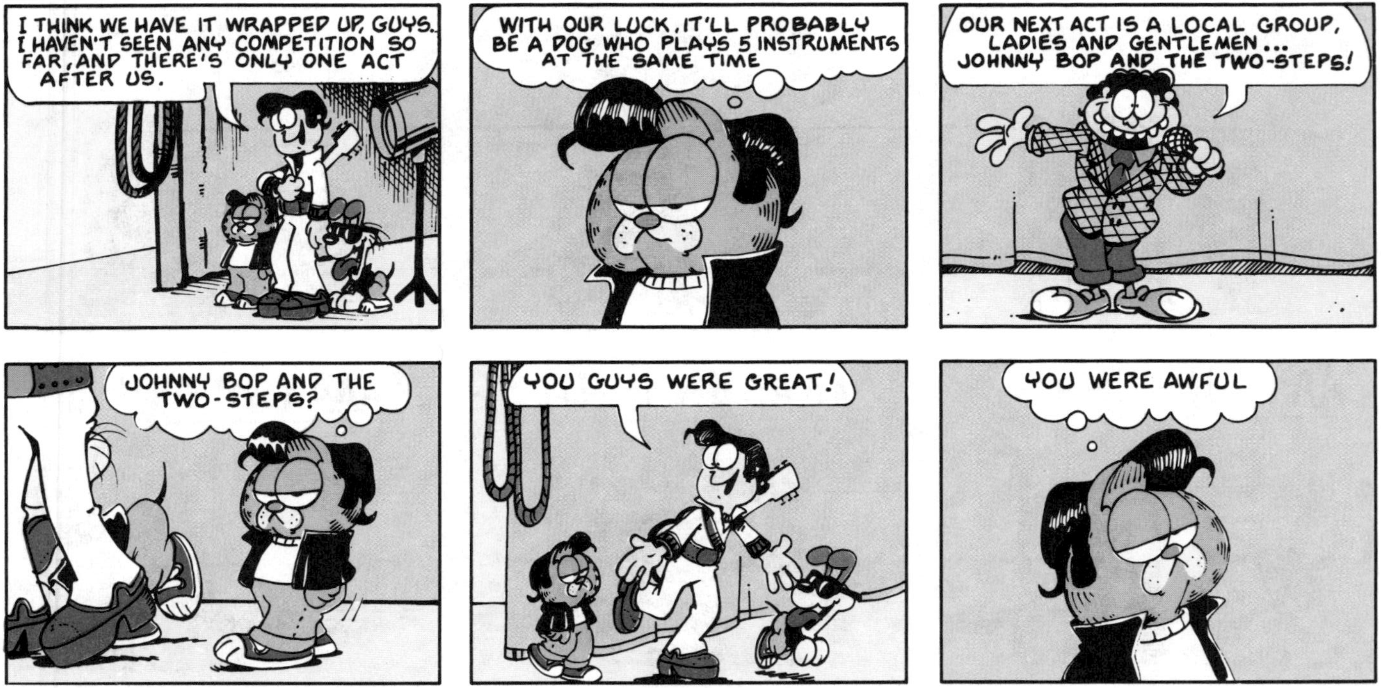
I THINK WE HAVE IT WRAPPED UP, GUYS... I HAVEN'T SEEN ANY COMPETITION SO FAR, AND THERE'S ONLY ONE ACT AFTER US.
WITH OUR LUCK, IT'LL PROBABLY BE A DOG WHO PLAYS 5 INSTRUMENTS AT THE SAME TIME
OUR NEXT ACT IS A LOCAL GROUP, LADIES AND GENTLEMEN... JOHNNY BOP AND THE TWO-STEPS!
JOHNNY BOP AND THE TWO-STEPS?
YOU GUYS WERE GREAT!
YOU WERE AWFUL

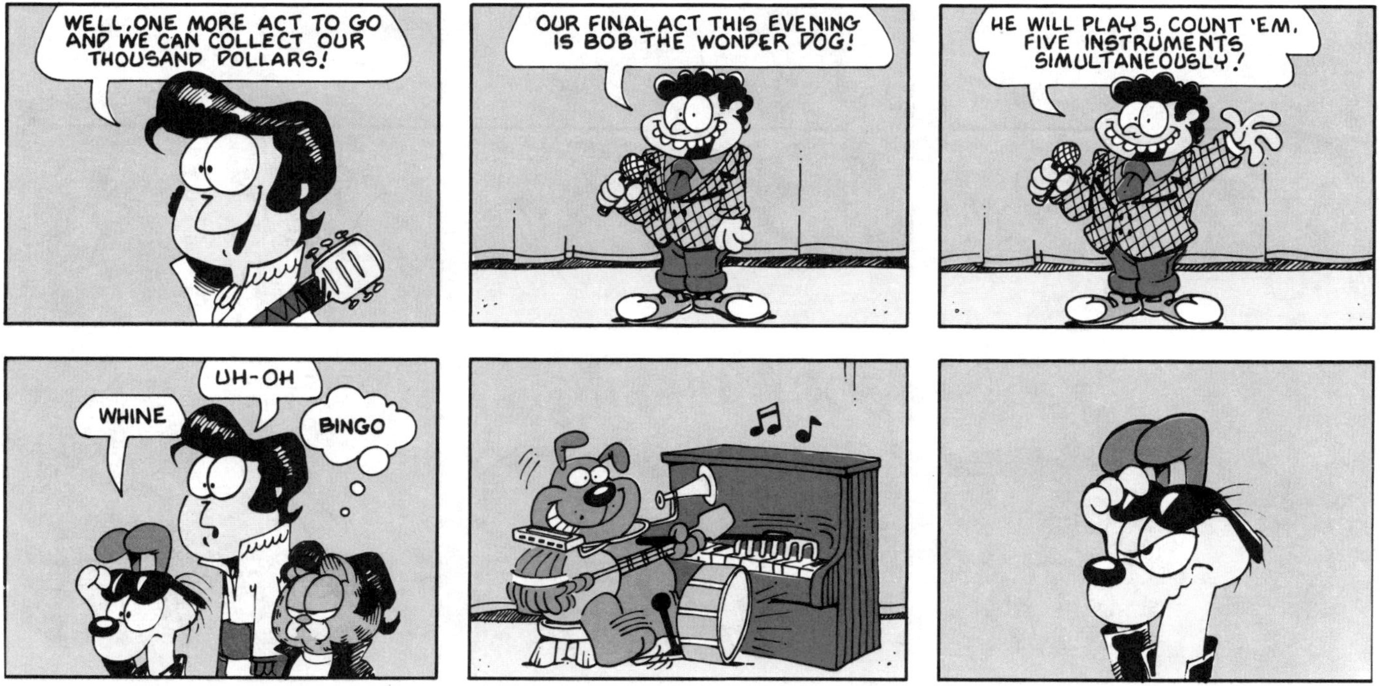
WELL, ONE MORE ACT TO GO AND WE CAN COLLECT OUR THOUSAND DOLLARS!
OUR FINAL ACT THIS EVENING IS BOB THE WONDER DOG!
HE WILL PLAY 5, COUNT 'EM, FIVE INSTRUMENTS SIMULTANEOUSLY!
WHINE
UH-OH
BINGO

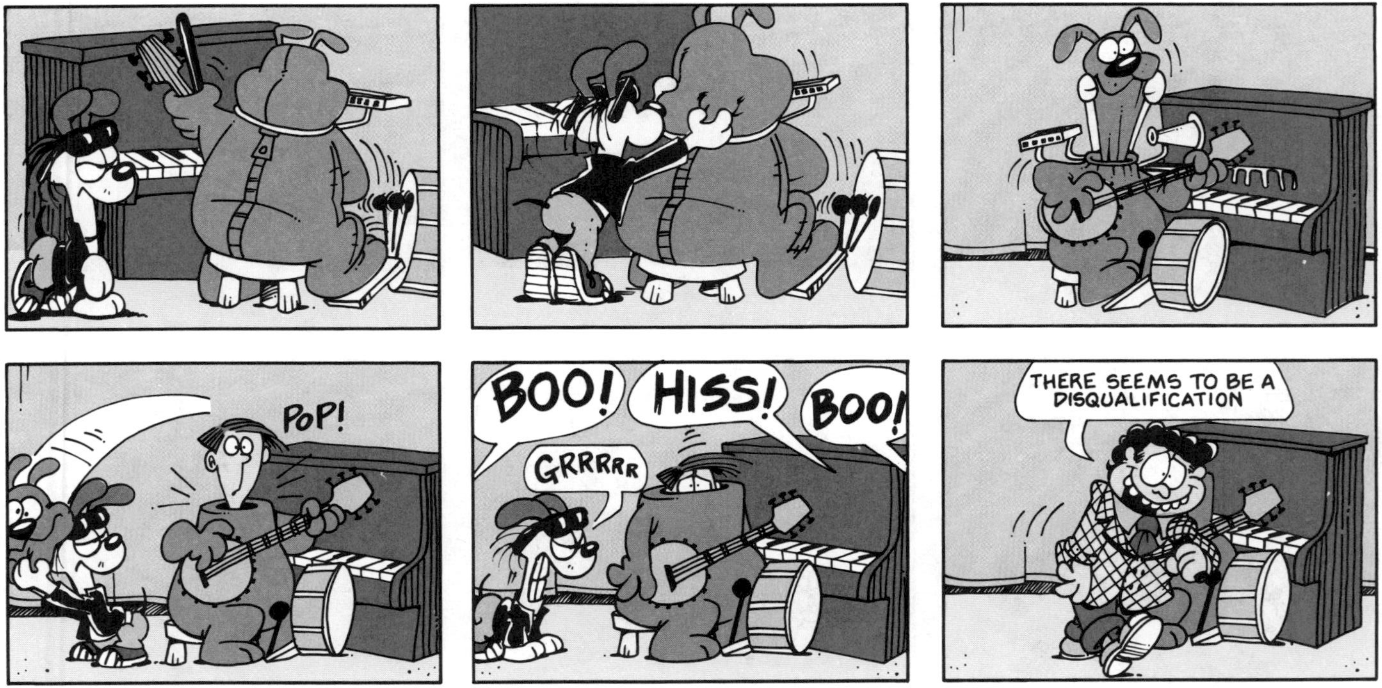

PoP!
BOO!
HISS!
BOO!
GRRRRR
THERE SEEMS TO BE A DISQUALIFICATION

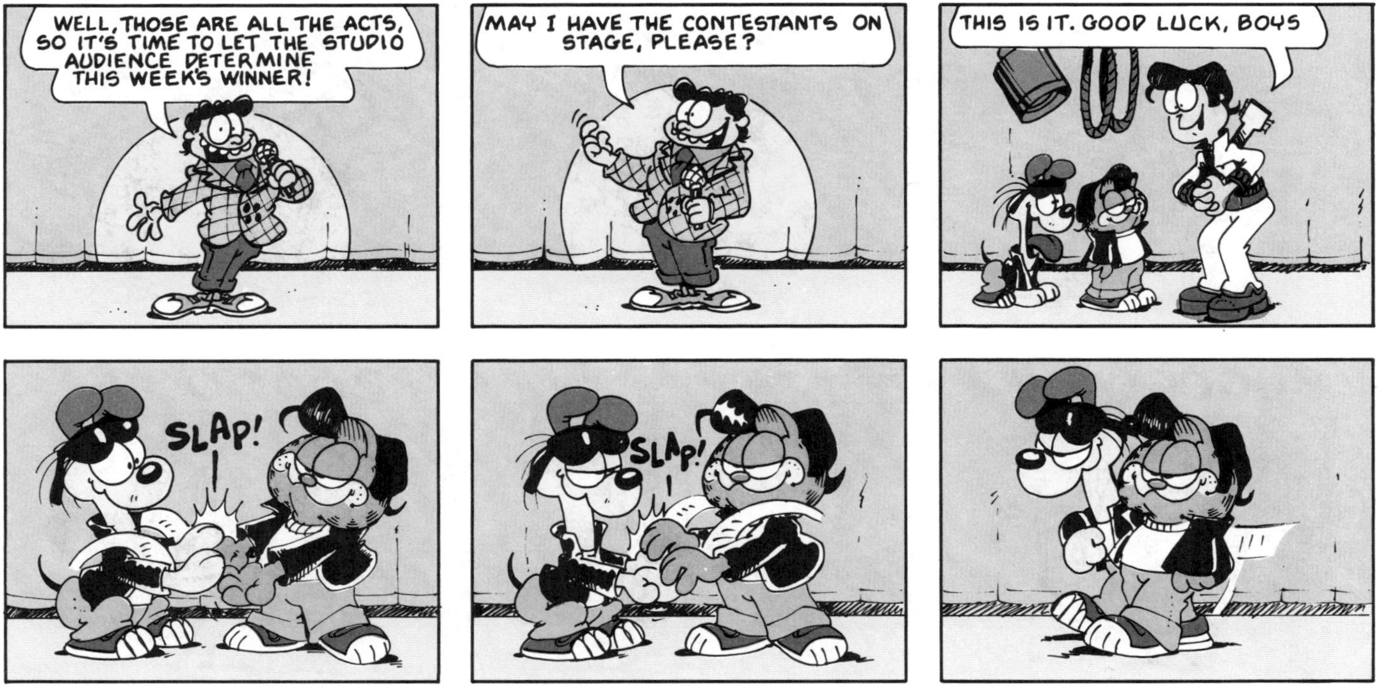
WELL, THOSE ARE ALL THE ACTS, SO IT'S TIME TO LET THE STUDIO AUDIENCE DETERMINE THIS WEEK'S WINNER!
MAY I HAVE THE CONTESTANTS ON STAGE, PLEASE?
THIS IS IT. GOOD LUCK, BOYS
SLAP!
SLAP!

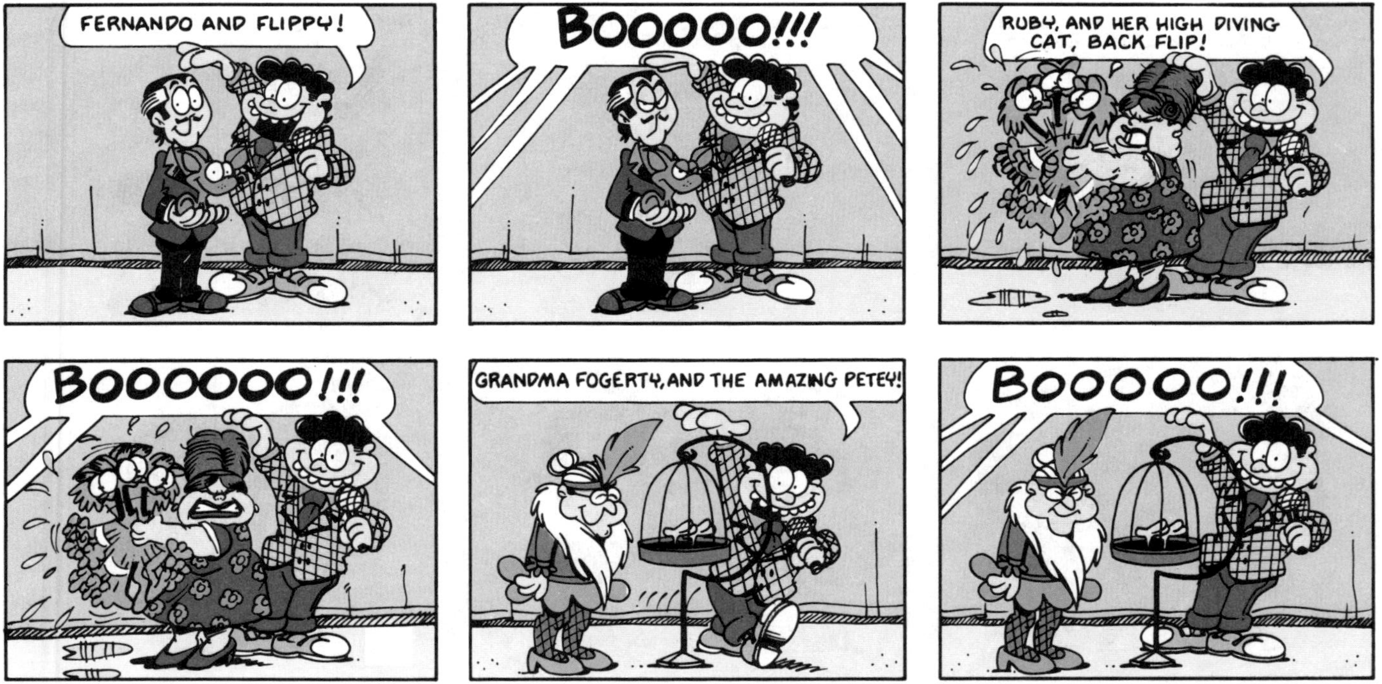
FERNANDO AND FLIPPY!
BOOOOO!!!
RUBY, AND HER HIGH DIVING CAT, BACK FLIP!
BOOOOOO!!!
GRANDMA FOGERTY, AND THE AMAZING PETEY!
BOOOOO!!!

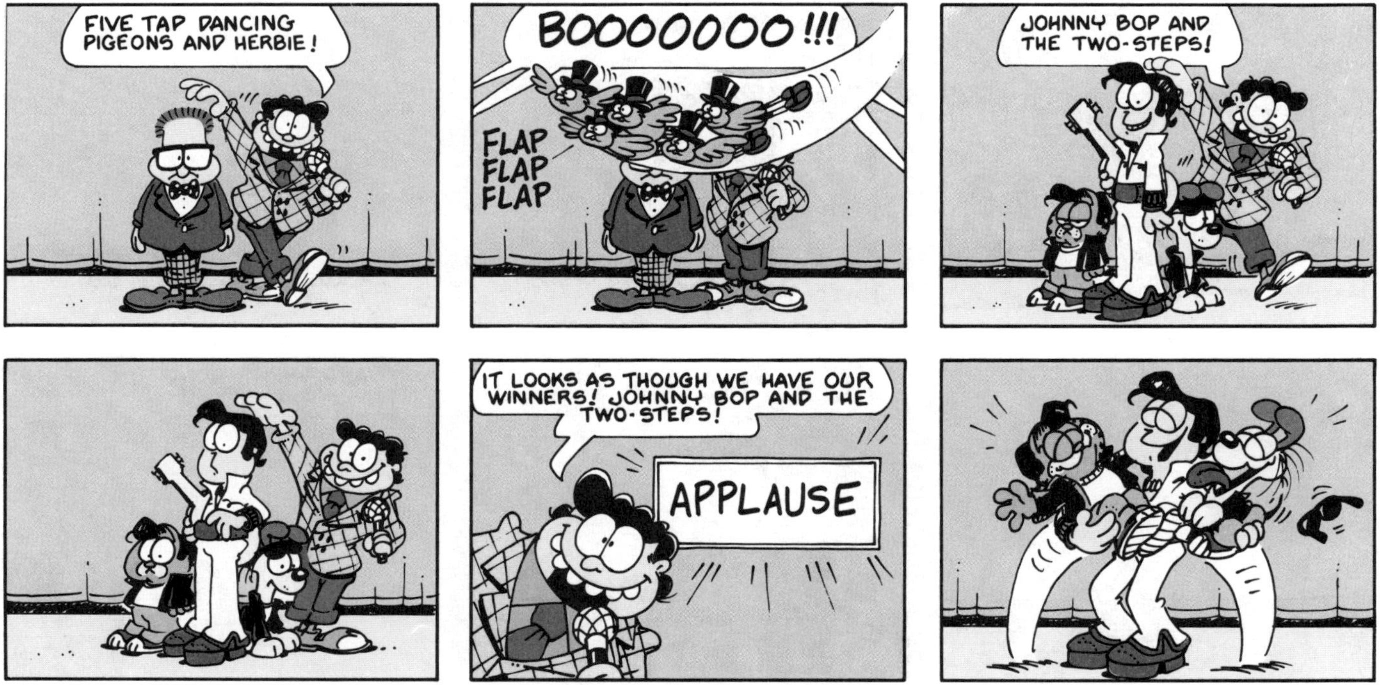
FIVE TAP DANCING PIGEONS AND HERBIE!
BOOOOOOO!!!
FLAP FLAP FLAP
JOHNNY BOP AND THE TWO-STEPS!
IT LOOKS AS THOUGH WE HAVE OUR WINNERS! JOHNNY BOP AND THE TWO-STEPS!
APPLAUSE

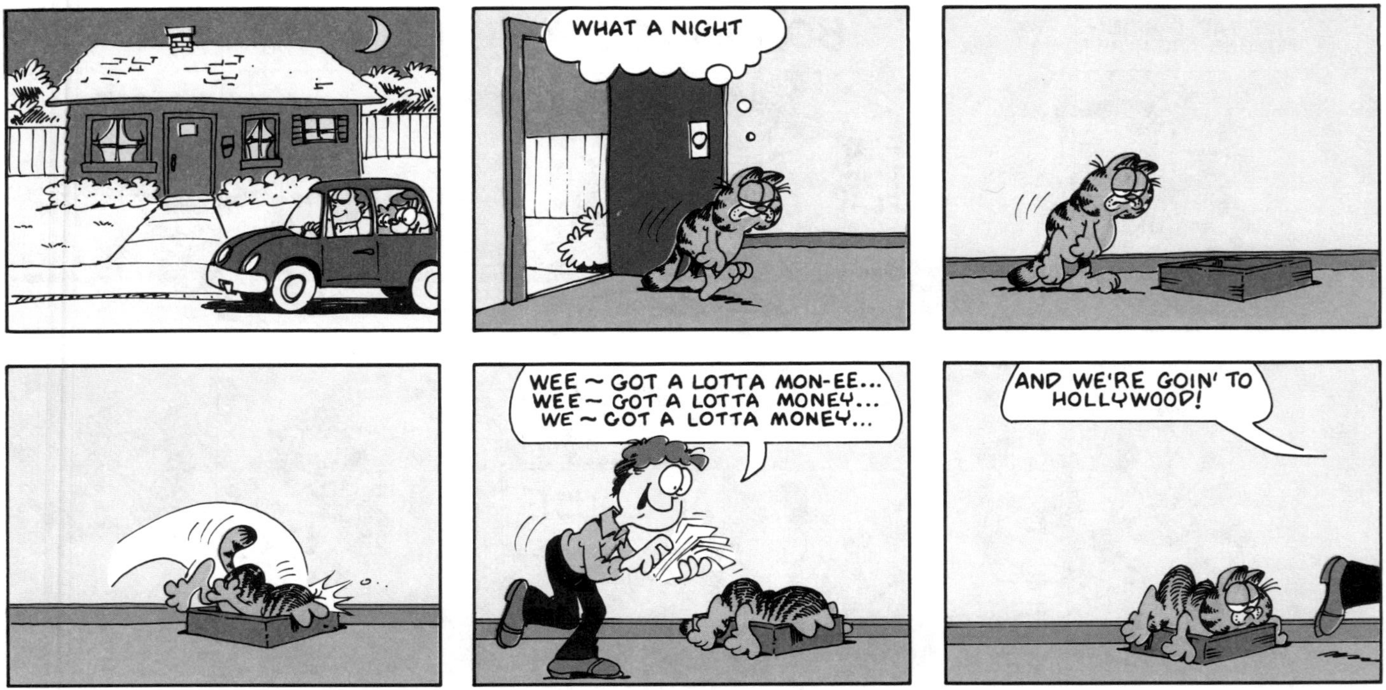
WHAT A NIGHT
WEE ~ GOT A LOTTA MON-EE... WEE ~ GOT A LOTTA MONEY... WE ~ GOT A LOTTA MONEY...
AND WE'RE GOIN' TO HOLLYWOOD!

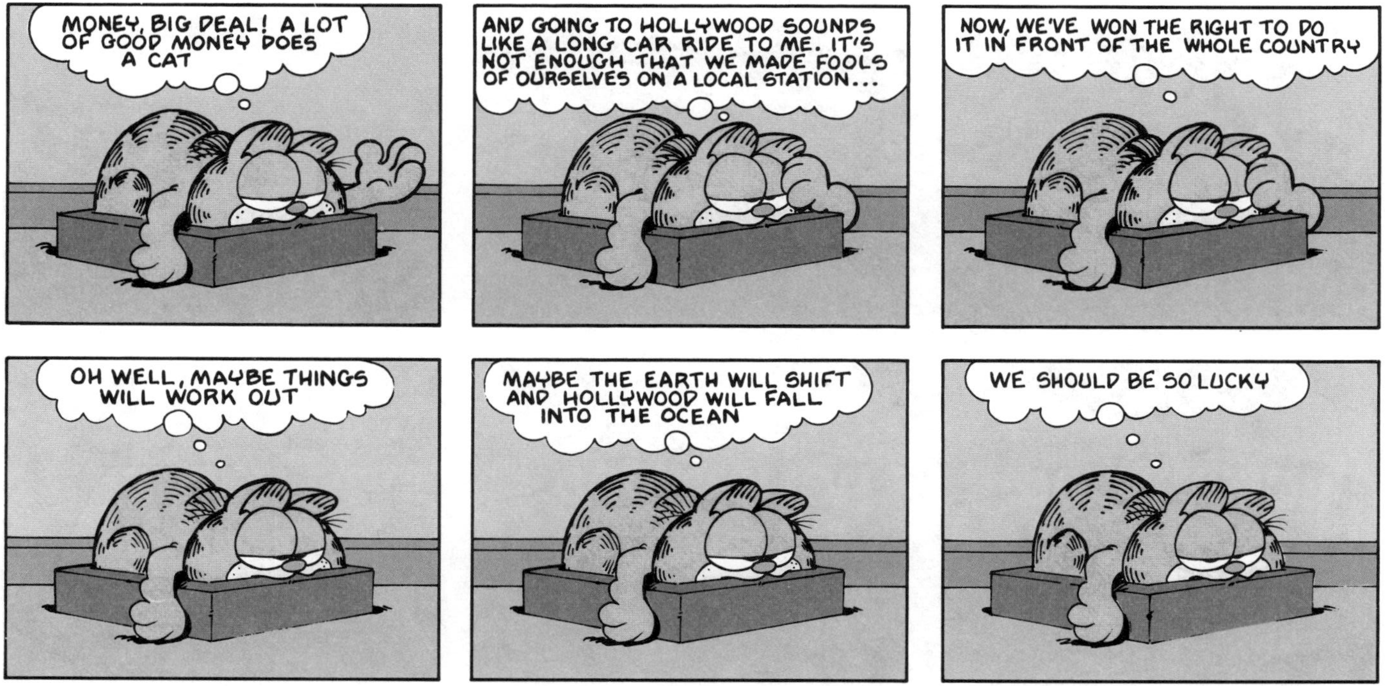
MONEY, BIG DEAL! A LOT OF GOOD MONEY DOES A CAT
AND GOING TO HOLLYWOOD SOUNDS LIKE A LONG CAR RIDE TO ME. IT'S NOT ENOUGH THAT WE MADE FOOLS OF OURSELVES ON A LOCAL STATION...
NOW, WE'VE WON THE RIGHT TO DO IT IN FRONT OF THE WHOLE COUNTRY
OH WELL, MAYBE THINGS WILL WORK OUT
MAYBE THE EARTH WILL SHIFT AND HOLLYWOOD WILL FALL INTO THE OCEAN
WE SHOULD BE SO LUCKY

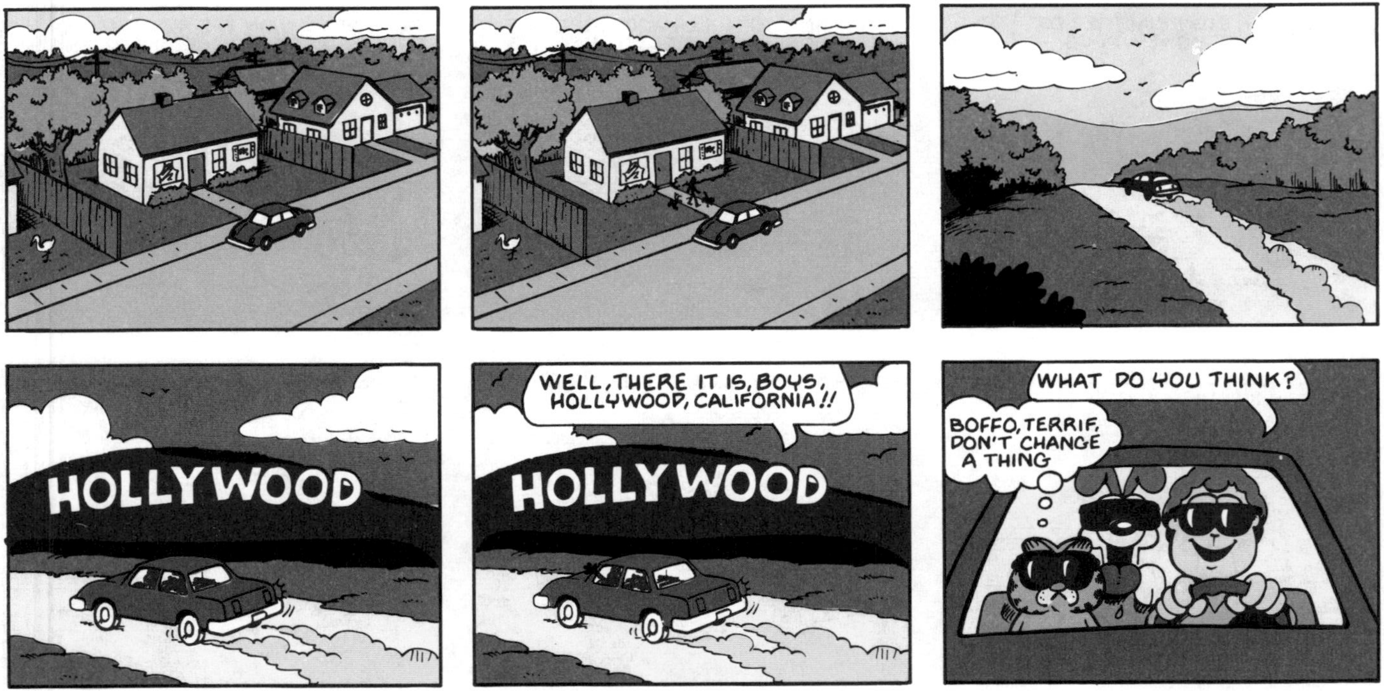
HOLLYWOOD
WELL, THERE IT IS, BOYS, HOLLYWOOD, CALIFORNIA!!
HOLLYWOOD
WHAT DO YOU THINK?
BOFFO, TERRIF, DON'T CHANGE A THING

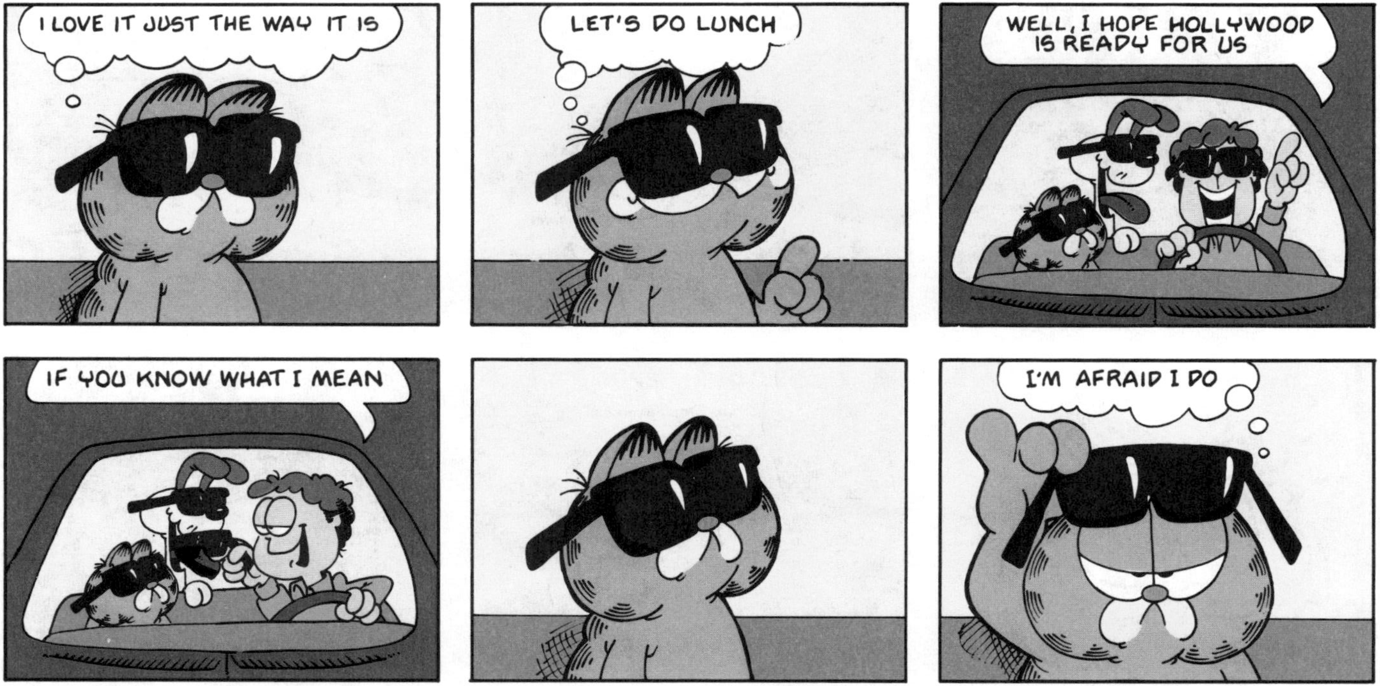
I LOVE IT JUST THE WAY IT IS
LET'S DO LUNCH
WELL, I HOPE HOLLYWOOD IS READY FOR US
IF YOU KNOW WHAT I MEAN
I'M AFRAID I DO

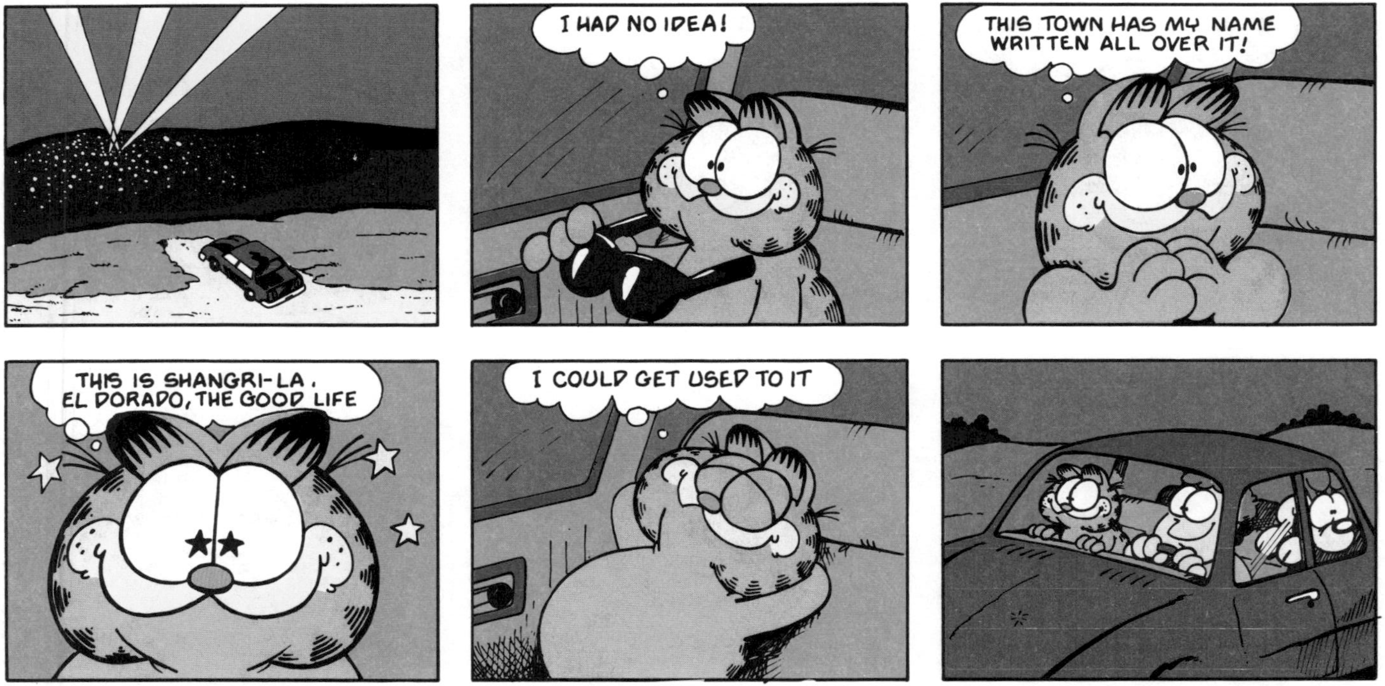
I HAD NO IDEA!
THIS TOWN HAS MY NAME WRITTEN ALL OVER IT!
THIS IS SHANGRI-LA. EL DORADO, THE GOOD LIFE
I COULD GET USED TO IT

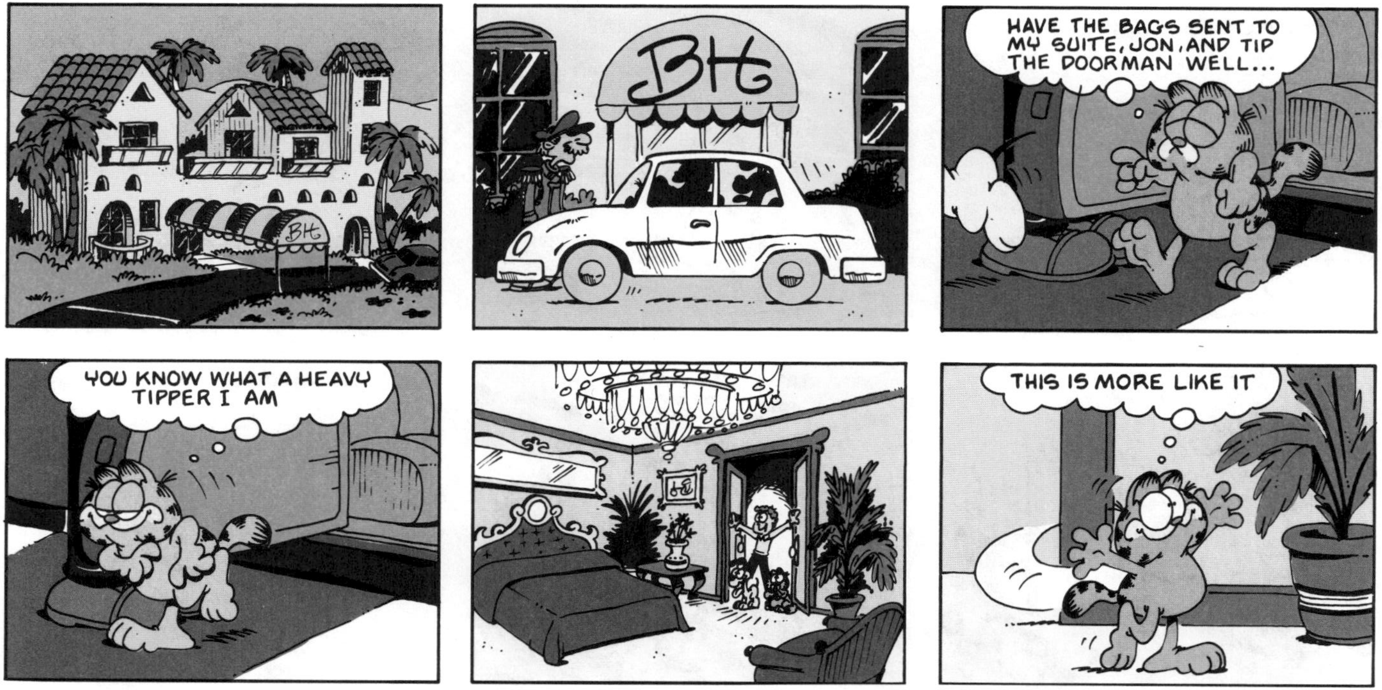
BH
BH
HAVE THE BAGS SENT TO MY SUITE, JON, AND TIP THE DOORMAN WELL...
YOU KNOW WHAT A HEAVY TIPPER I AM
THIS IS MORE LIKE IT

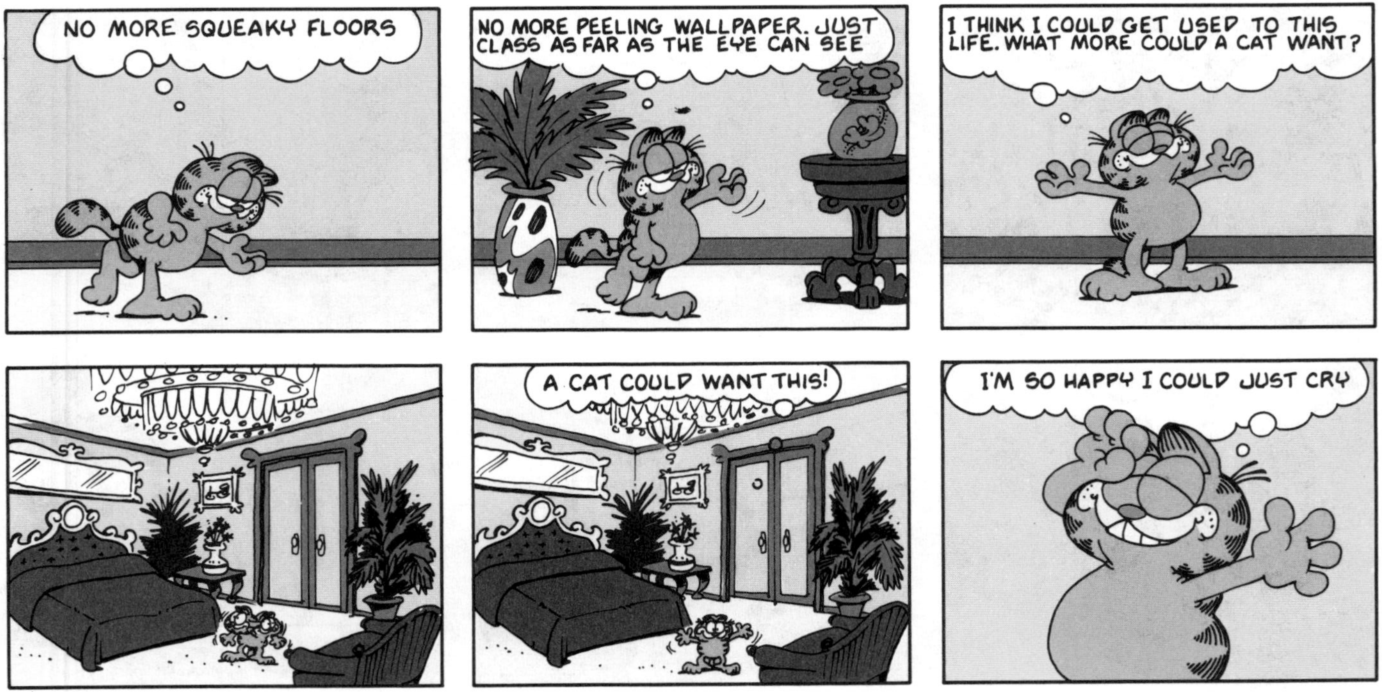
NO MORE SQUEAKY FLOORS
NO MORE PEELING WALLPAPER. JUST CLASS AS FAR AS THE EYE CAN SEE
I THINK I COULD GET USED TO THIS LIFE. WHAT MORE COULD A CAT WANT?
A CAT COULD WANT THIS!
I'M SO HAPPY I COULD JUST CRY

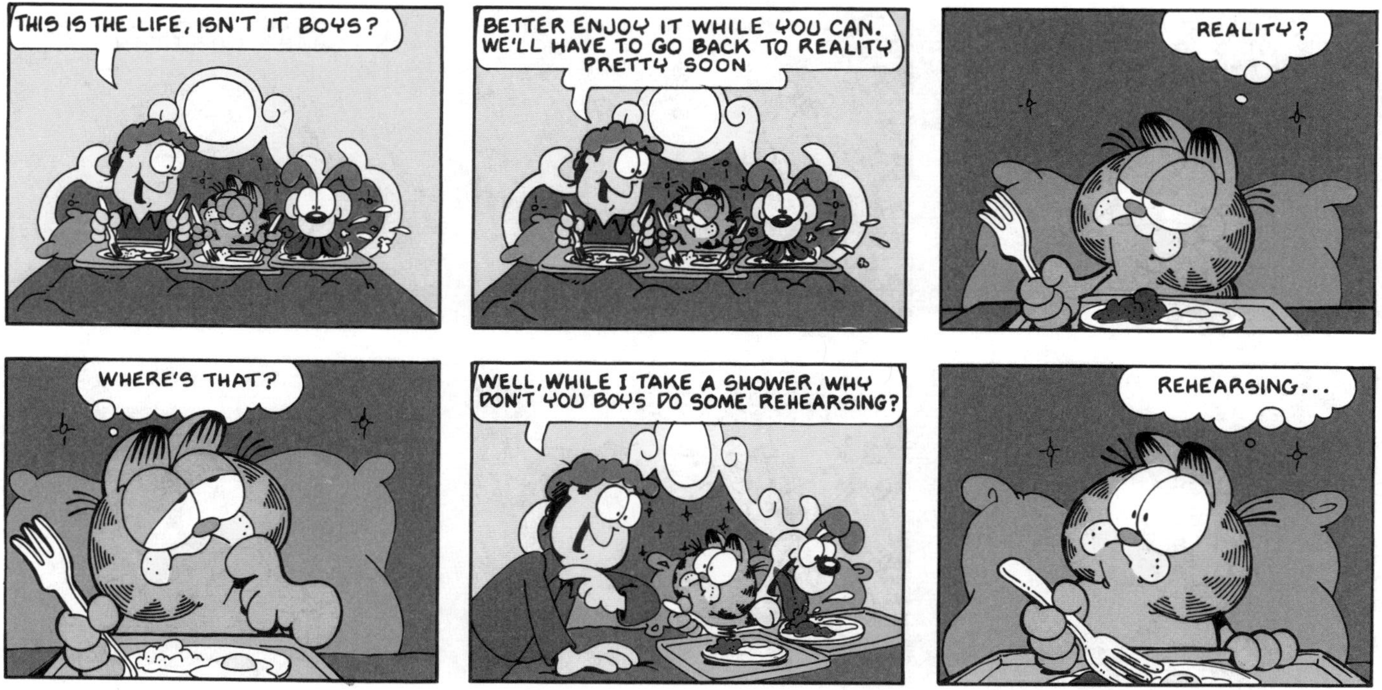
THIS IS THE LIFE, ISN'T IT BOYS?
BETTER ENJOY IT WHILE YOU CAN. WE'LL HAVE TO GO BACK TO REALITY PRETTY SOON
REALITY?
WHERE'S THAT?
WELL, WHILE I TAKE A SHOWER, WHY DON'T YOU BOYS DO SOME REHEARSING?
REHEARSING...

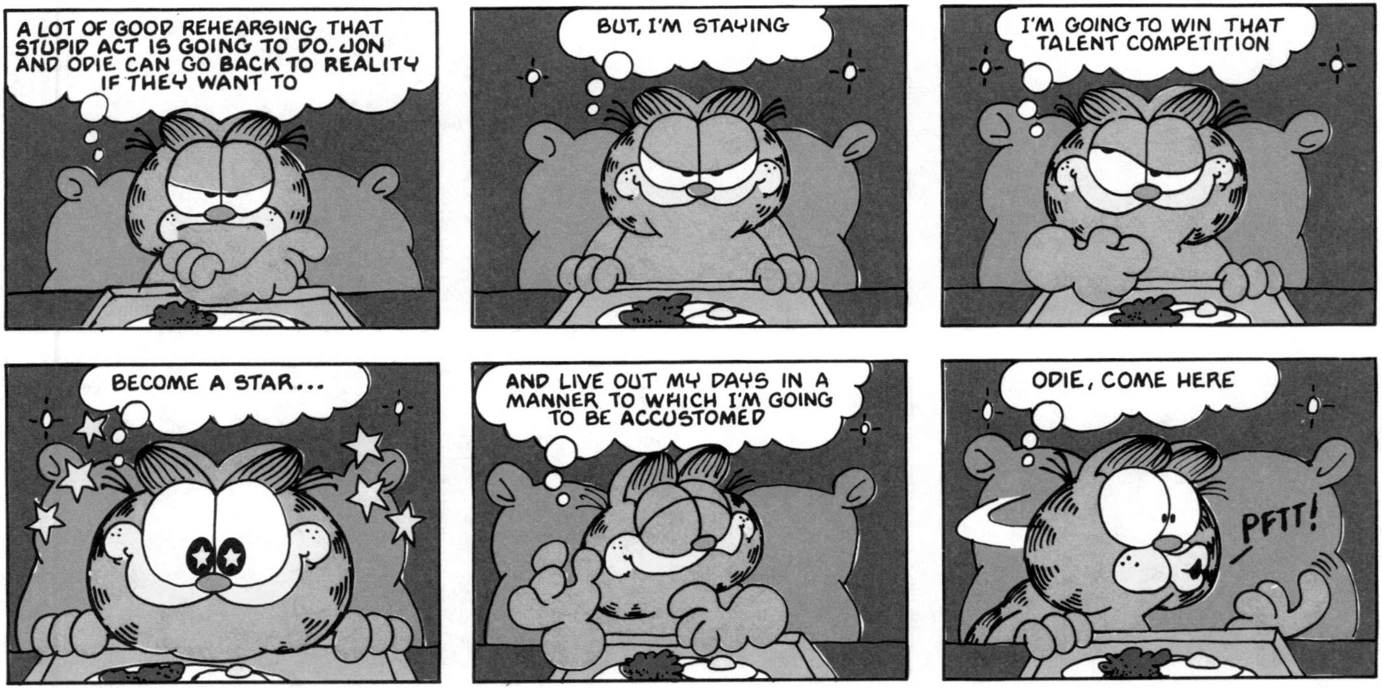
A LOT OF GOOD REHEARSING THAT STUPID ACT IS GOING TO DO. JON AND ODIE CAN GO BACK TO REALITY IF THEY WANT TO
BUT, I'M STAYING
I'M GOING TO WIN THAT TALENT COMPETITION
BECOME A STAR...
AND LIVE OUT MY DAYS IN A MANNER TO WHICH I'M GOING TO BE ACCUSTOMED
ODIE, COME HERE
PFTT!

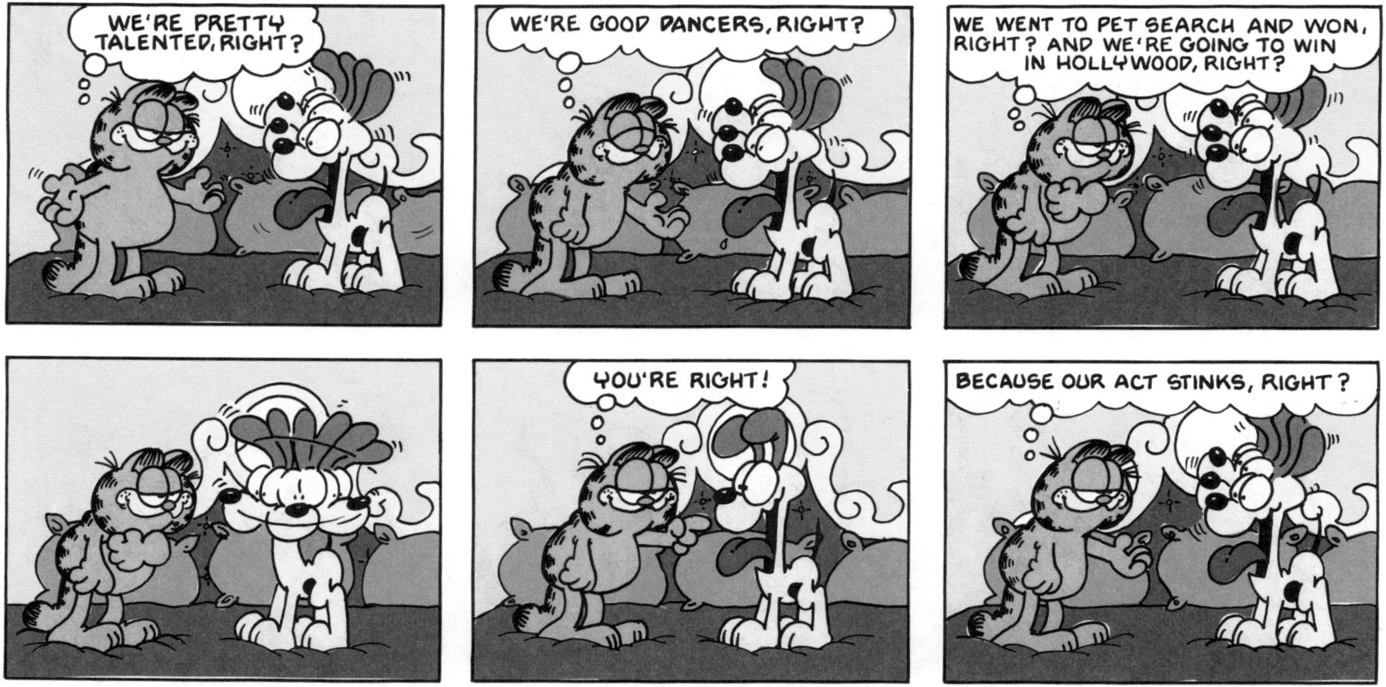
WE'RE PRETTY TALENTED, RIGHT?
WE'RE GOOD DANCERS, RIGHT?
WE WENT TO PET SEARCH AND WON, RIGHT? AND WE'RE GOING TO WIN IN HOLLYWOOD, RIGHT?
YOU'RE RIGHT!
BECAUSE OUR ACT STINKS, RIGHT?

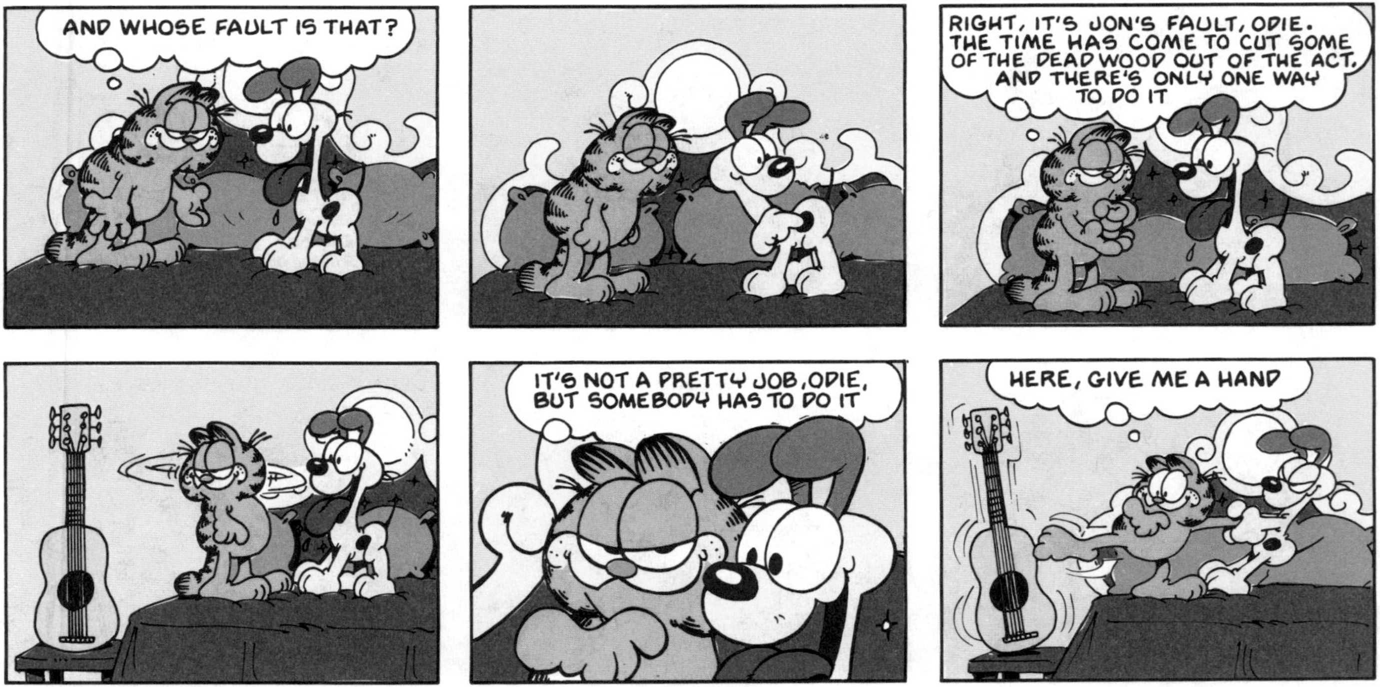
AND WHOSE FAULT IS THAT?
RIGHT, IT'S JON'S FAULT, ODIE. THE TIME HAS COME TO CUT SOME OF THE DEADWOOD OUT OF THE ACT, AND THERE'S ONLY ONE WAY TO DO IT
IT'S NOT A PRETTY JOB, ODIE, BUT SOMEBODY HAS TO DO IT
HERE, GIVE ME A HAND

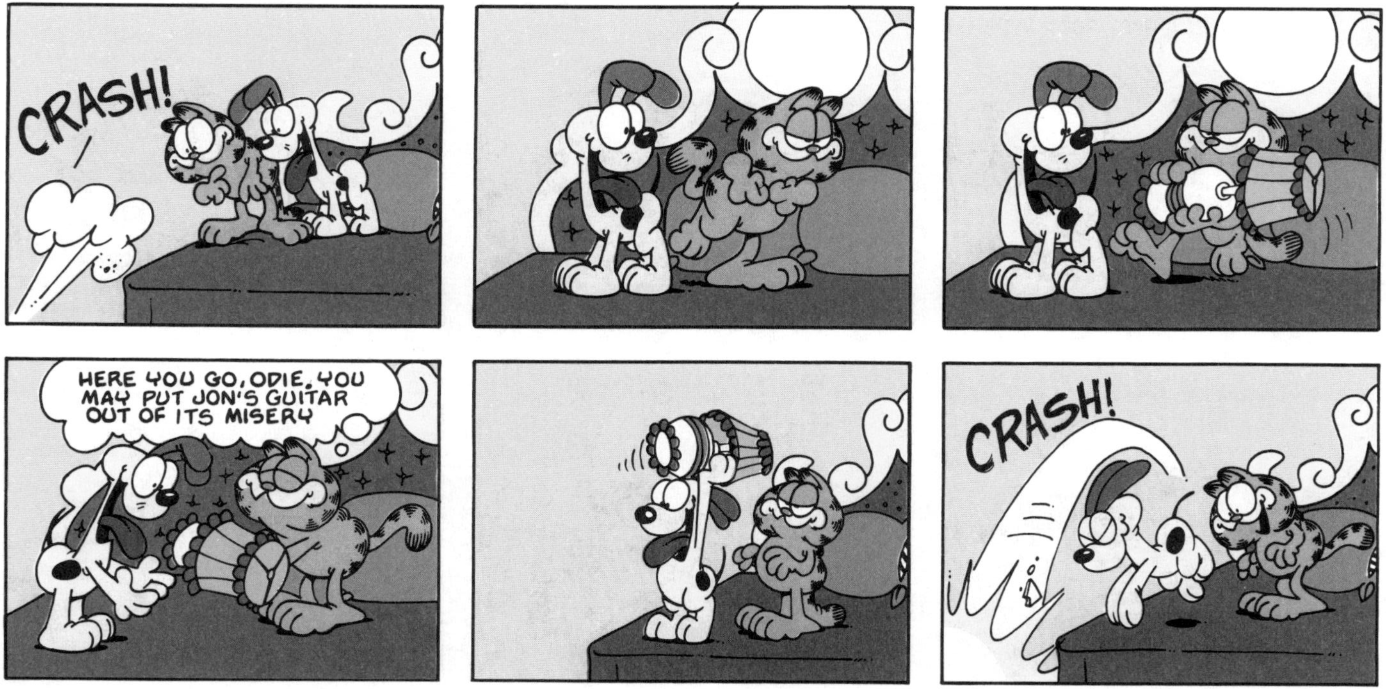
CRASH!
HERE YOU GO, ODIE. YOU MAY PUT JON'S GUITAR OUT OF ITS MISERY
CRASH!

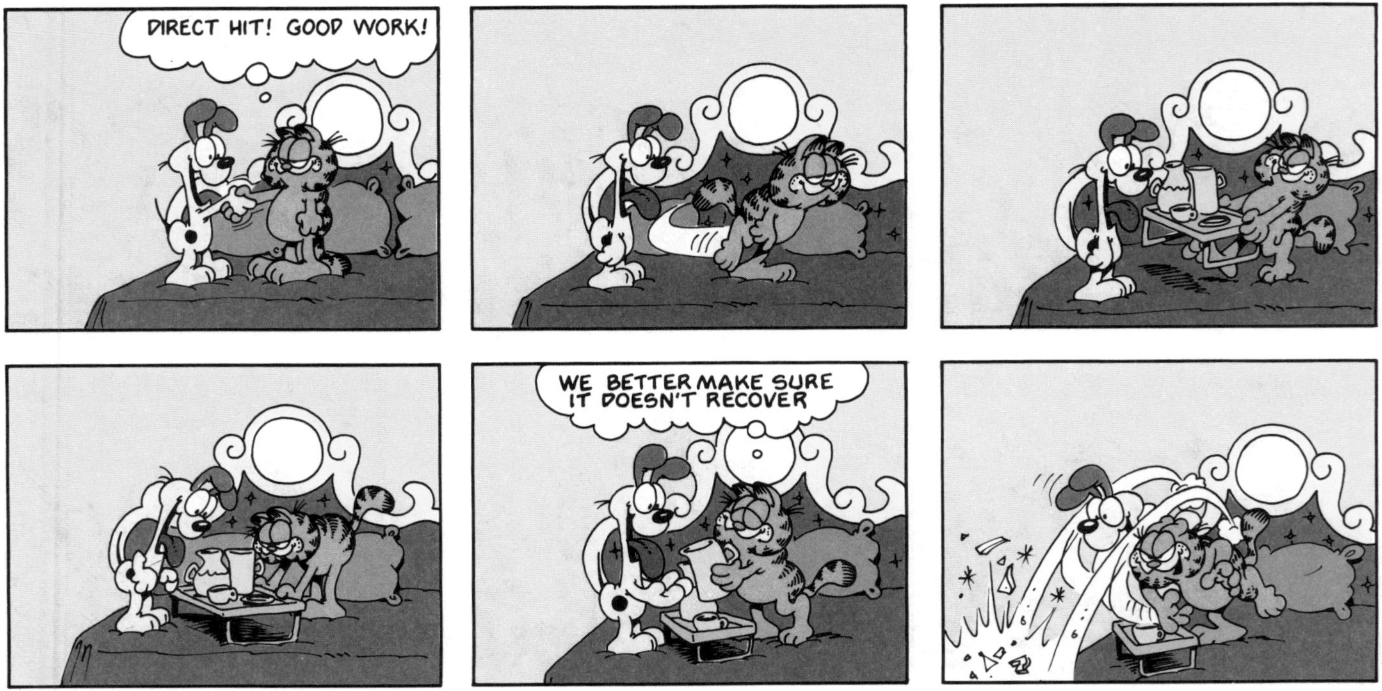
DIRECT HIT! GOOD WORK!
WE BETTER MAKE SURE IT DOESN'T RECOVER

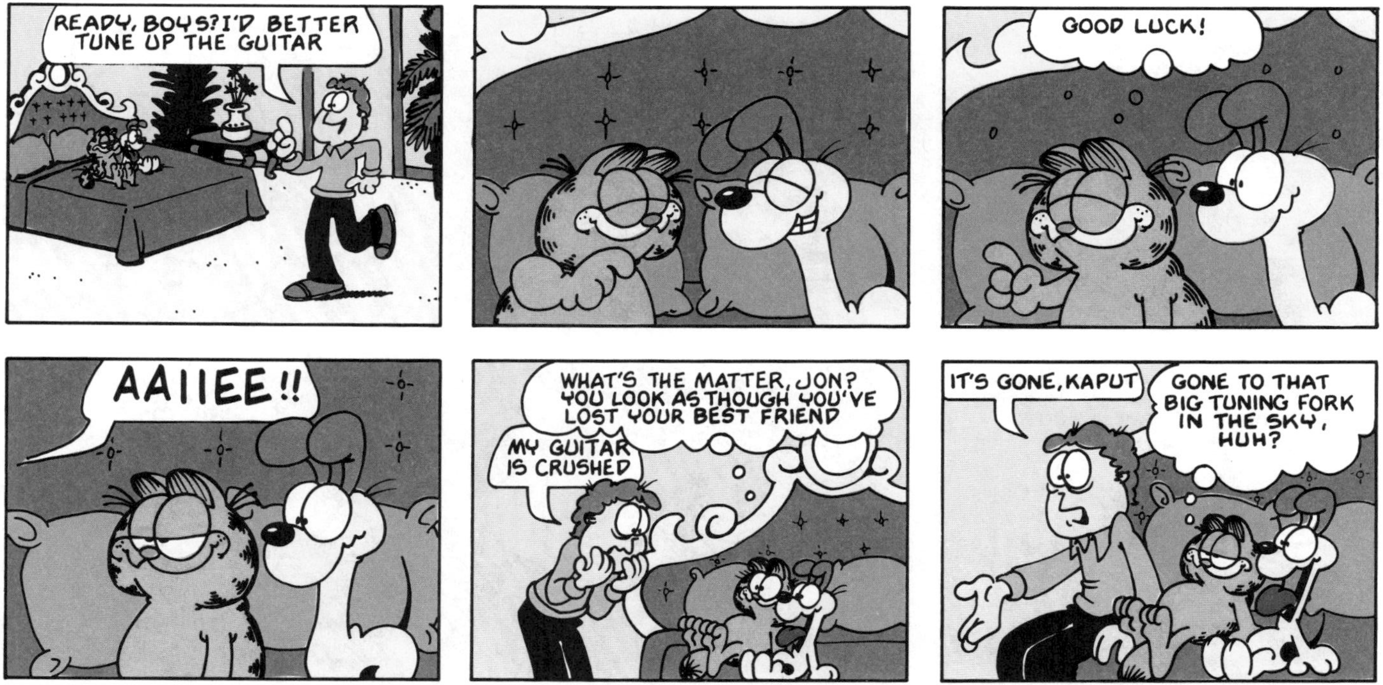
READY, BOYS? I'D BETTER TUNE UP THE GUITAR
GOOD LUCK!
AAIIEE!!
WHAT'S THE MATTER, JON? YOU LOOK AS THOUGH YOU'VE LOST YOUR BEST FRIEND
MY GUITAR IS CRUSHED
IT'S GONE, KAPUT
GONE TO THAT BIG TUNING FORK IN THE SKY, HUH?

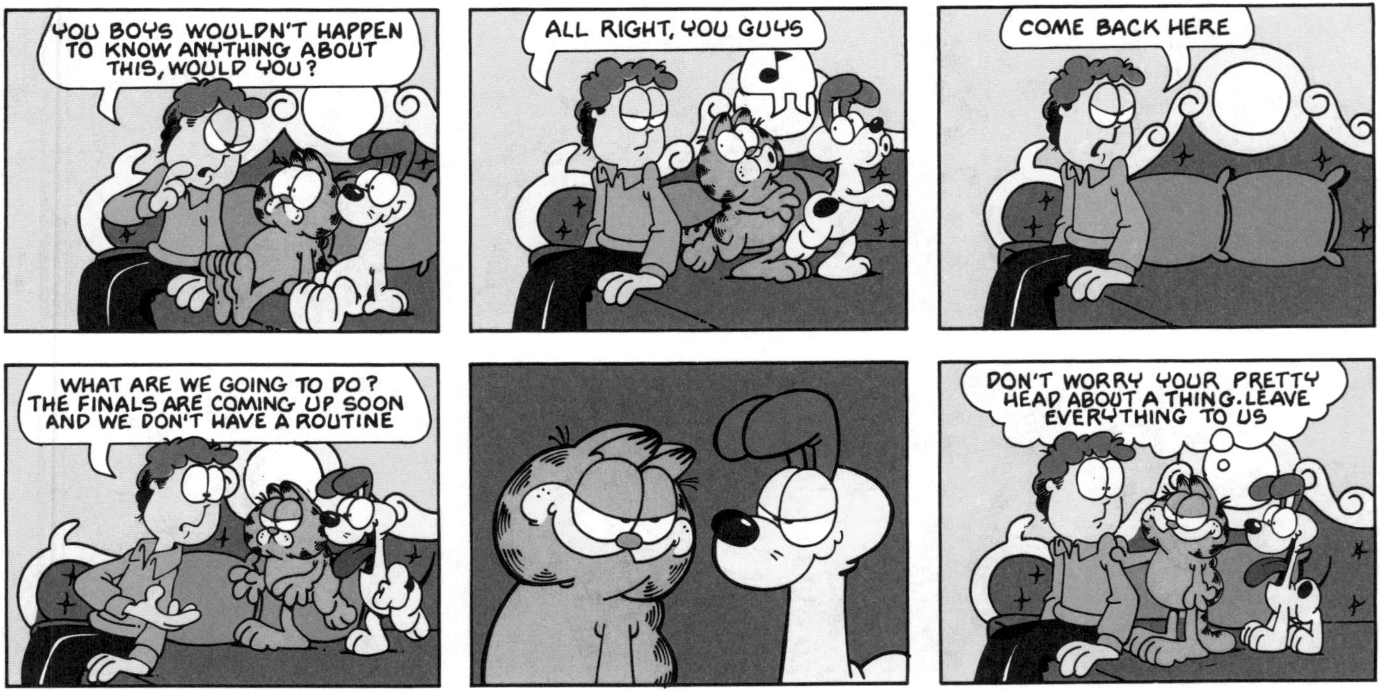
YOU BOYS WOULDN'T HAPPEN TO KNOW ANYTHING ABOUT THIS, WOULD YOU?
ALL RIGHT, YOU GUYS
COME BACK HERE
WHAT ARE WE GOING TO DO? THE FINALS ARE COMING UP SOON AND WE DON'T HAVE A ROUTINE
DON'T WORRY YOUR PRETTY HEAD ABOUT A THING. LEAVE EVERYTHING TO US

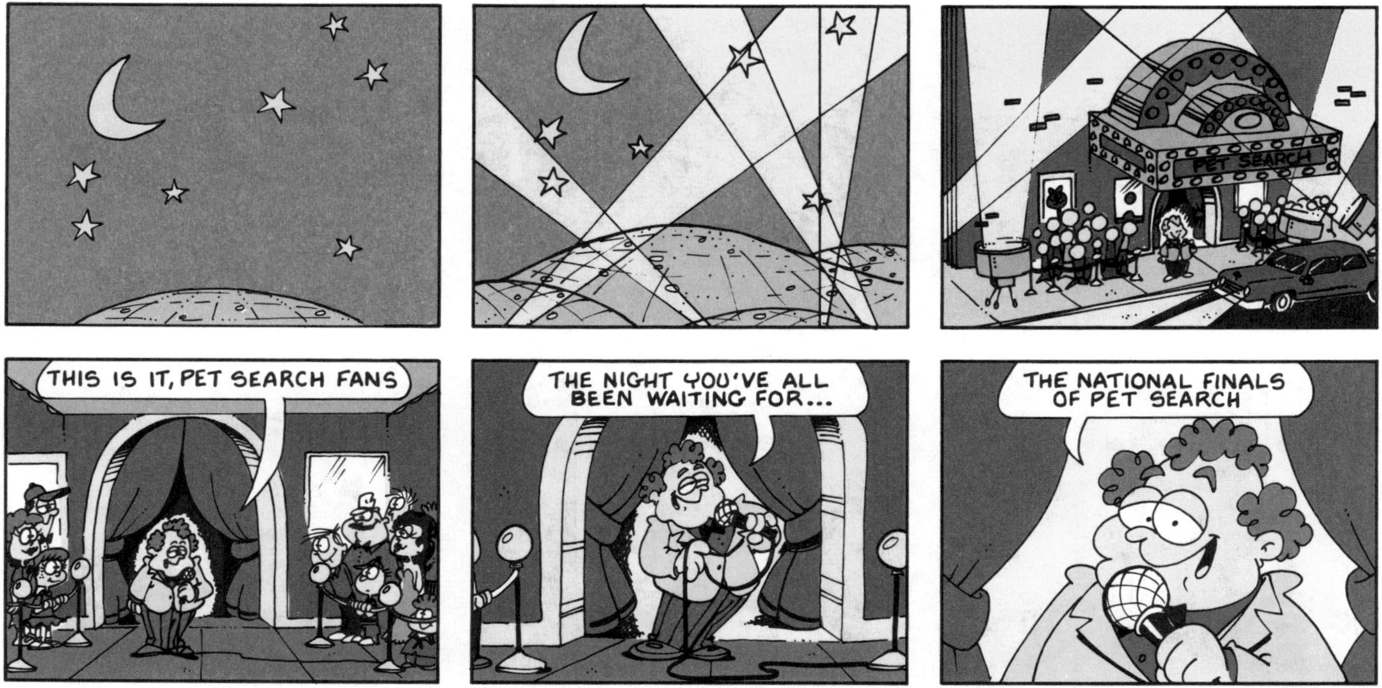
PET SEARCH
THIS IS IT, PET SEARCH FANS
THE NIGHT YOU'VE ALL BEEN WAITING FOR...
THE NATIONAL FINALS OF PET SEARCH

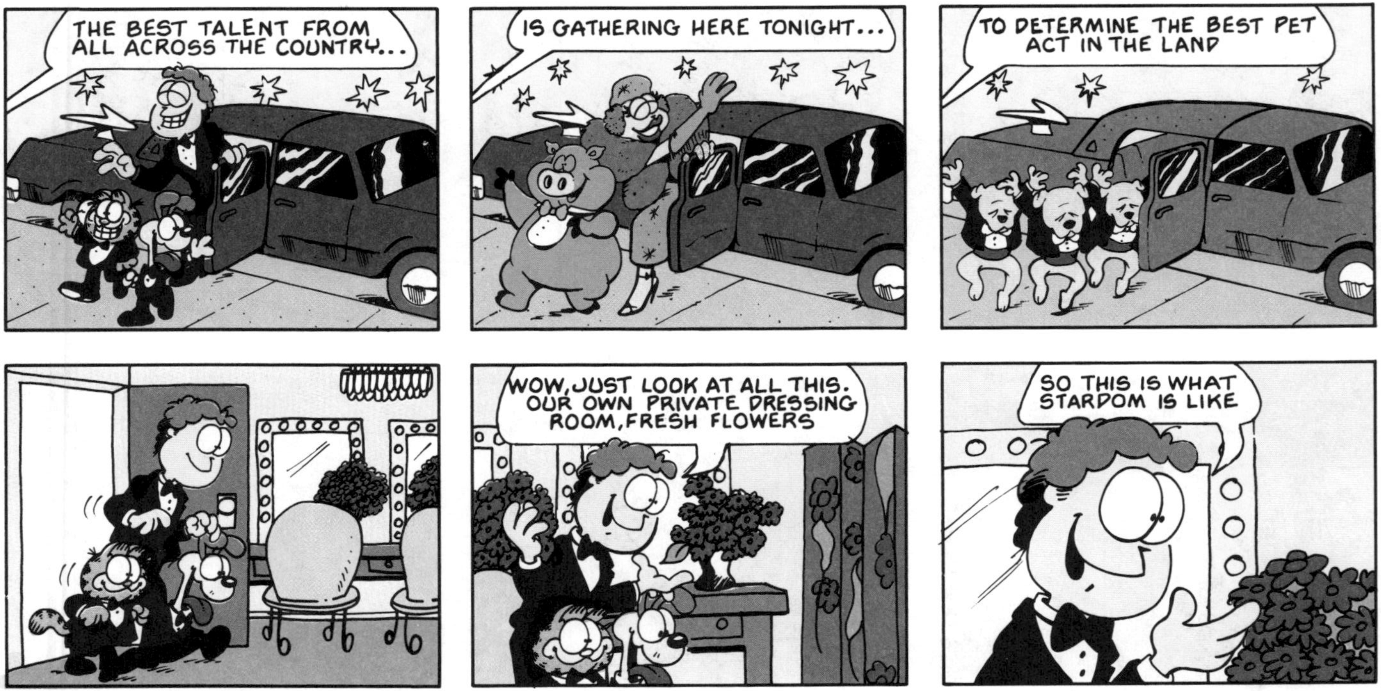
THE BEST TALENT FROM ALL ACROSS THE COUNTRY...
IS GATHERING HERE TONIGHT...
TO DETERMINE THE BEST PET ACT IN THE LAND
WOW, JUST LOOK AT ALL THIS. OUR OWN PRIVATE DRESSING ROOM, FRESH FLOWERS
SO THIS IS WHAT STARDOM IS LIKE

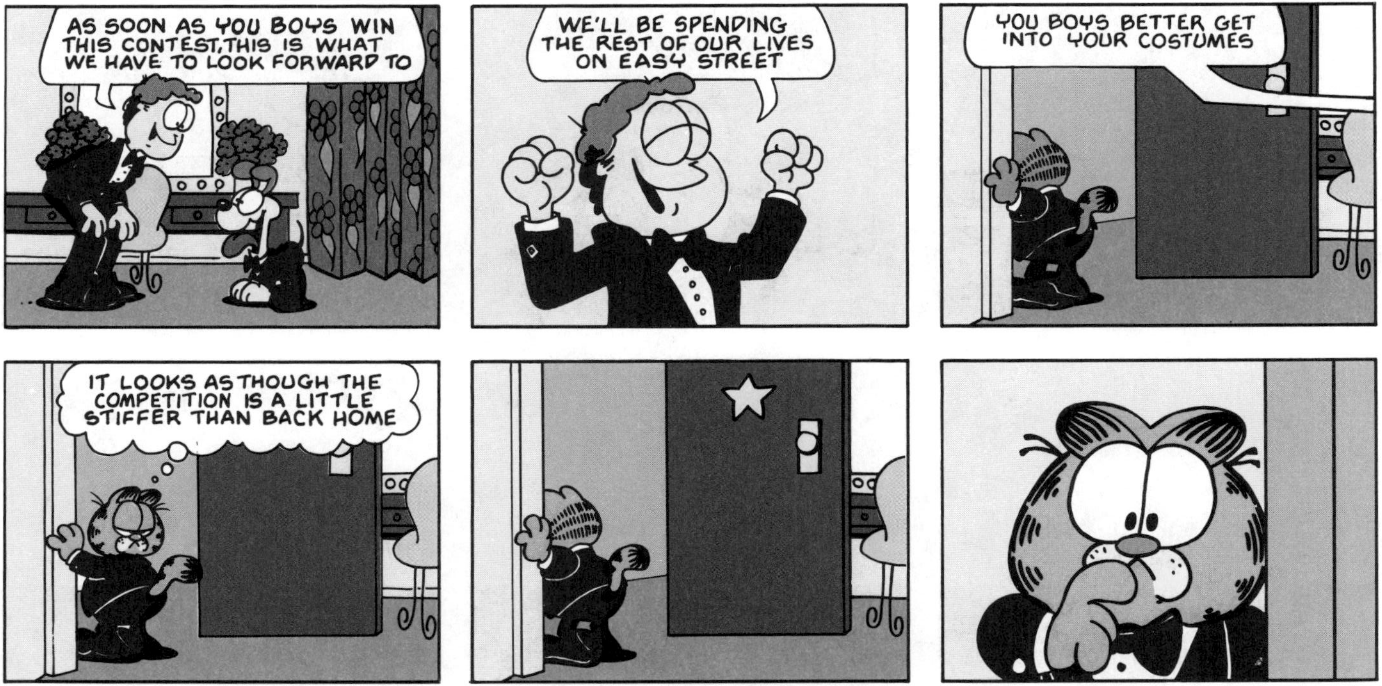
AS SOON AS YOU BOYS WIN THIS CONTEST, THIS IS WHAT WE HAVE TO LOOK FORWARD TO
WE'LL BE SPENDING THE REST OF OUR LIVES ON EASY STREET
YOU BOYS BETTER GET INTO YOUR COSTUMES
IT LOOKS AS THOUGH THE COMPETITION IS A LITTLE STIFFER THAN BACK HOME

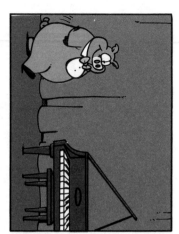

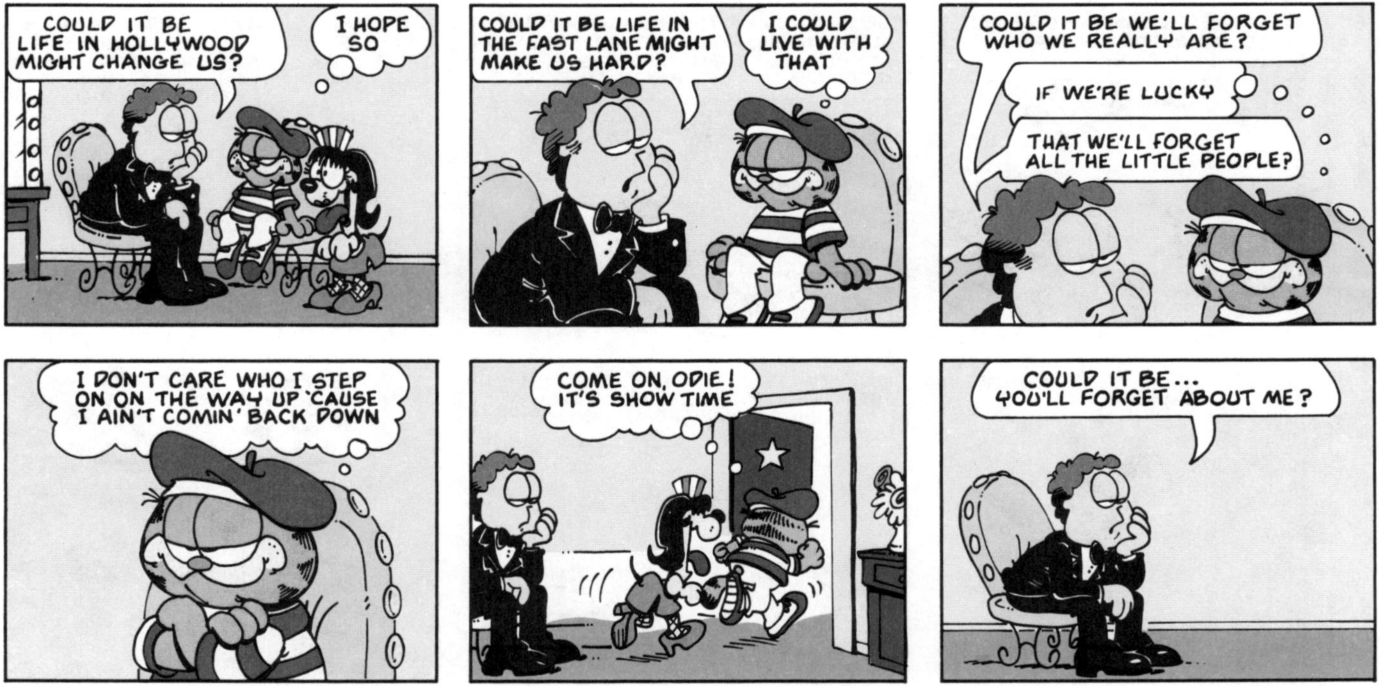
COULD IT BE LIFE IN HOLLYWOOD MIGHT CHANGE US?
I HOPE SO
COULD IT BE LIFE IN THE FAST LANE MIGHT MAKE US HARD?
I COULD LIVE WITH THAT
COULD IT BE WE'LL FORGET WHO WE REALLY ARE?
IF WE'RE LUCKY
THAT WE'LL FORGET ALL THE LITTLE PEOPLE?
I DON'T CARE WHO I STEP ON ON THE WAY UP 'CAUSE I AIN'T COMIN' BACK DOWN
COME ON, ODIE! IT'S SHOW TIME
COULD IT BE... YOU'LL FORGET ABOUT ME?

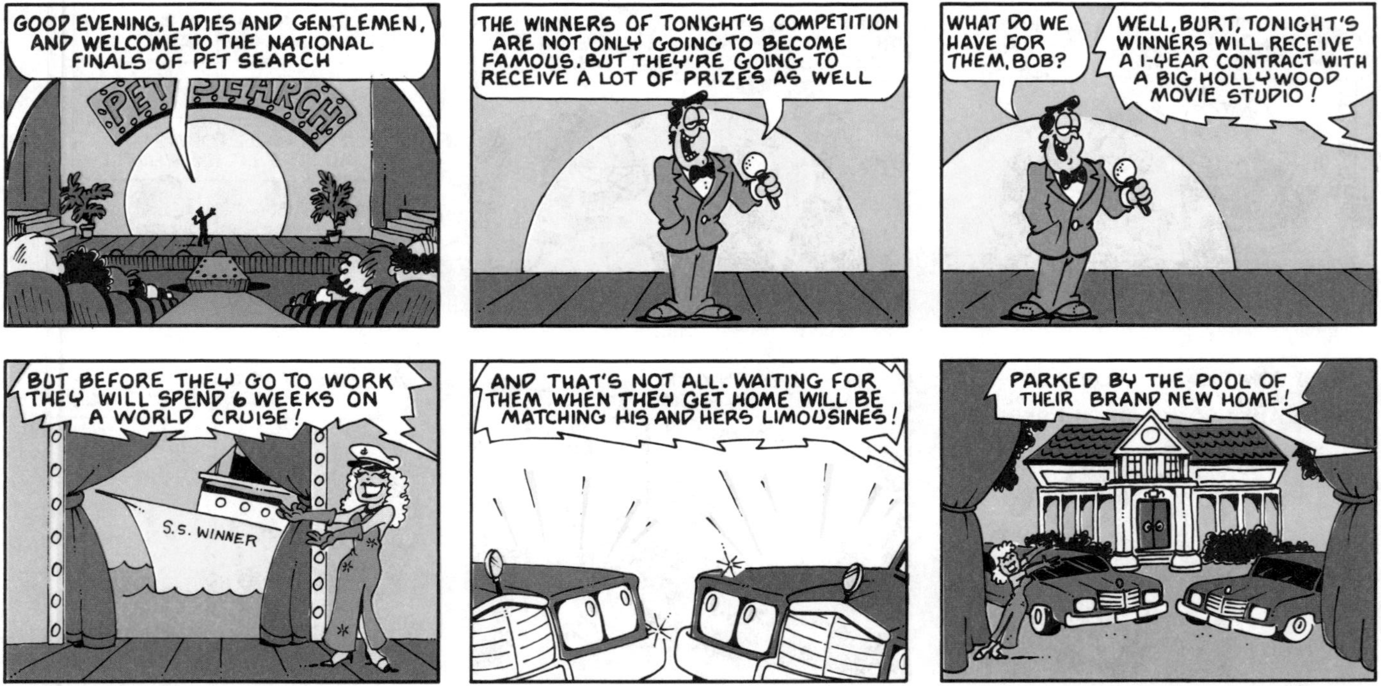
GOOD EVENING, LADIES AND GENTLEMEN, AND WELCOME TO THE NATIONAL FINALS OF PET SEARCH
PET SEARCH
THE WINNERS OF TONIGHT'S COMPETITION ARE NOT ONLY GOING TO BECOME FAMOUS, BUT THEY'RE GOING TO RECEIVE A LOT OF PRIZES AS WELL
WHAT DO WE HAVE FOR THEM, BOB?
WELL, BURT, TONIGHT'S WINNERS WILL RECEIVE A 1-YEAR CONTRACT WITH A BIG HOLLYWOOD MOVIE STUDIO!
BUT BEFORE THEY GO TO WORK THEY WILL SPEND 6 WEEKS ON A WORLD CRUISE!
S.S. WINNER
AND THAT'S NOT ALL. WAITING FOR THEM WHEN THEY GET HOME WILL BE MATCHING HIS AND HERS LIMOUSINES!
PARKED BY THE POOL OF THEIR BRAND NEW HOME!

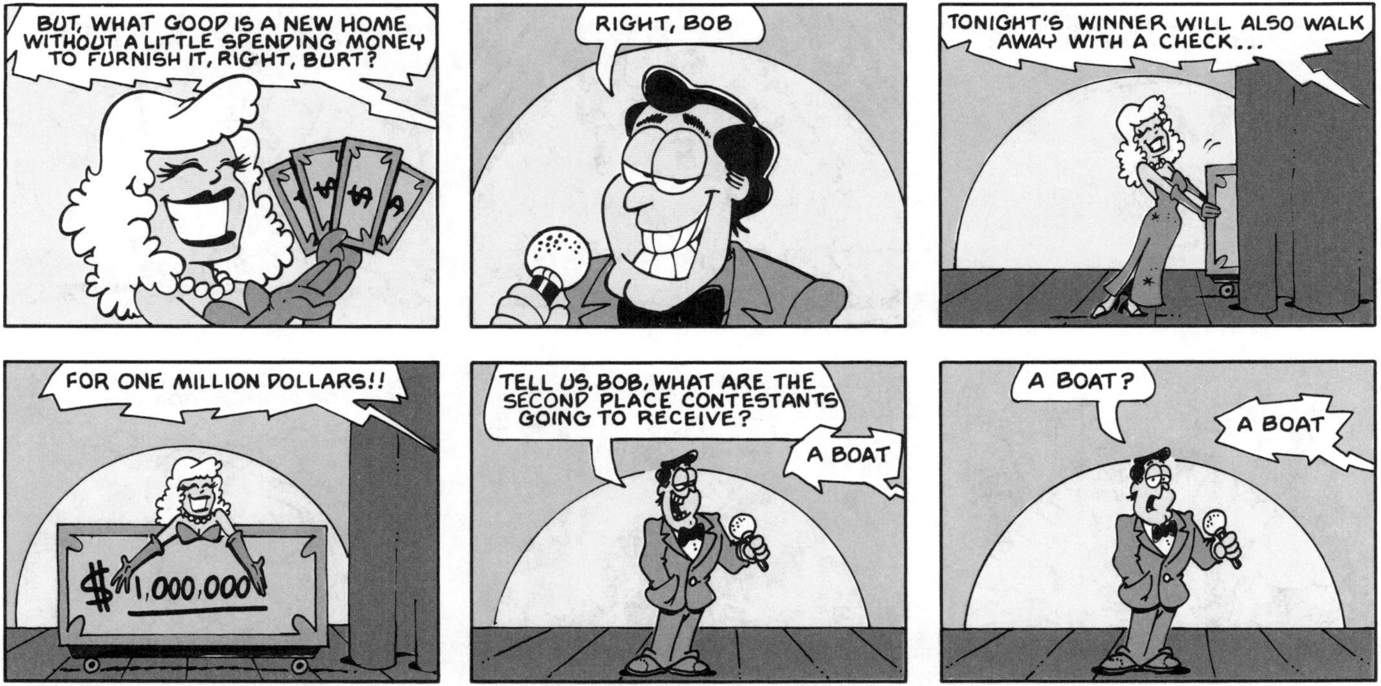
BUT, WHAT GOOD IS A NEW HOME WITHOUT A LITTLE SPENDING MONEY TO FURNISH IT, RIGHT, BURT?
RIGHT, BOB
TONIGHT'S WINNER WILL ALSO WALK AWAY WITH A CHECK...
FOR ONE MILLION DOLLARS!!
$1,000,000
TELL US, BOB, WHAT ARE THE SECOND PLACE CONTESTANTS GOING TO RECEIVE?
A BOAT
A BOAT?
A BOAT

THANK YOU VERY MUCH, BOB. NOW, LET'S GET ON WITH PET SEARCH.

THOSE CHICKENS ARE PRETTY GOOD

YES THEY ARE. WE MUST HAVE THEM FOR DINNER SOMETIME

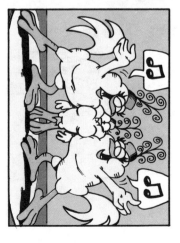

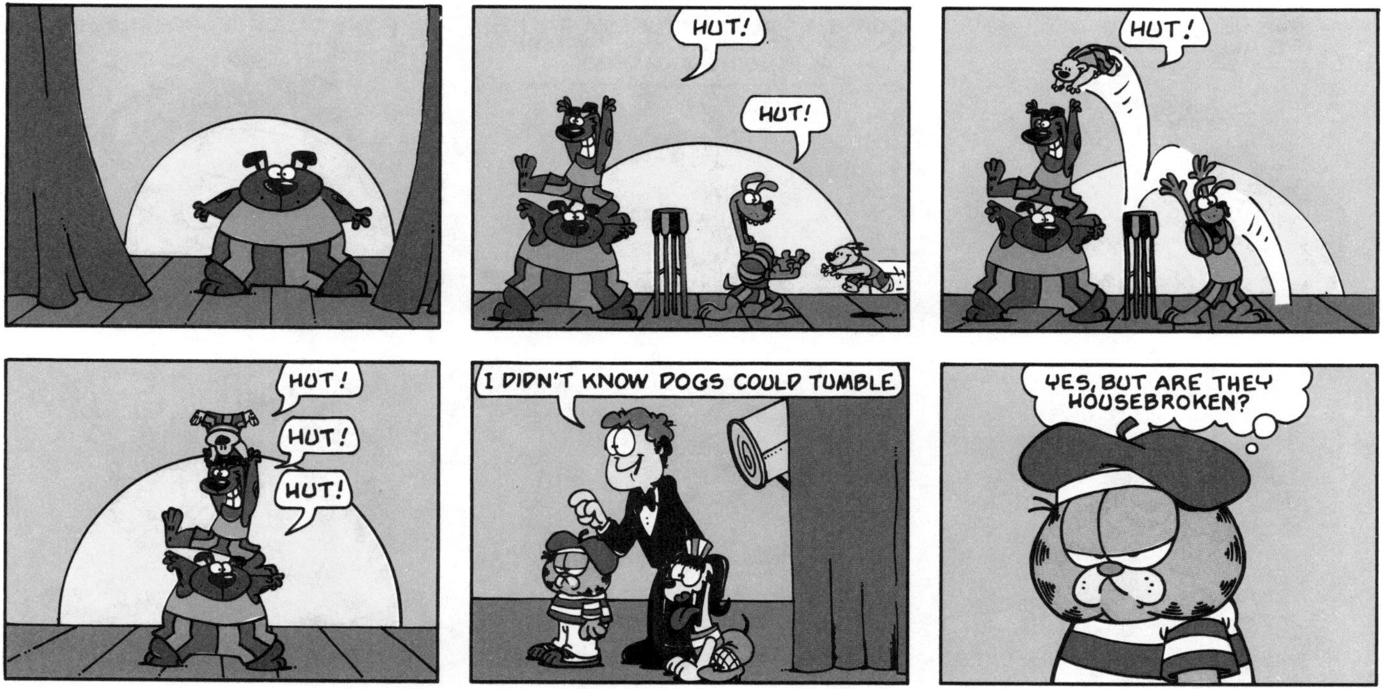
HUT!
HUT!
HUT!
HUT!
HUT!
HUT!
I DIDN'T KNOW DOGS COULD TUMBLE
YES, BUT ARE THEY HOUSEBROKEN?

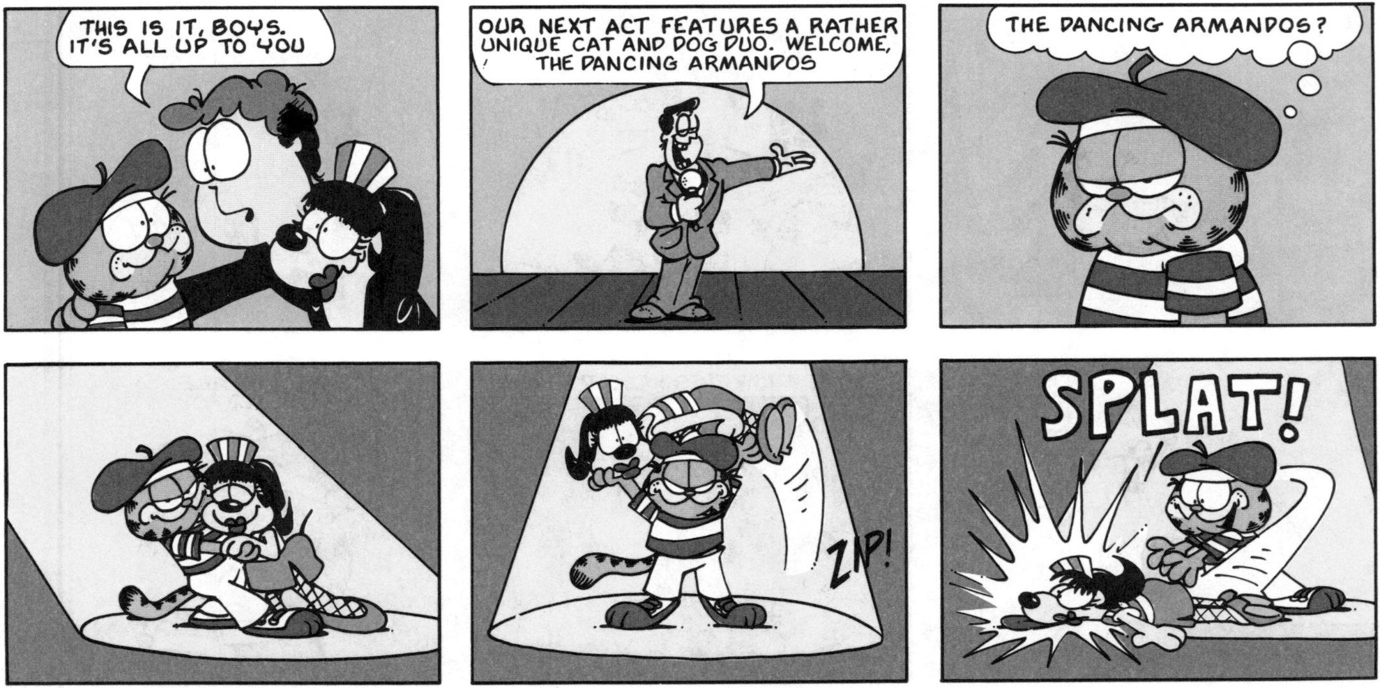
THIS IS IT, BOYS. IT'S ALL UP TO YOU
OUR NEXT ACT FEATURES A RATHER UNIQUE CAT AND DOG DUO. WELCOME, THE DANCING ARMANDOS
THE DANCING ARMANDOS?
ZIP!
SPLAT!

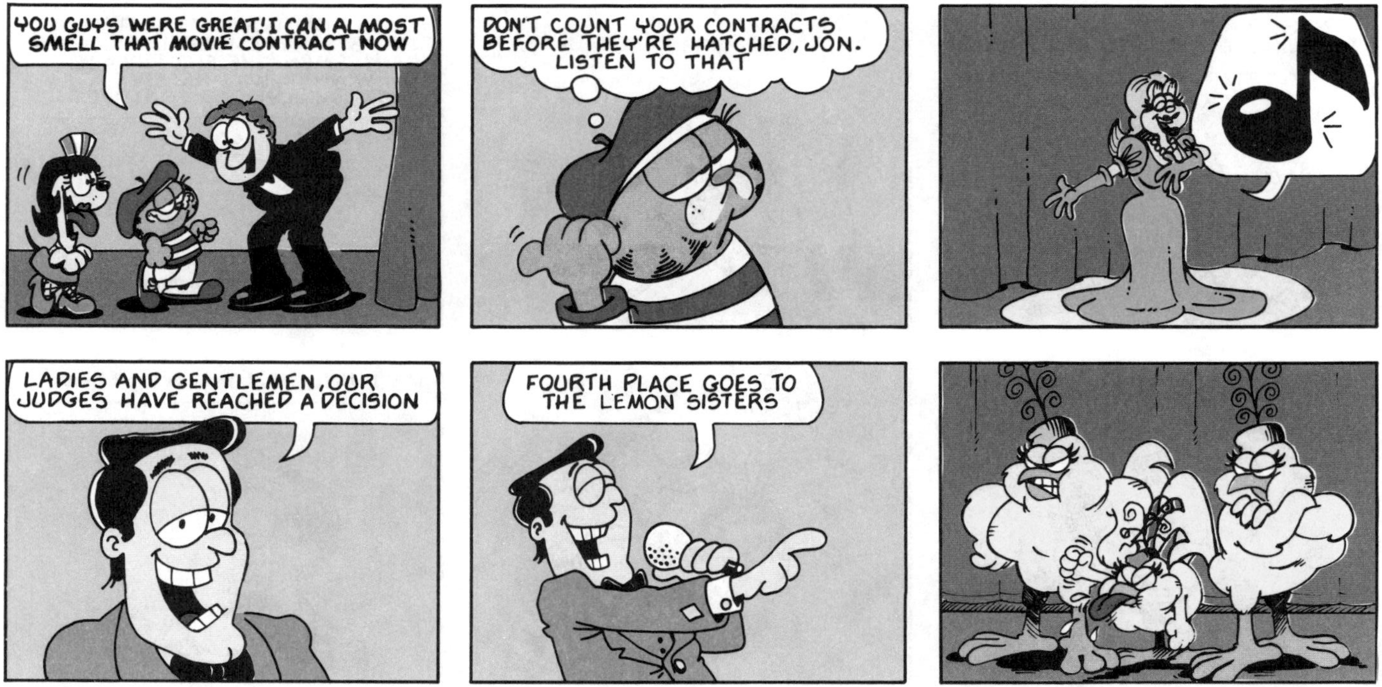
YOU GUYS WERE GREAT! I CAN ALMOST SMELL THAT MOVIE CONTRACT NOW
DON'T COUNT YOUR CONTRACTS BEFORE THEY'RE HATCHED, JON. LISTEN TO THAT
LADIES AND GENTLEMEN, OUR JUDGES HAVE REACHED A DECISION
FOURTH PLACE GOES TO THE LEMON SISTERS

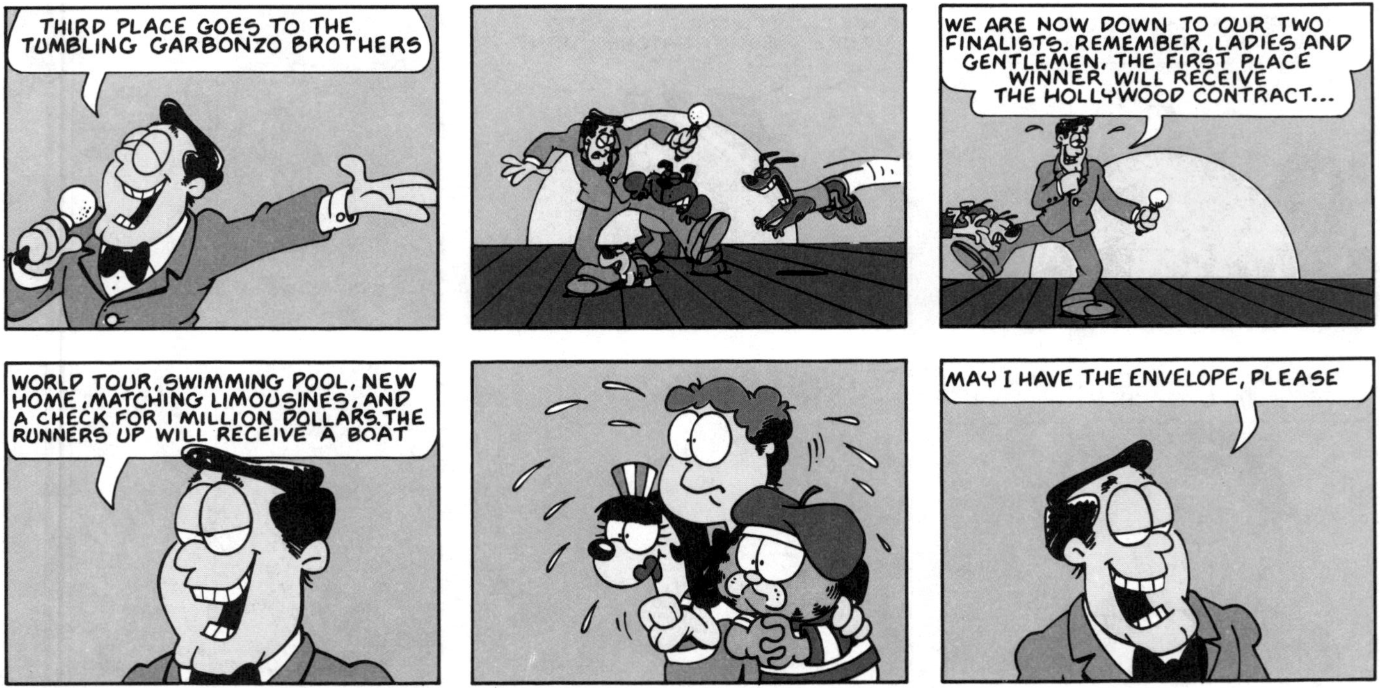
THIRD PLACE GOES TO THE TUMBLING GARBONZO BROTHERS
WE ARE NOW DOWN TO OUR TWO FINALISTS. REMEMBER, LADIES AND GENTLEMEN, THE FIRST PLACE WINNER WILL RECEIVE THE HOLLYWOOD CONTRACT...
WORLD TOUR, SWIMMING POOL, NEW HOME, MATCHING LIMOUSINES, AND A CHECK FOR 1 MILLION DOLLARS. THE RUNNERS UP WILL RECEIVE A BOAT
MAY I HAVE THE ENVELOPE, PLEASE

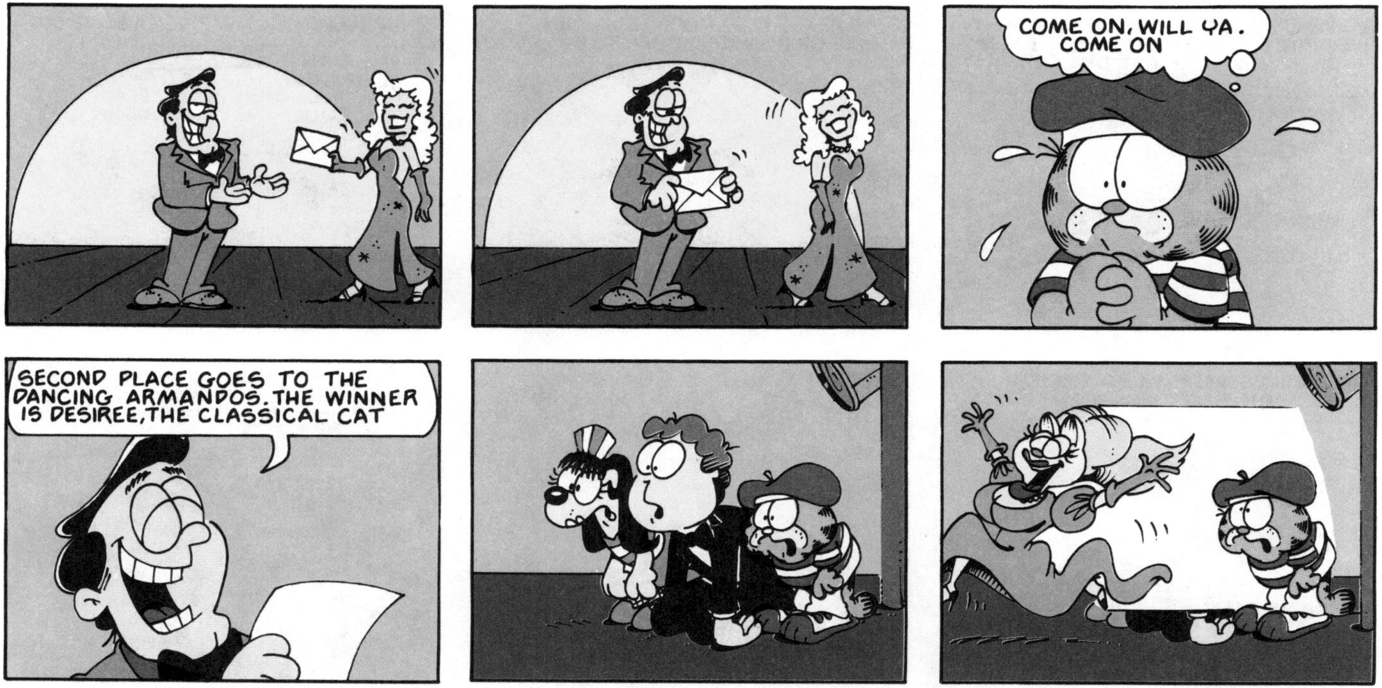
COME ON, WILL YA. COME ON
SECOND PLACE GOES TO THE DANCING ARMANDOS. THE WINNER IS DESIREE, THE CLASSICAL CAT

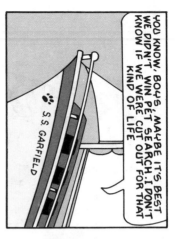

YOU KNOW, BOYS, MAYBE IT'S BEST WE DIDN'T WIN PET SEARCH. I DON'T KNOW IF WE WERE CUT OUT FOR THAT KIND OF LIFE
S.S. GARFIELD
SPEAK FOR YOURSELF, JON. SOME OF US WERE BORN TO BE GREAT
NEVERTHELESS, WE DID GET A BOAT OUT OF IT
RIGHT. THERE IS SOMETHING TO BE SAID FOR THE YACHTING LIFE. I COULD GROW ACCUSTOMED TO THIS
WHERE DO WE SAIL NEXT, BOYS? THE SOUTH OF FRANCE?
S.S. GARFIELD
I HEAR THE FIJI ISLANDS ARE PARTICULARLY NICE THIS TIME OF YEAR
MAYBE WE COULD DO SOME SURFING OFF THE GOLD COAST OF AUSTRALIA
S.S. GARFIELD
MAYBE WE SHOULD JUST SETTLE FOR A SIMPLE SPIN AROUND THE CARIBBEAN ISLANDS. WHAT DO YOU SAY ODIUS?
BARK!

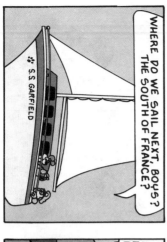

Why not live *extra* large? Gobble up two hilarious helpings of Garfield!

Garfield's Guide to Everything

Garfield Older & Wider

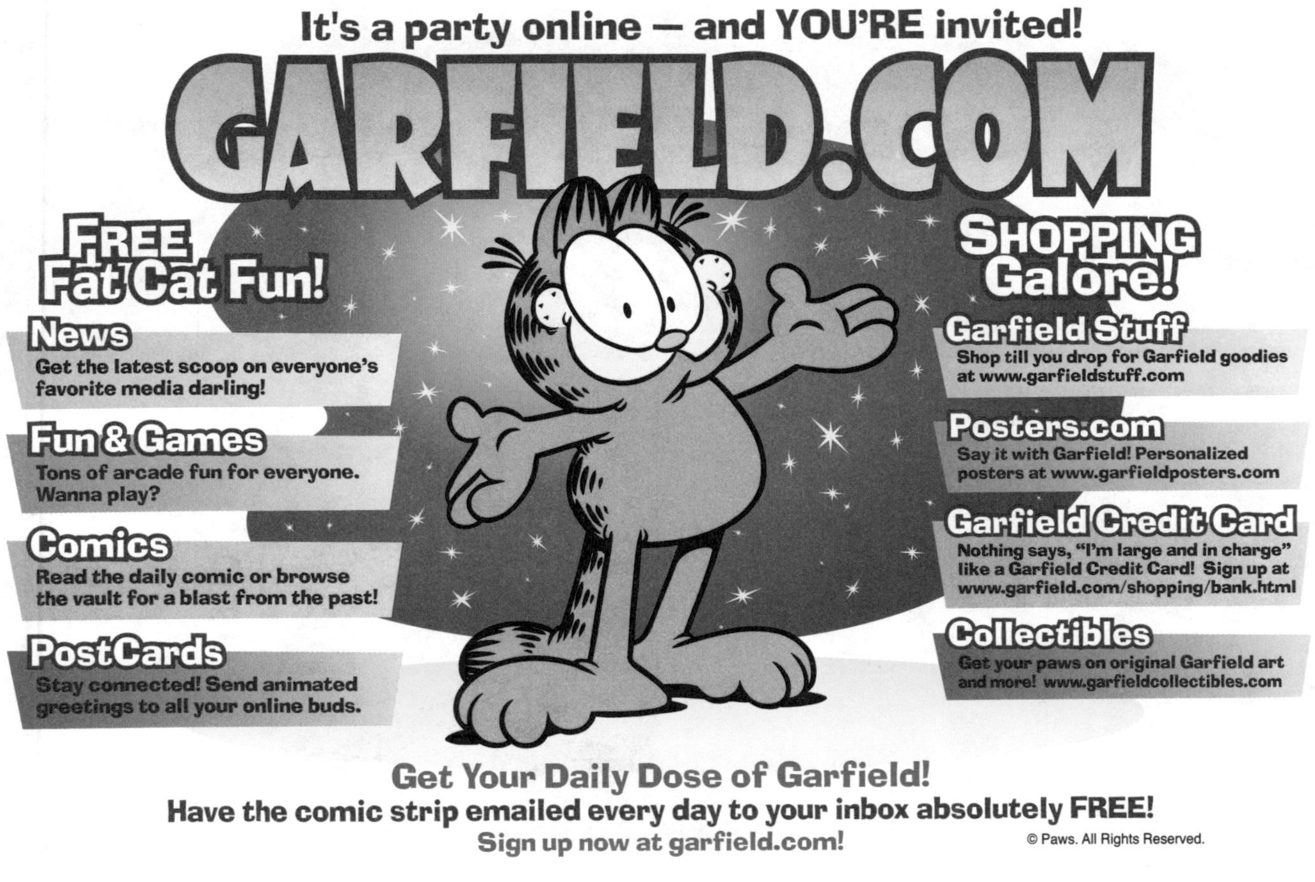
It's a party online — and YOU'RE invited!
GARFIELD.COM
FREE Fat Cat Fun!
News
Get the latest scoop on everyone's favorite media darling!
Fun & Games
Tons of arcade fun for everyone. Wanna play?
Comics
Read the daily comic or browse the vault for a blast from the past!
PostCards
Stay connected! Send animated greetings to all your online buds.
SHOPPING Galore!
Garfield Stuff
Shop till you drop for Garfield goodies at www.garfieldstuff.com
Posters.com
Say it with Garfield! Personalized posters at www.garfieldposters.com
Garfield Credit Card
Nothing says, "I'm large and in charge" like a Garfield Credit Card! Sign up at www.garfield.com/shopping/bank.html
Collectibles
Get your paws on original Garfield art and more! www.garfieldcollectibles.com
Get Your Daily Dose of Garfield!
Have the comic strip emailed every day to your inbox absolutely FREE!
Sign up now at garfield.com!
© Paws. All Rights Reserved.

HE PUTS THE 'CAT' IN VACATION.
GARFIELD TRAVEL ADVENTURES
This Never-Before-Available DVD Features Three Hilarious Garfield Specials: Garfield in the Rough, Garfield in Paradise, & Garfield Goes Hollywood.
Available To Own February 15, 2005!
©Paws. All Rights Reserved. ©2004 Twentieth Century Fox Home Entertainment, Inc. All Rights Reserved. "Twentieth Century Fox," "Fox," and their associated logos are the property of Twentieth Century Fox Film Corporation.
www.garfielddvd.com

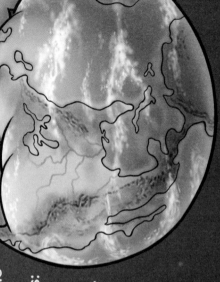

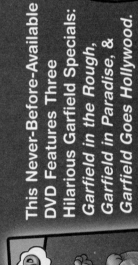